my son my son

my son my son

A father's desperate struggle

Chester Anthony

JOHN MURRAY
Albemarle Street, London

*This book is a record of events as the author recalls them.
Where necessary, names have been changed.*

© Chester Anthony, 1998

First published in 1998
by John Murray (Publishers) Ltd,
50 Albemarle Street, London W1X 4BD

The moral right of the author has been asserted

All rights reserved. No part of this publication may be reproduced in any material form (including photocopying or storing it in any medium by electronic means and whether or not transiently or incidentally to some other use of this publication) without the written permission of the copyright owner, except in accordance with the provisions of the Copyright, Designs and Patents Act 1988 or under the terms of a licence issued by the Copyright Licensing Agency, 90 Tottenham Court Road, London W1P 9HE. Applications for the copyright owner's written permission to reproduce anypart of this publication should be addressed to the publisher.

A catalogue record for this book is available from the British Library

ISBN 0–7195–5416 0

Typeset in Bembo by Servis Filmsetting Ltd, Manchester
Printed and bound in Great Britain by
The University Press, Cambridge

This book is dedicated to all those throughout the world (professionals and non-professionals), who, like Vivienne Gill, tirelessly and indiscriminately work for a better outcome for dysfunctional or underachieving children and their families. On behalf of all misunderstood, voiceless, educationally disordered children I thank you and hope that one day your combined hard efforts will bear fruit – appropriate tailored help for all children with special educational needs – and that you'll receive the support and recognition you deserve.

Contents

Prologue   1

Departing from the Centre   9

Pandora's Box   53

Secure, but not Safe   123

Answers   219

Epilogue   241

Useful Addresses   244

Acknowledgements   245

Prologue

ALEX HAD MADE A beeline for the tongs a thousand times before: whenever he and his brother Jason watched their mother curl her hair. At each attempt Sharon would say a resolute 'No!' Once or twice, as the tongs cooled, she had let him briefly touch them to see how hot they became so that he could understand that they were not a toy but could be dangerous. Alex was 3, Jason 4. When Jason had been quite a bit younger than his brother was now, he'd begun to respect a firm 'No!' Alex, however, still seemed to be utterly controlled by his own involuntary urges.

One evening, Sharon and I were in the kitchen cooking and tidying up. The boys were upstairs in the sitting room enjoying bouts of play and watching television, as well as having their usual minor sibling differences. Then we noticed they had gone unusually quiet: always a potential danger sign that I in time termed 'the noise factor', unless they were engrossed in one of their favourite television programmes. I crept upstairs to investigate. Jason was playing serenely by himself on the sofa, but Alex was nowhere in sight.

He was not in the bathroom, one of his favourite haunts, nor was he in the tiny spare boxroom. As I went upstairs towards the bedrooms, I caught the scent of a strange barbecue-type smell – the smell of burning flesh. There sitting at the top of the stairs was Alex. A freshly made, red-raw scar ran down the full length of his right cheek. It was about four inches long, and half an inch across its widest point, missing his eye by a whisker.

'What happened, son?!' I shouted in panic, as I rushed over to comfort him. Sharon and Jason must have heard me and ran up the stairs. Sharon was every bit as struck with anxiety and disbelief as I was. She pushed me out of the way, grabbed Alex in her arms and, barging open our bedroom door, sat him in her lap on the edge of the bed, horrified, while I scoured the dressing-table drawer for the petroleum jelly. Sharon held him tightly as I applied a large clump of gel to the wound. Alex hadn't made a sound or shed a tear until we started to fuss over his injury. Minutes later, as the pain took hold, he let rip and sobbed until he eventually fell asleep. Later he explained that he had taken the tongs out of the bottom bedside drawer where Sharon had packed them away safely, plugged them into the mains and switched them to the hot setting, but he could offer no explanation as to why he had done it. When I asked him why he didn't cry, he explained: 'Because you'd have told me off.'

Alex's injury was substantial enough to have made an adult cry, let alone a young child. Of deeper significance, though, was how anyone, even impetuous Alex, could pick up hot curling-tongs and put them on their own face. I was perturbed to the point of distraction, finding it difficult to reconcile how someone could do that to themselves. Did Alex not understand that the intense heat would burn him? Why he did it, and why he never cried, remained the most disturbing event of Alex's third year, and provided me with a mystery that I would not unravel for years to come.

The doctor explained that the scar might disappear because he was so young, or that it might fade considerably. Fortunately it did clear up completely within a couple of years, but the scar on my mind has remained ever since.

There was something definitely peculiar about Alex. By the time he was 7, it was difficult to remember what life had been like before it became dominated by his all-too-frequent acts of unacceptable behaviour. One typical and dangerous incident happened when I was perming Sharon's hair, my hands covered in cream. This time it was she who noticed the unusual silence coming from the sitting room and went downstairs to investigate.

'Oh my God, Chester. Chester, come quickly!' she screamed from the hall as the smell of burning wafted upwards. 'Alex has started a fire.'

On hearing the word 'fire' I must have taken all of two seconds to get down the two flights of stairs from our bedroom to the lounge. I saw the wastepaper basket alight, the flames almost touching Sherekhan, our tiger painting on the wall. A few feet away, towards the middle of the room, stood Alex. He was just starting to cry.

Without a moment's thought, I rushed back into the hallway, almost knocking over Jason in the process as I raced towards the bathroom. I grabbed a towel and thoroughly soaked it, then dashed back into the lounge where the fire was gaining strength. I threw the wet towel over the wicker basket and doused the flames. With a sigh of relief, I realised that this particular crisis was over – apart from the recriminations.

With a mixture of fright, anger and maternal concern, Sharon got hold of Alex and started shouting at him. I was angry too, but not that surprised by his behaviour, and joined in the verbal assault on our young son.

'You could have burned the house down.'

'What is the matter with you, child?'

'We could all be dead.'

'Why can't you behave yourself?'

'You can't be trusted on your own, not even for five minutes. People have to keep their eyes on you *all the time*.'

Faced with this onslaught Alex just cried and cried, whimpering between the tears, 'I'm sorry, Mummy. I'm sorry, Daddy. I promise I won't do it again.'

Jason stood transfixed in the doorway. By now, he was crying too. As I brushed past him, carrying the wet, charred remains of the basket, I snapped at him simply for being there. When the mess had been cleared away, Jason was allowed to remain with his toys and the television. Alex was ordered upstairs with us, where, shaken, I resumed perming Sharon's hair. Within minutes Alex was playing happily as though absolutely nothing had happened, but for the thousandth time we were left searching for explanations for his behaviour. At 7 years old he should have known better.

Not all Alex's misdemeanours were life-threatening, yet most were serious enough to give rise to genuine concern. Most children, Jason included, gradually learn the principles of cause and effect which govern life within family, school and the physical world. They may sometimes choose to ignore these rules, or break them under pressure, but they usually have a foreboding of the trouble this will cause. In Alex's case it was as though such rules simply did not exist, or at least had no permanency. Although he was perceived by his teachers to be bright and his IQ was thought to be normal, he failed to learn from experience. Often he was as shocked and surprised as others were at the results of his actions.

From the first day he went to nursery school, aged 3½, there were complaints. When he was 8 he was excluded from mainstream junior school, and that same year I stood before a High Court family judge who directed that family therapy must 'get to the root of this child's disturbances and frustrations'. His order has never been completely complied with.

As I write, Alex is nearly 17. By now, the amount of material that has been written about him is quite staggering. There are untold reports and files to be found on him in schools and special schools, a variety of children's homes and hospitals, open and secure units, at places all around the country. Latterly, and not surprisingly, the police have started to build their own portfolio on Alex as incidents occur wherever he lives. Everywhere he goes he somehow manages to divide people into two camps: those for him (usually the minority) and those against him (usually the majority). Like a pebble that has long since sunk to the bottom of a lake, causing ripples that seem to go on for ever, Alex remains the subject of talk years after he has left some establishments.

This book is the story of Alex's bizarre and sometimes tragic life, and my quest for the cause of his often disturbed, outlandish and eccentric behaviour. I wanted to tell it because I know now that there are other children, in differing degrees, like Alex. Their plight needs urgently to be highlighted. Early recognition and understanding is vital if they are to be helped. All too belatedly I've learned that this is indeed possible. For years, teachers, social workers, wardens, doctors, the courts – their remedies having failed – have, collectively, made Sharon and me feel that Alex is a one-off. He isn't.

No one should have to endure what this lad has been through. No parents should be forced to stand helplessly to one side while their child becomes increasingly and inexplicably violent towards others – or becomes the object of intense violence. It is a miracle that no one, including Alex, has died. I don't know what his future can be, but I am fighting to rescue it for him. Very recently, as this story will reveal, I have discovered there is light at the end of what has been a nightmare tunnel.

For many years I was mystified by my son's behaviour. I wanted to know: 'Why is he the way he is?' Try as I might, I could not find another child quite like him. I racked my brains about my own school days, remembering both friends and enemies, to see if I could recall a similar child. I couldn't. Yes, there were bad boys about – there always are. But I couldn't remember anyone like Alex.

Often I felt sorry for him. At times it appeared as if he simply couldn't help himself; at other times as if he were being wilfully disobedient. Oh, how he would get right up my nose when I felt his behaviour was deliberate! Sometimes I got angry – all too often, I admit with shame. I can only now appreciate this fully with the benefit of hindsight. Yet, amazingly, Alex was mainly such a happy kid. It was an immense pleasure to have him around when he was well behaved; he was a very funny, playful boy. I must admit: Alex confused me. I simply couldn't figure him out. I wanted to know why my son was so different, but answers were not forthcoming.

Not many parents ponder with seriousness the possibility of *their* little 'bundle of joy' becoming a major management problem in the future, and we were no different. Somehow other issues always seem to be more important: keeping a roof over the family's head; earning the money to pay the bills; providing enough food and clothing. Many working mothers and fathers can think of nothing they would rather do after a hard day than relax in front of the television, read the newspaper, or put their feet up and reflect on the day's talking points, before playing with the kids for a little while and then tucking them into bed. In this I was not much different.

As a parent it is easy to take one's own children's foibles for granted. I accept a degree of guilt here, especially when I was tired and not in the mood to listen to Jason's complaints about his younger brother. As with most siblings, accusations fly back and forth, yet they usually seem so trivial, just one small thing after another. And as soon as you listen to one child, then to be fair you have to listen to the other. Children can go on all evening with their endless tale-telling and attention-seeking demands, then at last they tire out and fall asleep. Yet it was at times like these that I was able to see my son as he really is: just an ordinary kid.

What went wrong? Where did my darling little boy disappear to?

Departing from the Centre

One

When a child's antisocial behaviour becomes a problem, or when such children are seen as different from their peers, yet not physically or mentally handicapped, people often want to know about the parents. They are interested to see if the parents' upbringing might hold any clues to their child's behaviour. Sharon's and my backgrounds have a good deal in common. We were both born in Jamaica in the mid-1950s and raised by our grandmothers after our parents emigrated to England in search of a better life.

Life in Jamaica in those days was good for me. For my first seven years I grew up in the downtown ghetto area of the capital, Kingston. This was one of the roughest parts of town and you had to be tough to survive. I don't have detailed recollections of this era but the family tell me that I became as rough as any kid in my environment and tougher than most. But I have no memory of any exceptionally bad experiences. I lived with my gran, two aunts, an uncle and at least half a dozen cousins; I was the second youngest. My uncle and aunt treated me as one of the family, but it's not the same as having your own mum and dad, is it? I had been left in the care of my beloved grandmother, Catherine, but since she lived with my aunt and uncle I suppose I was just as much their responsibility as hers.

In time I became too much of a handful for my ageing gran and she could no longer bear the responsibility. I have some scanty recollections of the adults speaking about my mother and father in England, and the next thing I knew, my hair was being cut – not that I had that much to start with. The barber gave me a 'skiffle': I was left virtually as bald as a cricket ball. They greased me from head to toe and I shone like a mirror. Then they dressed me in my best khaki suit – I was sure people could see their reflections in my face – but I didn't mind and took it in my stride. The adventure had begun.

I couldn't figure it out as a child – something to do with my uncle's job, I think – but he and my aunt seemed to live in two different locations: Kingston and Yuerton, a beautiful suburb in St Catherine's countryside, about thirty miles outside the capital. One of my few vivid memories of Jamaica is the journey between the two, with my cousins and me packed liked sardines in my uncle's black car. Now I was making this journey for the last time and didn't seem to care one bit. I remember feeling a sense of excitement. For the first time in my life the car went past downtown Kingston, past our other house, to Palezadoz – the airport. Then I started to become a little frightened because it seemed as if we were driving in the sea. The airport's approach road is a narrow strip of land about three miles long, on almost the same level as the Caribbean Sea. Next thing I knew, I was winging my way across the Atlantic. I was 7 years old.

I arrived in London in June 1963 and was reunited with my parents. Eventually I would realise that this was a common experience for many children of my generation who had been left 'back home' with grandparents.

I must have been a pragmatic little fellow, for I quickly settled into the English routine. The food, the climate and the people did not pose any problems; mind you, the joined-up houses were strange to look at and took a little getting used to. My 'new' family consisted of my mother and father, a much older brother and a much younger sister. A few years later another sister was born.

We lived in the East End of London. It was supposed to be a tough part of town, but I wasn't scared; it seemed like child's play compared to Kingston. In next to no time I was in the thick of it and fought with most of the so-called 'bad' boys in school. Dismissing them with ease, I quickly established my old Kingstonian reputation for being a good fighter.

I will not try here to do justice to the issue of children who grow up away from their parents and are then suddenly reunited. Suffice to say that my family experienced its share of the struggles of the sort not untypical among black families at the time. In addition, having a father who drank heavily did not make life easy for any of us, but my mother tried her best to compensate. She worked very hard as a hospital domestic, and saw to it that the bills were paid and we were fed. I became her assistant, so to speak, and was taught how to wash, cook, clean the house, assist with shopping and look after my younger sisters. Domestically, name it and I could do it, but what I truly hated the most were my regular trips to the launderette with bundles of family clothes.

Like many children, in time I developed a dual personality: one for home, the other for school. At school I was an all-round tough nut. I had my fair share of dressing-downs from the deputy headmaster and a good few canings too, though he was pretty tame compared with the teachers back home. However, I was never at any stage described as uncontrollable – my mother saw to that. There would be more than an element of truth in it, though, if I said that I failed to apply myself academically. Yet while not being a brilliant student, neither was I useless. English was my favourite subject but I never liked maths beyond the age of 14. I do have one major regret: that I foolishly walked out of school in the fifth form, never to return, because a teacher upset me. I thus left without qualifications. After a couple of very different factory jobs, I eventually got work in a garage and settled down to become a motor mechanic in earnest. In time I developed a reputation, not for fighting, but for being an able, industrious worker, and was therefore highly employable.

Sharon went through similar experiences. She and her slightly older sister Marva arrived in the UK in 1967 to join their parents, when Sharon was 10 years old. Unlike me she'd grown up in the country, and up until then had lived a typical country girl's village life. Her memories of that 'old' life are richer and more entrenched than mine. Thus it took her a little longer to adjust to London and for a while she pined for 'home'. I've heard it said often that girls are brighter than boys. Perhaps there is some truth in this, or maybe she was simply far more diligent in her studies than me. In any event she did well in school and repeated this success later in college, passing all her exams. When I met her Sharon was a happy-go-lucky, bubbly type of person. She was 20 and worked as a secretary in offices in the West End. I was 21 and got my hands dirty fixing people's cars. She was regarded as a skilled, reliable and friendly employee, and was well liked by her employers and colleagues. Our personalities seemed compatible, and the similarities in our backgrounds drew us together. Our courtship lasted for less than a year and then we married.

The following year our first son Jason was born. He was a handsome baby, with beautiful, perfectly formed dimples, and a full head of jet-black, half-curly and half-straight, hair. But, oh, he could cry, and what an appetite he had! He came into the world with all cannons firing, and gave new meaning to the term 'cry baby'. Howling and bawling, Jason's intention I'm sure must have been to try to let everyone in the East End know he was here. Sharon stayed at home to look after him and she hoped to return to work when he was older, but she became pregnant with Alex when Jason was about 8 months old.

Pretty soon it became clear that Sharon and I had different attitudes to raising children. She tended to pick Jason up each time he cried; I felt he should sometimes be left, as long as he wasn't hungry or dirty. Occasionally one of us would inflexibly defend our position and an argument would ensue, but most of the time we were happy and at ease, and I would hurry home in the evening to be with my family.

Spurred on by the success I was having at work, I decided to have a go at running my own garage. It moved slowly at first, but we always made enough money to pay the bills. Not being at all business-minded, when there was no work on hand my young assistant and I simply played draughts until there was something to do.

But as time passed and my reputation spread, the number of clients gradually began to build up.

Sharon, who was bored to tears with being at home all day, hankered for a prompt return to work. We'd felt Jason could be looked after by a childminder. Then she became pregnant again. At first she was depressed and wondered how we would cope in our tiny home. I tried to reassure her that we would manage somehow, and I promised we would move to a better place after the baby was born.

This pregnancy was even smoother than the first: everything went like clockwork. Sharon was in labour some 12 hours and, unlike his big brother, Alex had to be coaxed by the doctors to give his first cry. I was helpless throughout this ordeal, and when finally they handed him to me, tears filled my eyes as I held him and proudly walked a little way from the bed. Facing the window, with my back to Sharon and the nursing staff, I lifted him aloft in my arms and muttered softly to myself, 'My son, my son,' and thanked God silently – it was one of the happiest days of my life. I was particularly choked by Alex's birth because a traffic jam had caused me to miss the birth of Jason by just five minutes. I had vowed that would never happen again.

The gradual growth of my business ensured that Sharon did not need to return to work unless she so desired. I had no negative feelings about her wishing to go back because I often sympathised with how bored she must be, but the choice was always hers. As Alex got older she fluctuated between bouts of working and staying at home, usually stopping work because of her fears about the standard of care the boys received from childminders rather than any specific problems they had with Alex. In fact there weren't too many complaints about him save that he needed to be watched the whole time and was always trying to touch forbidden objects around their homes. This pattern continued until the boys reached school age. Our evenings and weekends were spent with the children, though I sometimes had to work late.

Jason had learned to walk at about 12 months. He was a very 'cryee', clingy baby who loved attention. He always wanted to be picked up and played with, and wouldn't wait a moment for his food when hungry. In fact he was so greedy that often I'd make extra portions of feed for him or thicken his milk with rusks just to fill him up and keep him quiet. I didn't mind looking after him to give Sharon a break. I'd help out in the mornings before going to work, and sometimes in the evenings and at weekends. He cooed, crawled and mumbled odd words, and did all the things babies normally do in their first year. Jason could be both a happy baby and a miserable one, with a face that many thought was far too pretty for a boy – especially when he smiled and his deep dimples showed. I felt he was a super-good-looking version of my father, who was generally regarded as a handsome man; however, most family and friends said he looked liked his mother.

Alex similarly met all his early milestones – some too early, Sharon and I jokingly remarked. He seemed to try to do everything too quickly. It's hard to describe, but he would often become over-excited and full of joy when he accomplished something, as if he were proud of himself and wanted to pat himself on the back. There are photos of him propped up standing at 4 months old, broadly smiling as he held on and didn't fall over. And when he started to crawl a month or two later, he was so eager that he went backwards before he went forwards. Then, as if revving an engine, slamming the transmission into first gear and suddenly releasing the clutch, he was off – roaring round the floor as though it were an open road. Alex was a very happy baby.

I have difficulty remembering another baby as happy as he. He was quite a contrast to Jason, who seemed to cry at the touch of a button – simply for being left alone in a room. As best as I can recollect, Alex cried only when he was in need, or occasionally when he wanted to sleep. He was not overly clingy, quite independent in fact, and was often content to be left in his cot playing with his toys. Family, friends and strangers, at least the majority, said Alex was the spitting image of me, though I couldn't see it – he was far better-looking.

Jason thrived on attention. He did not take too kindly to sharing his mum and dad with this new upstart. Sometimes he was quite rough with Alex and would push him out of the way or aim a slap at him if he felt Alex was getting more attention. Brothers and sisters of close age are often like this, so I'm told. For his first 15 or so months Alex took much of this in his stride, but began to retaliate more as he became older.

When not competing for toys, Mummy or Daddy, the boys enjoyed each other's company immensely. They were everywhere – touching this, interfering with that – and certainly kept us on our toes. They did not have an overabundance of toys like some children, but they had their fair share. Jason loved them and would play contentedly with a particular one for ages, but Alex seemed to get bored and would very quickly discard one toy for the next. Even before he could walk, he'd lumber over to Jason and make a nifty grab for the toy his brother was playing with contentedly. Well, this earned him a swift and unpleasant rebuttal from Jason: a push, a slap, a scratch, a bite, followed by an immediate retrieval of the item in question. One might have expected, in time, that these scuffles would see a pecking order established and Alex would eventually get the point. He never did.

Most of Sharon's days, when she was not working, were spent entertaining the boys; she'd play with them for hours, or referee between them until they had worn themselves out and were ready to sleep. Then she'd begin to cook the evening meal while they slept. But the niggling differences in our parenting styles were becoming more pronounced with time, and the sibling rivalry began to take a firm hold. Looking back, the signs of future trouble were already there. Not surprisingly, however, there is doubt as to the extent to which either of us appreciated this at the time. On the whole, our problems seemed normal ones. Our weekends followed the fairly unspectacular routine of an ordinary family: shopping, household chores, running errands, and visiting or entertaining friends. I was a working father trying to give as much support emotionally and physically as any man could to a family he loved.

Alex had started to become destructive when playing with toys. He'd regularly and deliberately pull them apart or he'd methodically smash them. When he was a year old, while visiting friends, an incident occurred that did not seem terribly significant to the others but it made a lasting impression on me. En route we'd stopped at a newsagent's to buy sweets; while in the shop, some toy cars caught my eye. Bearing in mind Alex's treatment of his toys, I thought, 'Those cars look strong,' and bought one each for the boys. I was sure this would keep them amused and that the cars would last. Halfway through the evening, amid the fuss and flattery that is heaped on children by adult friends who don't see them very often, I noticed that Alex's car was in several pieces. Somehow he had quietly broken it. But how? It had seemed much more substantial, but he also seemed to be perfectly content playing with the bits. I thought that quite odd. This incident made me aware of what appeared to be a pattern within the preceding three and a half months. Prior to this, no noticeable problem with Alex had existed.

Sharon and I found it difficult to agree on how to handle his increasing destructiveness. I sometimes confiscated a broken toy, which made him cry, while she wanted him to stay quiet and keep it. He was, after all, only about 12 months old. Sharon and I came to be at loggerheads over this. Most children have a favourite toy which they cherish. Alex had none. All toys received the same treatment – including any of Jason's he could lay his hands on. Privately I suspected that Alex had somehow sensed the contradictions in his parents' reactions and intuitively began to play on them. Alex, having gained centre stage, would then be picked up and fussed over by Sharon, even on occasions when it was obvious he was acting up.

Typical was the following: 'For God's sake, Ches, he's only a baby,' Sharon might say. 'I know he's only a baby, Sharon, but you can't pick him up every time he cries.' It is now fast approaching 9 o'clock. Sharon has been at home all day with the boys. I've been home for nearly two and a half hours. The kids should have been in bed by 8 and are already in their pyjamas. We've allowed them to stay up a little later because I came home late from work. The evening has been spent watching television and playing. I pretended I was a horse, and the boys took turns in riding me round the living-room floor. 'Sharon, it's nearly 9 o'clock; it's time the boys were in bed!' Sharon attempts to take the boys to bed. Jason offers no more than token resistance, but on this particular evening Alex starts to cry. He is in his cot. The crying gets louder and louder. Downstairs an argument develops as Sharon's intention to go and pick up the child is met with my disapproval.

Neither Sharon nor I, nor Alex, seemed to learn from this type of experience, which would be re-enacted many times over the following years. None of us would break our stance. I felt I was right. At times I would block Sharon's path to the child and simply let him cry until he fell asleep. As he grew older and more persistent, sometimes I gave him a light smack. When I did so, invariably after first crying louder Alex would quickly fall asleep. On other occasions Sharon would choose to stay with him, for ages if need be, until he fell asleep. Sometimes for a peaceful life I contradicted my stance and let the children come back down. Jason mostly kept out of these pantomimes, but would benefit from the reprieve earned by his brother's and mother's defiance and my eventual compliance.

Most toddlers want to touch things and put them in their mouths; for Alex this desire was insatiable. It wasn't simply a case of the usual scraps of food or sweets off the floor but quite literally anything: his mother's cosmetics, household cleaning chemicals, a metal screw, the edge of the settee, the remote control for the video. This was another reason to watch Alex closely, as he could have harmed himself with some dangerous substance. Even at the age of 13 the adolescent Alex would occasionally be seen sucking oddities. Yet there was a funny side to all of this. One evening I was in the sitting room with the boys, watching television, and dozed off to sleep. Sharon was in the kitchen cooking. Alex and Jason slipped out to our bedroom. When Sharon called them for dinner and found they were missing she also went upstairs. On pushing open the bedroom door she stumbled on a scene all too familiar to parents. The boys had plastered themselves with their own unique concoction of oils, creams and powders from her dressing table.

'Oh no, boys!' she cried, then called out, 'Chester, come here a minute.'

Of course we could not help but be amused. There is always a comical element to these dramas and what can you do but clean up the mess! They are, after all, only children. You explain to them why it is naughty. The tenth time you may even speak in a harsh voice and ban them from your bedroom. But still they get in again and meddle. In time Jason became less fascinated with these pastimes. And allowing for the 16-month age gap, we expected that Alex would do the same as he got older. He did drop some of his baby traits but it took him about a decade to do so. His last escapade with household items occurred when he was about 9 years old. And it is no joke when the bathroom is deliberately flooded with water, or a bedroom splattered with face cream and powder, or walls, doors and furniture defaced with scribbles, or important papers tucked away in a bedroom drawer are interfered with – but I'm rushing ahead.

As Alex grew older, Sharon and I occasionally became extremely upset and smacked him. I would never clear up his disasters, preferring instead to stand over and watch him, often in tears, clean them up himself. In my absence Sharon would sometimes do the same. More often than not, however, she'd simply voice her disapproval and then promptly proceed to clean up the mess herself – often while Alex played nearby or watched her do so. Her response might be common to some mothers, but it seemed utterly preposterous to me. I certainly couldn't imagine my mother dealing with any mess I had made.

'Sharon, let him clean it.'

'No, it would take for ever. Besides, he can't clean this up properly.'

'That's not the point! Nobody told him to make the mess, and it did not make itself. He should clean it up. So long as you keep clearing up for him, he will continue to make messes.'

Primarily for my benefit, Sharon might say something like: 'Alex, you really are a naughty boy. Look at all the hard work you have given Mummy.' This gesture didn't fool anyone, least of all Alex. Although both his parents are generally tidy and clean, he appeared to be unperturbed by creating havoc and his room regularly seemed like a tip.

Touching everything was the one trait Alex seemed least able to control. He'd simply rush at what caught his eye and play with it. As a baby his favourite word was 'no', yet when it was applied to him he never seemed able to grasp its meaning. If he wanted something he'd grab it. If resistance was met he'd fight for possession. His destructiveness was becoming deliberate.

Two

For me there can be little doubt that by the age of 3, Alex had begun to rule the roost. Most conversations at home were now centred on him. Hardly a day went by without there being some controversy, conflict or incident caused by his behaviour. By now he had truly mastered the art of getting right under other people's skin, and while no one knew for sure whether he did so deliberately, it certainly appeared so at times. Yet, contradictorily, he demonstrated an immense personal charm wrapped up in a bright, bubbly, extrovert personality, which made it virtually impossible for anyone to remain angry with him.

In a paradoxical sense he'd 'gradually exploded' into our lives almost without our noticing it. In so many ways we had a special child on our hands, but we did not know it. From the time he could crawl, peace in our household began to evaporate. To be flippant, he was like bacteria under a microscope: you see them multiply by the thousands right before your eyes. Alex too was everywhere, as though he had sprouted thousands of feet and hands. If you took your eyes off him for one second – he was gone. A very busy chap, he'd be away exploring some cranny or nook. 'Hyperactive' was scarcely the word: he was frantically on the go from first thing in the morning until he fell asleep at night. Watching Alex was a full-time job.

In time, the touching especially infuriated even the most tolerant and balanced of individuals, and his inability to control this caused the most discord. He simply could not resist the temptation to meddle with anything that caught his eye, especially if it was new or unfamiliar. He would go straight for it, as if it were a dangling piece of string before a playful kitten's eye. My son seemed totally unable to recognise the ownership of things by other people. Years later, it reminded me of an episode of *Star Trek* in which a super-powerful alien was causing havoc. Kirk, Spock and the crew of the *Enterprise* were powerless before it. The alien was about to do something to our sun, and the Earth and our solar system would have been destroyed. Kirk and the crew waited for death. Then with microseconds to spare, the voices of two even more powerful super-beings were heard: they were the parents of the creature. The punchline was that the mayhem had been caused by little more than a baby, equivalent to one of our toddlers; his parents had not yet taught him that other universes were 'out of bounds', that it was naughty to play around with other creatures' planets and suns.

My then prize possession, an expensive state-of-the-art quadraphonic music centre, was a magnet to Alex. He could not stop touching it. Talking to him or smacking his hand, I discovered, made little difference. When I was in the room, watching him closely, his burning desire to touch the machine could barely be contained, and as soon as I left he'd go straight to it. When I was out at work he would have a high old time. Finally he succeeded in breaking it. He shoved a screwdriver unceremoniously into its back: 'I was fixing it, Daddy.'

Friction and incidents that had occurred during the day sometimes spilled over into more disputes when I learned of them in the evening. I tried as best as I could to resolve these. You name it, I tried everything I could think of to make things work. I don't like to think of myself as an ogre, but I was firm where I felt strictness was required. In proportion to what I heard, I would respond accordingly, which meant that sometimes Alex did get smacked. Usually he was simply spoken to, softly or sternly. Sometimes he was not allowed to watch television, or deprived of something he liked to do or was playing with; sometimes he was sent to his room.

Alex's typical response, which will live with me *for ever*, was to act up. If he launched a 'spoiled brat' temper display, that would almost guarantee a smack from me. Somehow he learned that such displays didn't work too well with Daddy. They worked perfectly, however, in most other situations, enabling him to get his own way. He would pitch his outbursts to me perfectly: not outrageous enough to warrant a smack, but sufficiently annoying to guarantee a plea from his mother that whatever sanction I'd imposed be abandoned. I might have decided, for example, that he go to his room for 20 minutes. Alex would immediately start to cry and look to his mother for support with pitiful eyes, which demanded instant compassion and clemency, as he headed for the stairwell. If Sharon felt my punishment to be unjust, her reaction would soon be forthcoming. If she failed to respond, Alex would sit on the stairs or in his room and cry until she did. Sharon and I would sometimes become embroiled in an argument. That made me dig my heels in further and insist that the punishment remain in force.

It was Alex's outstanding ability to 'act up' that caused the greatest division between us. In those days, 90 per cent of the time Sharon seemed unable to see the reality of what he was doing. I felt frustrated because 90 per cent of the time I could. This exacerbated our differences in parenting. Our lack of unity served as fuel for more arguments. Intuitively Alex exploited, to his detriment, our inability to communicate. The whole process was quite fascinating in an odd sort of way. On reflection, I am still amazed at how simple and effective it was.

The pattern became established that if Alex couldn't get what he wanted he'd simply throw a temper tantrum. Some children seem to have a sixth sense for this; Alex had a seventh. When out in public, with strangers, friends or extended family, he soon played up. Invariably the results would be fighting if other children were involved; incessant crying, sobbing and fussing if responsible adults were around to take notice of him; or extracting sympathy from the adults with 'real' tears and insisting that he was genuinely hungry, or had a bad pain in his stomach, head, finger or some other part of his anatomy. These acts were so convincing that everyone responded. Eventually I learned to differentiate between Alex's little pantomimes and when he was in real distress. Sharon, like so many others, fell for his charm time and time again. Yes, he was utterly convincing. No responsible adult who did not know him extremely well could afford to ignore Alex's play-acting, thus he *always* got the attention he sought. Irresistible, too, was his cute little smile as he murmured, 'I *yuv* you, Mummy,' or, 'I *yuv* you, Daddy.' He would cry for an hour, or even two, for no other reason than being refused what he wanted. I am sure he sometimes forgot why he was crying in the first place.

Even today, privately, I silently stand in awe of Alex: his powers of manipulation are almost beyond belief – though now they are waning, especially the charm. At 3 years old he could get us to argue about almost anything. The irony of the situation was that I knew when we were being manipulated but couldn't stop it. I suppose our egos were just too big. Time and again I failed to prevent myself from being drawn into this negative cycle of events, but I was not alone. Alex has been able to divide even skilled professionals, sometimes into heated arguments. Naturally, Jason didn't stand a chance in figuring out what was going on. Thus unwittingly he too provided gallons of the fuel needed to keep family tensions running.

Yet insight into our family dynamics would be lopsided if I didn't highlight the amount of fun we shared in these early years. I'm sure at times we behaved more like four children than two adults and two children. I have vivid memories of such times. Every so often we would bundle into the car and go down to Petticoat Lane on a Sunday. After walking through the market we'd head straight for the Houndsditch Warehouse department store. There we'd usually check out the toys on the top floor. When it was the boys' turns for treats they never came away empty-handed. Sometimes on the way back they might even get an extra toy each: one that they'd seen on a market stall on the way to the Houndsditch.

Periodically, too, as the boys grew older we'd make trips to Toys 'R' Us in Wood Green's Shopping City. We played with them a lot. Often we went to the park and took them to the swings, slides and sandpit. We wrestled, played football and tickled each other silly. 'Tell us again, Mummy,' or, 'Tell us again, Daddy,' they'd beg as they eagerly waited for a favourite story to be repeated for the third or fourth time. We hugged and cuddled. Then sometimes out of the blue would come 'I love you' to whichever of us had captured that moment. But those precious occasions, many though they were, never lasted. They'd usually be spoiled before the day was out by another Alex incident, or there would be a fight between the two boys. Yet during those days the bonds of family love and parental affection were strongly cemented between us. Could they stand the test of time?

One of the most significant events in any child's life is when they start school or nursery. Thoughtful parents might prepare for this major development by engendering in the child a positive attitude. They might encourage a love of books by reading stories aloud, teach them happily to memorise the alphabet, mix them with older children who speak positively about school. The general idea is to help the child to look forward to it and enjoy the process of learning. Sharon and I did some of the above but half-heartedly, not in a planned or purposeful way. As it turned out, nursery school brought a new dimension to the difficulties of managing Alex, though we didn't fully realise this immediately. Up to this point, with the exception of a few childminders, coping with him had been mainly a family affair. That situation was about to change dramatically.

From the first day that Alex attended nursery school there were problems. When Sharon arrived to collect him, after just a few hours' attendance, she was confronted by teachers who told her that he had been involved in several scraps with different children. As time passed there were continual complaints about his behaviour. At first it was generally thought that he would adjust and eventually settle down, but this did not happen. Staff who watched him carefully noted he was a happy child, yet Alex was always in conflict with the other children. Primarily it was his old problem of taking their toys and, when challenged, fighting for them. He did not understand the concept of taking turns or sharing very well. The staff were concerned at the power of his attacks, which sometimes harmed the other children quite seriously. Whatever their sex or size, if angered

Alex would lash out and hit them just the same. Several other parents became angry, and disagreements arose between them and Sharon.

Some of the children were obviously frightened of Alex and avoided playing with him; others made complaints – repeatedly. Some staff came to dislike Alex; others kept a strict but caring eye on him. To maintain peace in the classroom they would attempt to remove him from any contentious situation. When this proved too difficult, some would simply give him the toy in question. Children who avoided Alex formed their own groups and excluded him, but he did not like this and would thrust himself upon them. He was quite unable to grasp his unpopularity, or why some hit him and others reported him to the teacher. Soon there were several groups closed to him, so he created his own.

Wherever Alex has been in school, there have usually been one or two other over-boisterous children like him, displaying similar but often less extreme characteristics. Like magnets, unavoidably they'd gravitate towards each other. Rough playing or fighting would ensue. A pecking order would be established. Alex, insofar as I could see, only ever understood that order when he was top dog. A state of either permanent compliance or permanent opposition would develop. Allegiances or enmities were formed. Alex was the one child who never gave in until he was top.

Whatever group he attached himself to or formed developed into one of generally unruly behaviour if it hadn't been so already. Teachers found him difficult to control; some kids found him difficult to get on with, others exciting. Unfortunately, this pattern would recur throughout his school life, but at the time it went largely unrecognised by teachers. Yet not all the incidents blossomed into fights. The vast majority of complaints were about his continually teasing and annoying other children. At this stage, no one suggested finding a way to arrest this process. Why should they? Alex was a 4-year-old child. So the whole negative cycle gained momentum and his power base now extended beyond the home.

When Alex was still at nursery school I started to notice the negative effect some television programmes were having on his behaviour.

Until then I'd considered prime-time TV to be mostly harmless fun and entertainment, but I began to change my mind and note with concern what avid viewers my sons had become. It wasn't some X-rated film that changed my thinking, but noticing the opposite effects that two very popular programmes had on Alex. These were *The A-Team* and *The Incredible Hulk*.

After watching *The A-Team*, the boys would re-enact the fight scenes. Alex modelled himself on the tough-guy character Mr. T. Fairly typical boyish reactions, you might say. But when items of furniture were broken, or thrown around the room, it was time to start worrying, especially as the boys' play-fights sometimes erupted into real ones. However, *The Hulk* had no adverse after-effect on Jason; not so in the case of Alex. It provided Sharon and me with our first evidence of Alex's showing genuine fear. He was absolutely petrified. He became stiff, frozen with terror, and gripped on to his mother or me, whoever was nearer, for dear life whenever Dr Banner changed into the Green Monster. His grip was agonising and desperate, and there he clung, motionless, until the monster disappeared. Yet contradictorily he always wanted to watch the programme.

With hindsight it is easy to see how damaging those programmes must have been to Alex. While *The A-Team* was on he was tough; during *The Hulk*, he was abject with fright. It took several months for me to voice my disquiet. In fact, for a while Sharon and I would threaten Alex with *The Hulk* when he misbehaved: instant improvement was guaranteed. Jason, however, did so just for fun, which would make his brother let out an urgent, frenzied scream. At last we'd found an effective weapon to use when he was naughty. 'The Hulk is going to get you if you don't behave, Alex,' Sharon or I would say.

After realising how terrified Alex in fact was, we stopped doing this, but I'd still allow him to watch both programmes as an easy alternative to avoiding another argument. Please remember that these were prime-time TV programmes aimed particularly at children. Millions of them looked forward to watching every week. And, despite his terror, Alex awaited *The Hulk* with eager anticipation. Not wanting to appear a killjoy, I joined the family unless I had something better to do. Alex eventually grew out of his fear when he realised that the monster couldn't get him.

The contrast between the boys' addiction to television and their strong aversion to anything even remotely academic was striking. The same children who could remain still and memorise TV scenes verbatim seemed unable to sit down with a book for more than a few minutes. Storytelling they could tolerate, but when it came to reading or writing themselves, forget it: this was almost a no-go area. This behaviour was more pronounced in Alex. Eventually Jason began to make slow but steady progress, although it was always difficult for him to discipline his mind. He had a distinct tendency towards daydreaming. As time wore on, however, Sharon and I became acutely frustrated in our attempts to tutor Alex.

For example, if a word began with the letter 'T', Alex might pronounce it with an 'F' or a 'W' sound. There was no rhyme or reason; he simply said whatever first came into his head. He did eventually learn his alphabet but developed a slight stutter, apart from which he spoke clearly. He did not appear to comprehend the correlation between the memorised letters of the alphabet and the phonetic sound each letter represented. Even when he was 9 or 10, he'd simply make a random guess at the words. We were frustrated but we never gave up entirely. In time we did succeed in also teaching him to count, read and write – but it wasn't easy.

My description of the boys' academic abilities might make it appear that they were backward, but this is not accurate and their teachers assured us this was not the case. Even some of those who disliked Alex described him as bright. Both boys were of at least average intelligence. Some said Alex was very bright. The problem was that neither seemed particularly interested in being educated. Alex preferred to misbehave and Jason to daydream. Later I became convinced that there was a link between the educational process and Alex's problems. Why else would such an intelligent child underachieve? Why would he behave socially in such an unacceptable manner?

In some ways, the person who was coming off worst in our family was Jason, with so much attention being centred on Alex. As the younger, Alex would quite often be given the benefit of the doubt when they quarrelled, which naturally made Jason resentful. A weird mixture of strong sibling rivalry, love and the need to be with one another prevailed between the brothers. Jason's character did not allow him wilfully to smash Alex's toys as Alex did his, so he had to find other ways in which to be spiteful. Realising that Alex was often in trouble, he would instinctively, when he felt the need, involve his brother in something naughty in the guise of play and be pretty certain that Sharon would believe him when he carefully laid the blame on Alex. Before long, Alex learned to reverse the system, and it was Jason who got blamed for Alex's deeds and earned retribution.

The only person who was able to get an objective inside view of our family dynamics at the time was my cousin Cyril. He was studying to be a chartered accountant and asked whether he could stay with us for a few weeks after he ran into accommodation problems. In the end he stayed for several months and, being an intelligent and thoughtful man, tried never to take sides when a row blew up between Sharon and me over Alex. But about four or five months into his stay, some incident with Alex at the centre had caused yet another family storm that had ended with Sharon upset, Jason upset, Alex upset and myself upset; yet within an hour Alex had done exactly the same thing as if nothing at all had happened previously. Cyril shook his head in despair and, taking advantage of the lull in hostilities, declared: 'This child will be the death of you two.' He continued, without allowing time for a reply, 'The seven devils that jumped out of Mary must have jumped into Alex when he was born.'

Cyril was not the type given to making sensationalist, superstitious remarks, and Sharon was privately disturbed by his comment. He must have felt very dubious and sceptical about Alex's future, but didn't wish to hurt our feelings by dwelling on his fears. At the time I didn't take much notice, but when Cyril left us I realised he was the one person who shared my view that there was something seriously amiss. Nearly every other member of our families insisted he would grow out of his outlandish behaviour, or contended that there was absolutely nothing strange in his behaviour at all.

It was easy to understand how Alex annoyed others or made them angry, especially as he got older. The complaints of adults came in thick and fast. His peers were naturally even less tolerant. Alex would fight them for their own toys, play with them, break them and, as he got older, take the toys home. We would dutifully return or replace them if broken. To complicate things further, Alex didn't appear able to differentiate mentally between small and larger children. Physically he knew the difference, but when it came to conflicts size did not deter him. He would, without thought, attempt to hit or fight an 8- or 9-year-old when he was only 3 or 4. On the other hand, he would not hesitate to hit a smaller child. His responses were very immature. Even if a baby wanted a toy Alex was playing with, that baby had better think again, for there was no way Alex would be giving it up unless he wanted to.

Painful as it was at times, I could not stop family and friends chiming in with their pennyworth of comments. Cuttings remarks stab at the heart of most parents when they are directed against their child. Unfortunately, Alex hardly ever failed to provoke them. Time after time he would be found pushing, fighting, biting, kicking, scratching his cousins and friends. Retaliation by the older children, or admonishment from adults, didn't deter him for long. The next conflict would probably occur later the same day. Wherever children were gathered, Alex would become overexcited and put himself, and us, right in it – again, and again, and again.

It seemed that he wasn't able to learn how to handle peer-group associations, yet being with other children was what he craved most. Everything would start off all right, then deteriorate rapidly. When away from other children and calm, he was absolutely adorable and always a pleasure to be with: a good companion. Relatively few people had the opportunity to experience this side of Alex, but those who have still hold a soft spot for him for this very reason.

When socialising, other parents nearest to Alex when something happened would sometimes revile him worse than if he were a dog. At other times they managed to contain themselves but only just: if you'd pricked them with a pin, I'm sure they'd have burst. With fury written all over their faces, some would march up to us to register their complaint. A relative might catch hold of him and smack him. How that could infuriate, when Sharon or I would never dream of smacking their child. Sometimes we wanted to lash back and point out that their children weren't perfect either. In fact, one of their little darlings may have started the fracas, but nine times out of ten Alex got the blame. So we'd try to keep him by our side – a hard thing for any child, but especially for one who couldn't sit still for five minutes. We'd hope he would sense the hostility directed against him and get the message, but he rarely did. Heartbreaking it was too, for sometimes Alex in his innocence would try to play with the very adult who, moments before, had shooed him away. Many times Sharon or I would look over, even in a crowded room, and see some parent chiding their child for playing with Alex. When they caught our gaze they would blush or fake a smile at us, so we'd sometimes make excuses and cut visits short.

In time, some kept their distance. We knew it was because of Alex. It used to amaze me how insensitive they could be. Most cutting were the remarks that were made in jest as well as in anger. 'If that boy was my child I would . . .' 'Why don't you send him back home?' 'If I had him for just one week, he'd be a different child.' 'What that child needs is a good . . .' 'When he grows up, send him into the army.' 'Just leave him with me for six months . . .'

Everyone seemed to have an opinion, but no formal debate about Alex had yet taken place. People were already divided: was he blatantly bad or could he help himself? Some blamed us, imagining his outrageous behaviour was encouraged at home. Others felt that all Alex needed was a good beating: 'That'll soon sort him out.' One believed that 'Alex is cleverer than all of you; he knows what he's doing'; that he was simply a manipulative, spoiled little brat, 'rotten to the core'.

So it came as no real surprise to us when Alex would complain that so-and-so had hit him, but we couldn't have an argument with them all. We usually tried to weigh up whatever Alex had said, in case he *was* being manipulative, and tried to mitigate problems wherever we could in a sort of damage-limitation exercise. But we're talking real life here and that wouldn't always work out. However, where we could make changes we did. Childminders, for instance, while not complaining wildly about Alex, had increasingly commented on his over-boisterousness when playing with younger children and animals. Eventually, primarily concerned for Alex, Sharon decided not to go out to work until he was old enough for full-time school.

Yet Alex also had his champions. 'Leave the boy alone; he's all right.' 'I like Alex; he's my kind of boy – take him or leave him.' 'There's nothing wrong with this boy; he's just lively.' 'You think Alex is bad: you should have seen me when I was a boy. I gave my old lady hell.' 'That boy is special. All the girls are going to like him.' 'He's so clever; he's really bright.' 'Give me Alex – any day!'

It was during these times that Sharon became Alex's public defender: her maternal instinct made her fiercely loyal. In the school setting this sometimes led her into conflict with parents and teachers. More and more I began to blame her for Alex's behaviour, while she blamed me. She thought I did not properly appreciate that Alex was only a little boy; that I was too strict and inflexible, and didn't show my son enough love. She believed Alex would grow out of his naughty behaviour and never viewed him in terms of being ill. After all, I had been a handful as a child, she'd remind me, and I'd changed; Alex would do the same. I observed how easily Alex could manipulate his mother.

I later came to believe that failure to break this deadlock was perhaps the greatest disservice we did to our son. I bitterly regret this. Relentlessly we held to our respective views and poor Alex became a casualty partly on our account. Intuitively, he had been subconsciously manipulating this deadlock between his mother and myself – I suspect probably before he could even walk or talk. Wherever he went he was always the centre of attention and he seemed to thrive on it. There was always someone bawling or shouting at him: is it any wonder Sharon became his public defender? Somebody had to, as I wasn't always sympathetic when he misbehaved.

Like Teflon, everything seemed to slide right off Alex and often we were left far more distressed. But even then I knew he must be hurting badly somewhere, deep down. Occasionally we'd get a hint of that pain, as if we'd caught him off guard, pondering his plight. Then he'd see us, look at us and smile – and his pain appeared to vanish. He had a sparkling enthusiasm that no one could damp down, an immense energy that no one could contain. His behaviour was not typical, and yet it was so close to normal that anyone not used to him, or meeting him for the first time, would think he was a little overexcitable – that's all. My apprehensiveness about him often left me out on a limb.

After the curling-tong incident, I knew something was wrong but had no idea what. I didn't know where to turn. I often felt frustrated and confused. My mother believed that Alex had inherited some of my father's traits, as he also used to fight a lot when he was young. If inheritance was the answer, I thought, why wasn't I like Alex? I had been a rough kid, but I hadn't give my family anything like this much aggro. Alex appeared to be in a league of his own. I could dismiss everyone else's comments as inconsequential; but why did Cyril, whom I respected, talk about devils? Could such a thing happen? Was Alex mentally ill? There was no premeditated malice in his actions: he'd simply do whatever came to mind. So many questions, and no answers. There had to be a more logical explanation, I thought . . . Thus went many a tête-à-tête with myself.

I tried to discuss the matter rationally with Sharon, without arguing, but our opinions still differed. I suggested we take Alex to our doctor to get a letter of referral to a psychiatrist. Sharon hotly opposed the suggestion. In pursuit of a quiet life I dropped the subject. Nevertheless, inwardly I remained deeply concerned about the eccentric behaviour of my younger son. Family opinion was stacked heavily against me, so I did not bother to seek medical advice. After all, Alex was only 4 years old.

Three

Alex was a handful, but he was still containable. Paradoxically, I did and yet didn't consider his behaviour to be an insurmountable problem. Had I felt it to be truly so, I'm sure I would have made stronger attempts to do something about it. It was as if on one level I sensed that my son had some serious problems, and yet on another I tried to ignore them since he was only a little boy. And on this latter level I hoped, like everybody else, that he'd simply grow out of it. I certainly hadn't contemplated that his unruliness was of sufficient severity to make me give up work. Perish the thought. I was trying to build up a garage repair business – a noble enough goal – and the whole family would benefit. So I had no scruples whatsoever about leaving Sharon, childminders, nursery, infant school and relations to cope. In fact it was sometimes a relief to be at work, and now and then I would think, 'Bliss at last.' I suppose many a husband has at some time had similar thoughts.

Although working for myself gave me greater freedom than when I'd been an employee, it also brought additional responsibilities, the chief of which was to get customers' vehicles mended speedily. That's what paid the bills and put bread on the table. If this required that I work late, then so be it. Sometimes work was slack and then in would come a customer with a five-hour job, two hours before I was due to go home. If I hadn't made enough that week it wasn't easy to turn up my nose at a chance to earn a few needed pounds, even if it inconvenienced me and my family. Sharon was sometimes far from pleased with me for working late. 'Why can't women understand that sometimes a man just has to work?' were my thoughts on such occasions. The only way round this dilemma was to let Sharon and the kids come to the garage. It's one of the advantages of being your own boss: no one can sack you. So it was that on some evenings and Saturdays my family came to work.

As business picked up, Sharon and the boys increasingly had the choice of either staying at home until I came in late, or coming to the garage to wait until I'd finished working. Hobson's choice, I know, but it was the best I could come up with. Sometimes it was the boys' behaviour that prompted Sharon to come, not a desire to be at the garage, and the children usually looked forward to it because for them it was more exciting. On several occasions Sharon rolled up her sleeves, put on a pair of overalls and insisted on helping in any way she could. It was during one of these sessions that Sharon and I were first forced seriously to consider an unsettling aspect of Alex's personality which hitherto had been spoken of only jokingly or in unhelpful speculation.

It was a Saturday, and I was under pressure to finish some work for my taxi-cab customers. The garage was unusually messy, with black grease and grime everywhere. We'd been busy that week and had not had time to clean up. It was not a good idea to leave the boys unattended in the office, because on previous occasions Alex had managed to break the typewriter and other delicate items of our meagre office furnishings. The only other clean space in the garage was in the back of one of the customers' cabs where they could amuse themselves with their toys.

From where Sharon and I were working we could hear the boys, and every five or ten minutes one of us would go and see what they were doing. On one occasion I'd barely returned to my bench when there was a loud crash of breaking glass. Sharon and I stopped working immediately. Our hearts pounded as we raced over to the taxi fearing the worst, that either or both children were horribly cut and covered in blood. We had no idea what could have happened but presumed they'd been fighting. Seconds later we saw there was no blood and both sons were fortunately intact, but the sliding glass panel in the cab that separates the driver from the passengers was shattered.

'What happened, Alex? What happened, Jason?' we shouted.

Alex remained silent with his mouth open.

'What happened, Jason?' I repeated.

Then came the most ridiculous reply I had ever received in my life: the kind that makes you doubt if you have heard correctly. In a soft voice Jason said, 'Alex touched the glass and it exploded.'

Almost before he had finished I interjected: 'What? You mean he hit the glass – and it broke?'

'No, Daddy!' Jason replied. 'Alex touched the glass with his finger and it exploded.'

Sharon and I stood there gobsmacked, looking at each other. A shiver went through us as similar thoughts rushed into our minds: Were Cyril or the others right? Did our son have a devil in him? Had something supernatural happened? We looked at Alex's innocent face, and then again at each other. Both of us remained silent in fear and disbelief.

For a brief moment it was like a weird scene from a horror film in which everything seemed to move in slow motion after Jason had said 'exploded'. We were trapped within a bubble of time, the four of us knew something odd had happened. Realising it was still our son passively sitting there and not some other being, Sharon asked Alex again: 'What happened?'

'I touched the glass, Mummy, and it broke,' he said, with a mixture of surprise and innocence.

Calmly, and in a low voice, I enquired, 'Show me how you touched the glass, son.'

'Like this, Daddy.' Alex gently touched another panel of glass with the index finger of his left hand.

Phew! Nothing happened! That panel did not explode. Sharon and I again looked at each other, this time breathing deep sighs of relief.

Make of it what you will. Neither Sharon nor I could offer an explanation for the mess we saw. Cube-shaped pieces of glass were everywhere. There were no cuts or bruises on either child. They had not been fighting. They had no metal implements or sharp toys that could have broken the window; there was no toy missing. They had not left the cab.

At the time of the incident I'd been working on black cabs for over ten years. In all that time I'd seen hundreds of taxis in various states of disrepair, but I'd never seen the partition glass broken on one that had not been involved in a road accident. Those panels, which slide open only about four inches to enable conversation between passenger and driver, are quite strong. Days later, when I'd had time to reflect, I decided that Alex must have moved the sliding panel very hard and broken it, but when I tried to repeat this action using a good deal of force, I found the glass impossible to smash. Without explaining why, I had several other mechanics attempt it too and none succeeded. So how did a 4-year-old boy shatter that glass panel? Not a single piece had been left in the groove.

I was forced to consider whether my son possessed some sort of supernatural power. I tend to be a middle ground man: someone who would rather listen to another side of an argument than rush off to form hasty opinions. Though I believe there are many things we do not understand about our world, and supernatural forces may indeed exist, I'd never before experienced anything like this. When Sharon and I heard that bang, followed closely by the crash of glass, we were at the taxi in seconds but we didn't see the event – only its aftermath. So we could never be sure what had really happened.

It was not something one could easily forget, and the serious question still remains unanswered: was the shattering of that partition glass an accident or a supernatural phenomenon? You can imagine, family and friends gave their views both for and against the notion of something spooky, but I tried to cope with the dilemma by shelving it in the back of my mind, though it kept coming to the fore and I remained disquieted by it. Sharon wanted to forget about the whole episode and pretend it had never happened. But a few months later, for me, questions about the paranormal came back into sharp focus.

It had been a typical Saturday evening at home. The family was lounging in front of the television. The boys had their usual rounds of playing, annoying each other and watching TV. Every so often they would get a little overexcited, go too far and get a bit rough with one another, and would thus earn themselves a light ticking off from Sharon or me. Eventually they were warned that they might be sent to bed if they continued.

Jason's ability to heed admonitions was akin to that of the average child who is able to realise when his or her parents are serious. Alex, however, was only able to do so for brief periods; soon he'd forget. A sharp object struck Jason on the side of his head. As if a coiled spring had been suddenly released, he shot into the air with an ear-piercing screech, and jumped up and down in excruciating pain – startling the four of us out of the relative quiet of that moment. His tears and screams flowed freely as he rubbed the side of his head intensely, trying to relieve the pain. Alex had gone too far. I smacked him and sent him upstairs to bed. He protested and cried to arouse his mother's sympathy, but on this occasion she was equally disgusted with his behaviour and did not go after him. When he realised he was not attracting any attention, and that Sharon and I were not arguing about him, he stopped crying after about 15 minutes.

This prompted a change of tack and I went upstairs to see him. There, trying to fall asleep, was a vision of a serene, beautiful little boy lying in the lower bunk bed. I looked at him and my heart melted. He was completely transformed from that aggressive, wild child of a few minutes ago. I picked him up and cuddled him. This was in no way unusual for me, but I would seldom do it so soon after he had been naughty. I'd always believed that that would give him confusing signals, though my heart frequently yearned to show him affection when I had to be firm. Traditionally I'd reserve such tenderness for when we played, or when he'd made a positive effort to obey some request or instruction; and, of course, for when he was reasonably behaved. But on this occasion I broke my usual pattern and sat in the tatty armchair in the boys' room with him snuggled up against me.

Demonstrating my love, concern and deep affection for my son, my voice quivered as I asked, 'Son, Daddy doesn't understand! Please tell me why you do the naughty things. I want to understand. Daddy loves you, son, and Daddy doesn't want to smack you, so why do you do the bad things?'

Alex looked me in the eye, and from the comfort and safety of my arms he slowly and softly said, 'Daddy, I don't want to do naughty things.'

'Then why do you do them, son? Do you like to be told off, or sent to your room, or smacked?'

'It's the bones, Daddy!'

'The bones?' I repeated with surprise.

'The bones keep knocking in my head, Daddy.' Then he continued, 'I don't want to do naughty things, Daddy, but when the bones touch, that's when I do them.'

'I don't understand what you mean by bones, son,' I said, wishing he could elaborate.

'Daddy, if the bones don't touch, I don't do naughty things. But when they bang against each other they go "CLANG CAL-ULANG" and I do naughty things.'

I was utterly unprepared for this revelation and was deeply touched by it. I comforted my son and hugged him even tighter. 'Never mind, son, never mind. If the bones are going to "knock" again, son, you must tell Daddy – OK?'

'OK,' Alex said, clearly relieved he'd explained his problem to me.

For the next half hour or so I stayed upstairs until he fell asleep on my lap. After tucking him back in bed, I went down and, when Jason had gone up too, told Sharon what Alex had said. Quietly we sat and deliberated as to what he could have meant by 'the bones', but failed to see how we could pursue the matter further. Hot on the heels of the glass incident, the notion of our son possessing some supernatural power no longer seemed so far-fetched. And did all this explain his burning his face with hot tongs and not crying?

I know now that Alex had been attempting to tell me what was wrong with him, but there seemed no way to interpret his words meaningfully. And he never did tell me that the 'bones' had knocked again, though his episodes of extreme antisocial behaviour gained even greater momentum when he turned 5 and went to infant school.

'School-days are the happiest days of your life.' I'd hoped those words would prove true for Alex: as if to say that going to school in itself would miraculously make a difference, and that mixing with teachers and other children would somehow straighten him out. My simple optimism may have been misguided, but there is something about us human beings that makes us shy away from the unpleasant realities, hoping that our worst fears will not be realised. So when work-time came I switched off from home life, and it was easy for me to expect the teachers to switch on to the educational issues involving my son and deal with them. Isn't that what schoolteachers are supposed to do?

So what of happy school-days for Alex? I'd be very surprised if the majority of staff at his nursery school were not overjoyed when they no longer had to cope with him. Needless to say his reputation had gone before him to our local infant school, which Jason already attended, but as I knew in my heart of hearts and as the school was about to discover, no amount of advance warning could truly prepare anyone for Alex. They needed to experience him first-hand.

Throughout the summer holidays Alex knew, because it had been firmly etched on to his brain, that whenever the time came for Jason to go to school he'd be going too. So he couldn't understand why, when the day came, Jason was going to school without him. Sharon thought the matter had been resolved when she explained to him that he'd be starting the next day with all the other new children. She had duly taken Jason to school, then she and Alex returned home, and since she wasn't feeling very well she went upstairs to lie down. At about 10 a.m. I received a phone call from a panic-stricken Sharon. A neighbour had rung the doorbell to alert her that the street door was open. Then she had realised Alex was nowhere in sight. I told her I'd come home at once, but no sooner had we hung up than the school phoned Sharon to tell her Alex was there. They asked her to collect him.

It transpired that Alex had taken his mother's door keys while she dozed, put on his shoes and coat, and determinedly walked to school. Although Alex might be praised by some for his enthusiastic initiative, at the time it was frightening for us. He had had to cross a busy road which, before and after school, was supervised by a lollipop lady. Fortunately he negotiated the crossing successfully and unaided. Not for one moment did he consider the possible consequences of his impulsiveness: he simply did whatever gripped his mind.

Of course daily incidents followed. He enjoyed playing with the other children at school, but hadn't learned how to do so acceptably. After many complaints the headmistress found it simpler to keep him with her at the first sign of trouble. Being sent to the head teacher was supposed to be the ultimate sanction, but this happened so often that she began to give him little jobs to do, and thus unwittingly turned what should have been a punishment into a privilege. Such was the effect of Alex's charm.

Around this time, Sharon and I decided to try to use a childminder again. She wanted to return to work and someone would be needed to take the children to and from school, and look after them until about 6 p.m. We tried to learn from the concerns expressed by previous childminders, and ruled out those who had very young children or animals because of Alex's tendency to play too roughly. Eventually a woman was recommended who had two children, a boy and a girl, slightly older than ours, but the arrangement came to an abrupt end when she accused Alex of 'leading her children astray'.

Sharon was just settling into her new job. It seemed unfair that she should lose it so we agreed I would change my work routine to take and collect the boys from school. Depending on how pressurised I was at work, I'd either go home with them or straight back to the garage to finish off a job.

As the months went by complaints about Alex's general unruliness from teachers and parents became stronger, and any hoped-for settling down did not materialise. Sometimes, when I was collecting the boys in the afternoon, children waylaid me to relate what Alex had supposedly done to them earlier that day; at other times it was their parents. He would vociferously contest these accusations, offering his version of what he claimed the other child(ren) had done to him. He seemed to have an excuse and answer for everything; nothing was ever his fault. And yes, when given a fair hearing sometimes Alex was completely exonerated, but mostly not. On one occasion, as I parked my car I caught him red-handed when I saw him run over from one side of the playground to the other and kick another boy in the back. Alex had not seen me, and the lad had simply been standing with his sister, waiting for their parents to collect them. The attack was completely unprovoked. Teachers claimed Alex often did such things. Virtually every school-day for his two years in the infants, Alex was involved in one sort of dispute or another. By the end of that time he had earned the reputation of being a bully, unsociable and acutely disruptive in class.

To me it was as if Alex believed subconsciously that he ruled the school; that from the moment Sharon or I deposited him and left he was in control. He was in his element and without a watchful father he could do virtually as he pleased. And he did! Generally speaking, his teachers were no match for him in that they were easy to manipulate. He quickly discovered ways to frustrate them, including the head teacher, using his usual technique of playing one party off against the other. Occasionally he'd undergo a beating from an older child, but mainly Alex got his own way.

The escapist bliss I'd sought at work was a mirage. Just as a thick dawn fog loses its battle under the blistering attack of a determined morning sun, so my mist of peace was quickly to disappear. Increasingly I'd get phone calls at work about Alex's behaviour, some of them from the school. Thus, even at work, Sharon and I were constantly worrying and fretting over Alex. But the bulk of the pressure fell on me, for I was always contactable (so much for the joys of running your own business). I became increasingly frustrated by this, and resentful: getting in touch with me in a crisis or out of sheer frustration became the norm for almost anyone involved in Alex's care.

As the years passed I somehow evolved into the ultimate weapon or saction that many people would use against my son: 'If you don't behave yourself, I'm going to tell your dad.' The pressure on me became almost unbearable. It was as if Alex respected no one but me. Many sons dote on their father but Alex's admiration seemed exceptional. In his world, no other authority seemed to exist. I didn't engineer this, appreciate it or pander to it. On the contrary, from day one I had tried to instil a proper sense of respect for other people and their property in both my children. For all that, it was as if I alone could reach parts of Alex's brain that no one else could. The connection between us seemed almost uncanny. It was something stronger than any normal bond – as if we were sympathetic twins. I did not like this 'ultimate-weapon' status that had been thrust upon me, but what could I do? I was his father. The buck stopped with me and I had to bear my responsibilities.

I couldn't stop loving my child, although I was unable to tolerate some of the things he did. Sharon and I tried our utmost to ensure that he experienced the good things in life too – not purely in material terms, but also in giving of ourselves to both children to make them feel loved and secure within the family. We made every possible attempt to teach Alex the lesson that if he behaved nicely, others would be nicer to him. When Sharon or I had those positive one-to-one moments with him – and there were many – he seemed to understand and always promised to behave better. But it was as if something consistently prevented him from sustaining any kindness.

Swimming had become a weekly routine. The boys looked forward to it each Saturday and it gave me an opportunity to make myself available exclusively to them. From time to time, however, I had to exclude Alex as a form of punishment. One such day was when he teased an overweight girl of about 12 until she burst into tears and left the pool. My response to Alex was: 'If she is going home, you are going home too.' I was upset that the girl, who had done nothing to him, should lose out because of my son. The price paid was that we all lost out – very unfair to Jason, as he himself protested. Another day ruined!

The girl's mother complained to me that it had taken her two years of encouragement and coaxing to get her daughter to go swimming again because of previous cruel jokes by insensitive children like Alex. I'd asked him to leave the girl alone but he ignored me, as he sometimes did in public places. Later, on the way home, he remained unrepentant and still found the whole episode terribly funny, even after I'd explained to him what the mother had said. He was unable to grasp the unkindness of his actions, that he'd unjustly hurt someone, and so I banned him from swimming for the next two weeks. Sometimes I was at my wits' end as to how best to cope with each incident.

As mentioned earlier, neither Jason nor Alex took well to academic study, but Jason had developed a love of drawing; he was comfortable with that. His efforts were always considered to be good and frequently earned him praise. This made Alex feel distinctly neglected and he eagerly sought similar praise for himself, so whenever Jason began to draw, Alex too would put pen or pencil to paper. The difference, however, was that what he produced consistently distressed me, though I did not make this obvious.

He was unaware that the pictures he drew were the ugliest I'd ever seen produced by a child. Most children between the ages of 5 and 7, if asked to draw a picture of a man or woman, will attempt to make some representation, no matter how peculiar or vague. Even if it is only a 'matchstick' effigy, it will be distinguishable by its dress, long hair or a moustache perhaps. Some feature will tell you whether it is intended to be male or female. Not so with Alex! What he drew seemed to me to be sexless: monstrous outlines of faces with no features other than two eyes set wide apart. I found them deeply disturbing.

He'd never take more than a few minutes to draw his pictures, while Jason devotedly laboured away. Alex's pictures resembled the face of a whale when viewed straight from the front with its body not visible. It is difficult for me to describe them, but to me they were horrible. From the time he progressed beyond scribbles, the sketches remained the same. Very gradually the monstrous features became less pronounced, and Alex's portrayals began to take a more human shape; but still only comparable to those of a much younger child. 'That's Mummy,' or, 'That's Jason,' or, 'There's the man,' he'd say. Try as we might, we could rarely see any similarity. Sometimes we'd catch him murmuring happily to himself while he drew, as very young children often do. It was the repetitiveness of the drawings that struck me and increased their impact, especially when he tried to explain them. Unsettling myself further, I'd often think: 'If this is what Alex "sees", then something must really be wrong.' For documentary purposes I wish I'd saved one.

Sometimes I simply shook my head in the privacy of my own thoughts as Cyril's words leaped back to my mind. They didn't seem quite so far-fetched now. But all this pales into insignificance compared to Alex's most dangerous exploit that year.

Friday evening was the one evening of the week that I regarded as my own. I would normally go to the kick-boxing gym for a workout. While I was going through my routine the phone rang. This in itself was not an unusual event, but when one of the lads shouted, 'Ches, it's for you,' I immediately feared something must be wrong. Naturally my thoughts went straight to Alex.

It did not seem too serious when I heard Sharon say, 'Ches! Alex has fallen off his bicycle and hurt his leg.' She wanted my opinion as to whether she should take him to casualty. I felt relieved, reasoning that the injury could not be that bad if she was so unsure. She explained what had happened.

'I was on the phone speaking to Marva and told her I must go because I could hear Alex fussing in the garden.' She had found Alex lying on the ground with his bike near by. Both boys told her that Alex had been riding his bicycle, and fallen off and hurt himself. He was lying on the concreted section of the garden near to the door, whimpering slightly but not crying. Sharon asked to see his hurt leg. His left shin was slightly swollen and reddened. Having decided the injury was not serious, Sharon declared: 'That serves you right for playing so roughly. Now get up and come inside.' When Alex replied, 'I can't walk, Mummy,' Sharon's first thought was that this was another attention-seeking ploy. When he didn't move she picked him up and carried him upstairs and placed him on the settee. An hour later he was still whimpering and quite obviously in pain. That's when she rang me. I told her she was the person on the spot to assess the true nature of the problem. If she was uncomfortable about it I suggested she drive him to casualty and I'd join them later. If not, we'd take him to our doctor in the morning if he didn't seem better.

Usually on these Friday evenings when I was at the gym, Sharon and the boys visited her parents. That's what she'd been discussing with her sister, in among their usual chit-chat. She decided to go ahead and visit her mother while keeping a special eye on Alex. He said he wanted to see his grandmother and demonstrated his enthusiasm by limping around, but when Sharon's mum saw Alex's leg she ordered him to be taken to hospital at once. So Marva and her son, Alex's gran, Sharon and Jason all escorted him to casualty.

Unaware of this I got home about 10.30 p.m. and settled down to wait for their return. After several hours Alex was finally seen, and Sharon and the boys returned in the early hours of Saturday morning. After the boys were tucked in bed, Sharon explained how the boys had told her mum and sister and the nurse the same story she'd told me earlier on the phone. In due course, Alex's leg was X-rayed, then they waited for him to be seen by a doctor. Again he told the same story.

The X-ray showed Alex had sustained a serious fracture to his shin. The doctor was convinced that such a fracture could not possibly have been caused by such a fall. He returned to the cubicle and looked Alex straight in the eye: 'Alex, you did not receive this injury by falling off your bike, did you? Now tell me, son, what really happened?'

Maybe it was the towering authority figure of a doctor in a white coat, or the excruciating pain he was feeling, but six hours after the event Alex finally told the truth: 'Jason told me to jump out of the window – so I jumped.' I was stunned, but allowed Sharon to continue. I could hardly wait for morning to come to question the boys myself.

To understand the implications of this event you need to visualise the layout of our house. It was built on three storeys, the bedrooms on the upper floor, the lounge and bathroom in the middle, and kitchen and dining room on the ground floor. The kitchen door led to a concreted area about six feet by fifteen. The rest of the small garden was lawn. The telephone was in the hall next to the stairs between the entrance to the dining room and kitchen.

The boys had been playing with their bicycles in the garden. Sharon was in the lounge watching television when her sister telephoned. They'd become absorbed in conversation, only to be interrupted by the need to call in Alex for misbehaviour. He was sent upstairs to the lounge. Sharon continued on the phone; Jason remained in the garden. The boys now talked through the partly open window. Soon Jason was exploiting his advantage by teasing Alex. He was out in the garden with the bikes, and Alex was stuck upstairs. He asked his mother whether he could return to the garden. She said yes, on condition he promise to behave. However, within minutes Alex was in trouble again and Sharon had to call him back in. Vigorously protesting, stamping his feet and crying, he had to be returned bodily to the lounge. Sharon resumed her conversation with her sister. Alex interrupted them three more times, requesting then demanding to go back outside. Sharon was adamant and back upstairs he was sent. Jason continued to taunt Alex through the window, a fact of which Sharon was unaware. Jason told him he could fly out like Superman (their all-time favourite film hero) and goaded him into doing so. Realising he could not get past his mother, Alex promptly climbed out of the window and 'flew' – straight on to the concrete slab below. It was a drop of about ten feet. He could easily have sustained brain damage or broken his neck had he struck his head. Maybe the pain didn't register straight away.

Oblivious to her offspring's shenanigans, Sharon continued with her telephone conversation. Jason managed to persuade Alex to say he had fallen off his bicycle. Alex agreed, knowing he was also in the wrong for climbing out of the window. It was not until several minutes after the event that Sharon, alerted by the whimpering, went to see what was going on and assumed that Alex had crept past her on the stairs.

After hearing all this I was speechless. Yes, I realised Alex was capable of almost anything, but I found this hard to believe. We deliberated for a long time. Was there nothing Alex wouldn't do? Any child who is prepared to jump through a first-floor window, for no other reason than because he wants to be in the garden, has to be taken seriously, I thought, and must be in need of urgent help. And having jumped, what ordinary kid could fail to cry – for nearly six hours – after fracturing a leg?

This incident finally jolted me into action. It topped the shattering of the glass and the burning of his face: this was dangerous stuff. I felt that I'd somehow neglected his needs. Guilt racked me for not doing what I had long since felt was right. I'd chosen the easy way out because nobody agreed with my view that all was not well. Now my mind was finally made up and I was determined to seek professional help. I felt ashamed that I'd allowed five years to slip by – wasted time in which my son could quite easily have seriously injured himself. Enough was enough, and something had to be done.

Sharon protested at my renewed suggestion that Alex see a psychiatrist, but I didn't care and so was surprised when she decided to accompany us the day I took Alex to our doctor. Dr Khan was not particularly helpful that morning. I tried to explain Alex's behaviour to him, but he assured us that Alex was a normal little boy, that boys often play rough and do foolhardy things, and he was ready to show us the door. But I was in no mood to be patronised; I wanted my son to see a psychiatrist and needed the doctor to agree to it. He was not amused by my insistence and made a superficial examination of Alex – lasting in all about one minute – then declared: 'Fine boy, fine boy!' Alex's leg was in a plaster cast. We'd just told the doctor he'd jumped out of a first-floor window, and this was all he could tell us. I continued to insist on a referral. Reluctantly he agreed and said he'd write to a good psychiatrist attached to a local clinic.

Following this visit Sharon felt completely exonerated by Dr Khan's attitude and comments. I sensed he had not grasped the full seriousness of Alex's situation. How can you see a person for only a few moments and then make a complex professional judgement? We'd been experiencing difficulties with our son for five years; he'd seen him for five minutes. Several weeks later, notification of the promised appointment dropped through our letter box. The whole family was to see a child psychiatrist, Dr Singh, for an initial consultation. During the weeks leading up to the appointment Alex caused several bitter arguments and I'd had enough. I talked of leaving home, of sending Alex to Jamaica or putting him in the care of social services. I didn't mean it, but we were all frustrated and the strain was beginning to bite.

It also didn't help that Alex was now a celebrity at school. Hobbling around on one leg provided the perfect excuse not to work and earned him extra attention, but that didn't stop him getting into trouble. And with his fractured leg, everyone seemed to be talking about how he'd done it. There was always some chatty Nosy Parker dispensing unrequested advice. Take Cynthia, for instance. Her son Chad went to the same school and his behaviour partly resembled Alex's in so far as I could discern. She felt Chad was being victimised and was unfairly treated because he was black. Sometimes when Sharon or I collected the boys we'd see Cynthia intensely engaged in conversation with other mothers or teachers about something to do with her son. 'My Chad this . . .' or 'My Chad that . . .' she would say, always defending his position. Never did it occur to her that 'her Chad' was sometimes a bully who caused trouble too. So it wasn't long before she was also defending Alex in the playground.

She may have meant well, but she and those like her emboldened Alex in his misdeeds. I eventually asked her politely to mind her own business. Some of her attitude undoubtedly rubbed off on Sharon, and I found myself arguing with her over keeping this meddlesome person, and those like her, out of our lives. A battle of wills seemed to have been developing between me and Alex, and I was losing. I wanted him to behave in a certain way and, in my absence, he behaved in whatever way he wanted, spurred on by busybodies like Cynthia. With the involvement of the wider community after he started nursery school, it seemed to me that almost everyone had become an expert on Alex – all with conflicting opinions.

Dr Singh quickly noticed the disunited approach of our parenting. She indicated we were key factors in the continuing difficulties with Alex, urged Sharon to support me more and went on to offer Alex weekly therapy sessions. Now it was I who felt exonerated! Sharon promptly dismissed her as a 'stupid old woman' and refused to attend further sessions. At our meeting with Dr Singh Alex did not fail to live up to his reputation, and Sharon and I did not miss our cues. The resulting family debate provided an instant insight into the family's dynamics. Dr Singh had drawn her conclusions from this.

Once again I had to rearrange work to take Alex to his weekly appointments. Alex hated those sessions and did not want to go, but go he did throughout the next year. On the three or four occasions I was unable to take him Sharon deputised; each of these times Alex played the doctor up. On the final visit, almost a year after the original consultation, Alex successfully manoeuvred the two women into a heated argument. An angry Dr Singh told Sharon not to bring Alex back. That was music to Sharon's ears, since she had no intention of doing so.

Sharon and I may not have been the perfect couple but we did try. For sure, our disagreements didn't help our son, but neither, unfortunately, did Dr Singh. Alex's year with her, far from modifying his behaviour, seemed to make it progressively worse. Besides – she never did tell us what was wrong with him. I was frustrated and disappointed, not just because the therapy had ended in no positive result, but mainly because Dr Singh had allowed herself to be drawn into conflict with Sharon. Alex had won again. He'd achieved his short-term goal not to see Dr Singh. Both women had been successfully manipulated by a 6-year-old boy.

Pandora's Box

Four

You know when something is really wrong when the headmaster positions himself at a vantage point in the school building – the way they sometimes do in order to observe what's going on in the playground – and his eyes are focused most of the time on your son. This became a common practice for Mr Dixon after Alex followed Jason to junior school. It was in the same building as the infant school, so he was presumably well briefed about the kind of behaviour he could expect from Alex and may even have witnessed some of it. Nothing, however, could fully prepare him for being responsible for Alex five days a week.

A mature headmaster, he might well have thought he'd seen it all as far as rough kids of primary-school age were concerned. It was no doubt his experience that, if treated with firmness and skill, in time such children would mellow and settle down to a reasonable degree. I'm sure he expected Alex to do so; deep down I knew this wasn't going to happen. For Alex, a bigger school simply meant more children and therefore more excitement, with the added bonus of big brother Jason being there.

At the very beginning of his first year, Alex's relationships with his peers started to turn sour. He was still excitable and charming, but now when he was ordered to the head's office his personality no longer won him any special privileges. Instead he was duly disciplined. Not that this stopped him from getting into further trouble – far from it. Within about six months, many children at the school were wary, even frightened, of Alex, and the teachers were beginning to tire of him. Naturally they didn't say as much directly, but we could tell by their tone and facial expressions as they related whatever he was alleged to have done that day.

Alex had never been deliberately cheeky to adults. True, his boisterous behaviour in the company of children and his incessant touching of forbidden things meant many adults found him difficult to cope with, but he was seldom directly rude or insolent, as far as I'm aware. In fact, with his childish innocence and charm still intact, he largely came across as being quite affable to many, tolerable to be around provided he didn't get too overexcited. All that changed at junior school. Increasingly he began to adopt the feisty attitudes of some of his less-well-brought-up peers. Since there was no authority figure in the school whom he intrinsically respected, he became more and more brazen until some teachers felt he was being wilfully obstreperous and began to dislike him. He seemed to have a nose for trouble, sniffing it out wherever it was happening in the school, and then rocketing himself right into its midst.

Disruptive behaviour during lessons, fighting and bullying in the playground, inability to concentrate during lessons, poor to nonexistent school work and almost daily removal from class: all boded ill for Alex's future. When the head asked to see Sharon and me it came as no surprise. Alex had successfully frustrated all the staff who had attempted to instil in him some kind of normal school routine and attitude about appropriate behaviour. Once again he had subconsciously set his own agenda and manipulated those around him to his detriment. His accredited 'bright intelligence' and average IQ clearly weren't working well for him.

I remember thinking that it would only be a matter of time before something was bound to give way; that the patience of outsiders – non-family members – would eventually wear thin. Sharon and I were in desperate need of answers but were no closer to finding out what was wrong. There were many occasions when adults felt that Alex had been deliberately winding them up. For instance, he might repeatedly ask them questions to which they were sure he knew the answers. This was the sort of behaviour an adult might expect from a child under 5, but Alex was by now well past his seventh birthday. The sharp contrast between his increasingly mannish attitude in some circumstances and his childish behaviour in others proved too much for less perceptive teachers and adults to tackle, and it often provoked hostile reactions.

I cannot recollect whose decisions it was to call in an educational psychologist to see Alex, but neither Sharon nor I objected.

Mr Dixon had tried unsuccessfully to lessen the difficulties my son was experiencing and causing at school. I felt sorry for him; his face often looked haggard and worn. I tried to empathise and console him with the knowledge that Alex was difficult at home too, hoping that he would better appreciate that Alex had not come from a 'bad' family in the context that the term is generally interpreted, but that profound difficulties emanated from Alex himself.

About three meetings took place over a period of time with the educational psychologist, who suggested fresh approaches which the school and we the parents might like to try. This double-barrelled tactic aimed to foster in Alex a more positive attitude towards his school work and general behaviour. We all co-operated with the suggestions. By the final meeting, however, the psychologist and the headmaster seemed to be recommending that Alex be moved to a school where he could be assessed for special educational needs. The way they explained how things would work seemed perfectly reasonable to me. At some stage Alex was to go to a special school for a two-term assessment and then return to his present school with extra support if necessary. Sharon was none too keen on the idea – she'd been listening to blabbermouth Cynthia again – but when I voiced my approval of the arrangement she reluctantly agreed not to scupper the plan. We knew nothing of special schools or how they worked, and imagined they were to help children with educational difficulties to catch up. Alex would get extra tuition with his school work. Thus, with mixed feelings, we interpreted this as a positive move.

While the turbulence in Alex's school life was gathering momentum, the odd paranormal (I use the word very loosely here) happenings continued too. I had been on a trip to America and brought back presents for the family. Jason got a small portable combined radio and television set, which he adored, and for Alex I bought a beautiful, and fairly expensive, radio-cassette player. It had instantly caught my eye because of its unusual brightly coloured design. I hadn't seen anything as attractive in the UK and felt that even Alex would cherish it. Unfortunately, within a week of my return, the radio developed a fault and stopped working. I was very disappointed. You see, Alex *did* like it, and he didn't dismantle or in any way abuse it. I was unhappy for him and upset with the department store that had sold it to me, but I could hardly take it back to New York for an exchange or refund. I tried fixing it myself but to no avail. When I was about 14 I had made a transistor radio (a somewhat crude and clumsy monstrosity, I must admit) out of lots of little components fixed to a piece of hardboard, by following the wiring instructions of a circuit diagram – and it had worked. But I knew I'd be unable to fix this complex modern radio as the fault wasn't immediately obvious – rundown batteries, perhaps, or a broken or loose wire.

Some months later, Alex was playing upstairs and Jason was downstairs in the kitchen with us. When we heard music playing loudly above, it didn't click immediately that the sound couldn't be coming from my music centre since Alex had already succeeded in breaking that. As I climbed the first flight of stairs all I was concerned about was telling Alex to turn down the noise. Then I realised the sound wasn't coming from the lounge. I found Alex in the middle of the room he shared with his brother, with toys, clothes and story books strewn all around him. I was about to shout, 'Turn it down!' when I realised, astonished, where the sound was coming from. Alex barely raised his head to acknowledge me, then returned his gaze to the toys he was playing with, saying in a rather matter-of-fact way, 'I have fixed it, Daddy.'

I was dumbstruck. The incident remains special because I was in the house when it happened. It carried more weight for me than similar oddities that others had reported. In all cases the common denominator was Alex 'fixing it', and nobody else being present in the room when he did so. Nothing of earth-shattering importance was ever mended – electrical bric-a-brac lying around the home or chucked away in some drawer or cupboard. Kiddies' pocket computer games, small radios, a hand-held car-alarm control all seemed to fix themselves in Alex's presence. Isn't that enough to make one wonder?

Alex's fascination with fire remained a constant cause of anxiety and worry. Similarly his preoccupation with sex, or the opposite sex, troubled me immensely. He continued to damage his own toys as well as other children's and adults' property. Above all, his desire to dominate every situation involving his peers strengthened. Hardly surprisingly he and Jason continued to clash, and Sharon and I continued to argue over his care. The need for adults to set firm demarcation lines, to tell him what he could and could not do, was still overwhelming but he rebelled against all boundaries and sorely tested those who set them. Then one day I had to make the difficult decision not to take him with me on a special day out that had been planned months before. It was coming to the end of his first year in junior school. He would soon be 8 years old.

It was a Saturday and I was participating in a martial arts tournament with my team-mates in a neighbouring county. It was to be a large event and several hundred people were expected to attend; audiences are typically made up of families and friends of the competitors. I'd planned to take Sharon and the boys, but she didn't enjoy the sport and did not want to come. However, the boys' faces lit up at the prospect of going with me, but without Sharon to keep an eye on them it seemed unwise to take Alex. Because I was competing I knew I'd be unable to watch over him closely, so I decided that without Sharon, Alex couldn't come.

My decision was firm, and reached a week or so before the tournament. It was not intended as any sort of punishment, being wholly based on past experience of Alex in crowded situations. It seemed imprudent and irresponsible for me to take him. Sharon and Alex protested – Alex with many tears and promises – but I would not budge an inch.

As the tournament drew closer, Sharon's and Alex's pleas grew louder. Moved by the tide of sentiment, even Jason joined in and begged that his brother be allowed to come; still I wouldn't change my mind. Finally the Saturday morning arrived. We got up early and Alex bawled the house down: non-stop crying as Jason and I got ready. Sharon continued to argue that it was unfair, then said that Jason should not be allowed to go either.

'Let them both go, or let both of them stay.'

'Why don't you come, and the problem's solved?' I said.

When Jason's position appeared threatened, he started to cry too and pleaded that I allow Alex to come. Alex wore pitiable expression after pitiable expression, and howled from the heart as he made every promise under the sun: 'Please let me come, Daddy. I promise I'll behave myself. I'll be a good boy, Daddy; I promise I'll be good.'

I reeled off a string of past misdeeds: 'What about the time when you . . . or the time you did . . .? It's no use, Alex, you'd best stay home.'

I've always tried to maintain a consistent approach to rearing the children: good behaviour deserves reward, persistent bad behaviour deserves punishment. That's how I was brought up in Jamaica and by my parents. My children were not allowed to get whatever they wanted whenever they wanted simply because they demanded it or threw a tantrum. To me it was important that Alex learn this. I tried to let the boys know where they stood with me by not sending them confused signals. If I said 'Yes', then usually I'd stick to it; if I said 'No', I usually stuck to that too. Jason accepted my stance and was as comfortable with it as the average child; Alex never did and, by whatever means necessary, would always try to get his own way.

I caved in. 'OK, Alex, you can come; but if you give me any trouble down there, I'm going to smack you, OK?'

'Yes, Dad, I'll behave myself. I'll be good.'

The torrent of tears trickled to a stop. Soon Alex's face was beaming as he hurriedly washed and dressed with the help of Mum, both acting quickly in case I changed my mind. They didn't know that what had tipped the balance was not so much Alex's tears as my guilt over the fact that I'd agreed to take along two of the boys' playmates, yet was willing to exclude one of my own. That didn't rest well with me, especially when Alex was begging and crying his heart out to come.

Soon we were on our way to pick up the other children who were ready and waiting. Alex behaved impeccably – but not for long. No sooner had the car reached a point in the journey where he sensed I was unlikely to turn around and head back for home than he started to become restless and annoy the others – overexcitement no doubt. Immediately I threatened to abandon the trip and turn off at the next slip road. This instantly produced sad faces and pleas of unfairness from all, followed by more promises from Alex. I was already beginning to regret I'd not had the gumption to stick by my original decision. However, I pressed on for the benefit of the other children and because I didn't want to let down my team-mates.

When we arrived at the sports hall there were already four or five hundred people present, including many youngsters. The crowd was to swell as the day wore on. Alex was in his element – this was even better than school! Within an hour I'd already had five or six complaints about him. He raced around the hall, bumping into this and charging into that. I wanted to go home and blamed myself for bringing him. Friends tried to keep an eye on him for me and my team-mates pleaded that I stay. Any moment my name would be called for me to compete and to leave now could have resulted in the disqualification of our team.

As the programme of events got into full swing the crowd grew to in excess of a thousand people. There were swarms of children playing and milling around, and Alex was having an absolute field day. By 5 o'clock he'd had at least half a dozen full-blown fights with different boys, and ruffled quite a few parents; and there were a good four or five hours to go before the tournament was over. In addition, throughout the day a total of about 30 adults and children, mostly strangers, had sought me out to complain about what Alex had said or done; some were very abusive. Security staff had found him in off-limits areas; he had broken a window, upturned a parked motorbike, and was found on several occasions tampering with the organisers' presentation equipment and prizes. After each incident he had been ordered to stay with me or frogmarched back by one of the lads from our club. Shortly thereafter he'd slip away and mingle with the crowds while my attention was caught up in the noisy, electric atmosphere, watching others compete.

I don't think he was capable of calculating behaviour, but I'm sure Alex instinctively understood that I was not going to hit him while we were at this venue, nor was I going to leave once the competition had started. He seemed utterly unconcerned about what might happen later, or about my obvious disapproval of his blatant disobedience. He may have 'forgotten himself' because there was so much there to excite him, but this was not the only reason for his rudeness. He seemed to be dishing out to me, and just about everyone else who attempted to correct him, the kind of insolent disobedience he'd become accustomed to serving up to his teachers – simply because there was a large crowd present. The only options I had were to threaten a severe disciplining for his relentlessly disgraceful behaviour once we got home, or to leave immediately. I wish I'd left.

That evening I sat Alex down and explained why he was going to be punished. I gave him a few strokes of the belt, as I had done before on very rare occasions when I felt it had been necessary. Naturally he didn't enjoy it. Neither had I enjoyed the sting of the belt from my relatives in Jamaica, or from my mum, or 'six of the best' from the deputy headmaster's cane at my East London primary school. Alex hollered and screamed at the top of his voice before I even touched him. He usually reacted like this when given a moderate smack with the hand. I aimed for his bottom, but his wriggling meant that I struck him on his legs and arms as well. He knew I was serious and struggled, making enough noise to arouse Sharon's objections. Whenever I received a good tanning from my mother or father I always resented it bitterly, but it did me no lasting harm and arguably a lot of good. However, for years I've accepted it was wrong to punish Alex in this way, for it didn't work out in his case; but at the time I felt the situation warranted it. I also believed he was acting up because he knew his mother was in the house, and that his accompanying melodrama was as much designed to secure her intervention as it was a reaction to any pain. I disciplined my son not because I hated him, but because I loved him, and on this score offer no apology.

The following day, Sunday, the matter was over with and the whole family went swimming as planned. That evening we visited relatives. On Monday it was back to school as usual.

Most weekday evenings I collected the boys from school. This particularly evening we'd barely been home 20 minutes when there was a knock on the front door. I was greeted by a man and a woman who introduced themselves as social workers. They'd come because they were investigating an anonymous allegation of child abuse and asked to see the boys. The social workers refused to give further details and continued to insist on seeing the children, who shortly came to the door anyway. I remained calm and invited them in. When they asked to see Alex alone I co-operated, and Jason and I left the room. While they were alone with Alex I phoned Sharon at work and told her what was happening. She was furious.

After seeing Alex for some 20 minutes, both the social workers decided he was not walking properly. They said he was limping and should see a doctor. Alex had been at school all day without anyone noticing he had a limp. They then requested my permission to remove his trousers for a closer inspection. I not only gave permission, but also helped remove the trousers so that they could examine his leg and hip. Their next request was more of an order than a proposal: that Alex should be taken to our doctor. I said I'd take him in the morning but they insisted I take him that evening.

I pointed out that there was nothing wrong with Alex, who was by now playing with his brother. Still calm, despite their measured antagonism, I pointed out that the family had gone swimming the previous day and Alex's body had been in full public view. I attempted to show the illogical nature of their innuendoes, reasoning that swimming baths would be the last place I'd take my son if I'd battered him and had anything to hide.

A few moments later Sharon walked in and asked, 'What's your visit about?'

'Your son was heard crying on Saturday night.'

She did not deny the children were smacked on occasions: 'But not to injure or lame them.'

'There are scars all over his body,' one said; the other: 'He is limping.'

'That's ridiculous!' was Sharon's response. Like me she also pointed out he'd been fine at school and was not complaining of any pain. Despite her further protests they continued to insist that Alex be taken to our own GP for an examination. She was none too pleased with the uninvited visitors and told them so. They beat a hasty retreat, but not before pointing out that they were 'only doing their job' and reiterating that Alex should be taken to our doctor that very evening. I saw no advantage in getting angry, despite being deeply offended by their insinuations and unwanted intrusion.

Memories came flooding back to me of a then recent news item that had received media attention: a black man had battered his young child to death. The social services concerned had been severely criticised for not interceding. The attitude of these two social workers, however, made me feel they'd already decided I was guilty. I remember thinking to myself that they might be, quite wrongly, regarding this as 'their' big case and, unlike their colleagues, had no intention of making mistakes. I felt I was being tarred, quite unjustly, with the same brush as that other father.

At the surgery Sharon explained to Dr Khan what had happened, unaware that the social workers had already been in touch with him. The doctor questioned her about Alex; she co-operated with him fully, and lamented that Alex was a difficult child for whom we had been trying to get help; that we had been to see Child Guidance but that no one seemed to want to know. He was very concerned that social services were not carrying out the investigation correctly; that they should be trying to get help on how to control him and understand how best his behavioural needs could be met. A thorough physical examination followed, during which he found only some faint red marks. Dr Khan concluded that the child had not been ill-treated and could not see any signs that he had been abused in any way. His verdict was that no child abuse had taken place.

Sharon asked, 'Could a bruise like that [referring to the faint red marks] give anyone the right to claim that my child had been battered?'

His reply was an emphatic 'No!' and he continued: 'But like I said before, social workers have a very odd way of carrying out their investigations.' He added, 'I know how you feel. I, too, have children of my own, and if this was happening to me I would feel the same way you do.'

He asked to see Alex alone and questioned him for a while, after which he called Sharon and Jason back into his room. 'As far as I am concerned there is nothing to worry about,' he said, and explained that he had to report back his findings to social services, 'But you can hold on until I have done so.' She and Jason returned to the waiting room.

After a few minutes the doctor returned and glumly told Sharon, 'The social workers want your son to be put in hospital – tonight – for a check-up.'

'Why? You've just told me there is nothing to worry about, so why do they want to put him in hospital?'

'I don't know either.'

The doctor decided to contact the social worker again. After a few minutes he came back and told Sharon, 'It's all right for you to take the kids home.'

About two hours later and way outside normal office hours, the social workers' team leader called to see us. He asked similar questions to the earlier two, spoke about Alex's behaviour – past, present and future – and told us that we should 'use our hands' to smack Alex. He also asked whether the child had been taken to see the doctor, and again we went over the weekend's events. We thought that would be an end to the matter but couldn't have been more wrong.

After he left, Sharon and I reflected how strange it was that we had been trying to get help for Alex for nearly three years without anyone particularly caring, but because I had punished him with a belt we'd had three social workers visit in one day. The team leader had given the impression that he would do something for Alex very quickly. It was a pity that this situation had to happen, he said, before they realised the problem we were having, but, 'If in the end we get the right help, it will be worth it.'

That same evening Sharon commented that their actions did 'more damage than any good to the situation'. Neither of us knew what was in store. The following day, social services returned.

It was a hot June summer's evening. Sharon had collected the boys from school and was at home with them. She had made them a sandwich then settled in the lounge to read the newspaper with the television on in the background. Jason went to fetch himself a cold drink from the kitchen, and he noticed a police vehicle and other cars pulling up outside the house. 'Mum, some police are outside!' he shouted. Alex went to investigate.

'Alex, move yourself from the window, it's nothing to do with us.'

'Yes, Mummy, there is police outside,' Alex blurted back.

Sharon glanced outside and saw the police officers sitting in a van. She called the boys away from the window, and the three went back to watching children's cartoons. Then she heard a knock on the door and went to answer it. It was about a quarter past six. Confronting her with a broad smile was the female social worker from the previous day, with the team leader and another one or two social workers in the background. This time they'd brought reinforcements, and were accompanied by two or three police officers. Shocked and surprised, Sharon asked, 'What do you want?' As if bringing a piece of mundane good news, the female social worker greeted her in a bright and cheerful voice: 'Hello, Mrs Anthony.'

'What's all this? What are you doing?'

'We have come to take the boys.'

'Take what boys?! Why? What for?'

'Because you failed to take them to hospital.'

'Well, I did take them to the hospital, didn't I!' she said, meaning our doctor.

Sharon could not believe what she was hearing. She was incensed, deeply offended and momentarily numb with disbelief, but then snapped with anger and began cursing the social workers bitterly, especially the smiling one. Sharon suspected she was behind it all because of their heated words the day before. The team leader, a slight figure of a man, looked more like a second-in-command as he stood by impassively. Sharon insisted that nobody was leaving until I came home, and in a brief but frantic phone call told me what was going on. I downed tools and left work immediately.

In the meantime a noisy scene erupted both inside and outside our house. The boys cried and screamed that they didn't want to go with the social workers, while Sharon remonstrated with them for the trouble their behaviour had caused while trying to get the boys ready. She said later that the police appeared sickened by the actions and attitudes of the social workers. One officer, reacting in a human way to her deep distress, tried to calm her down. After a while he put his arm around her and said, 'Look, love, let them go. You might as well let them go with them.'

Sharon later told me, 'The policeman had a tough look on his face, as if he was angry with them – but he couldn't say it.' He told her the boys were being taken to the local general hospital. She asked why, addressing her comments to the social workers who did not reply. Finally the policeman said, 'For further examinations.'

'But I took him to my GP and he told me everything was all right.'

The female social worker replied, 'Because you initially refused to take him to your doctor.' She was referring to their meeting on Monday.

'If I had refused, how then did the doctor examine him?' No answer came. Sharon was furious, later protesting that the boys were being 'treated like little criminals – at that age – being dragged away by police and without their being asked or even knowing why'.

I drove the short distance home on autopilot, turned the corner into our street, and was confronted by an unforgettably distressing sight. A crowd of neighbours and passers-by had gathered, watching eagerly the drama unfolding on my doorstep and through the open front door. It was unusual to see such excitement in our relatively quiet street. I could hear my sons crying. Two police vehicles and other social workers' cars cluttered the road outside. An officer stood guard near the door, while his colleagues and social workers were crammed on to the small pathway. The crowd whispered as they saw me arrive, and parted so I could gain access to my home.

When Alex saw me all hell broke loose. 'Daddy! Don't let them take me.'

Prior to my arrival, the social workers had been trying unsuccessfully to get the boys to co-operate. Jason and Alex were enraged and wept profusely, running about the house in a futile attempt to escape and hide, even though at the prompting of the police Sharon, highly distressed, shouted at them that they must go. The social workers seemed particularly anxious to get them away before I arrived, but their attempts to 'help' the boys along had met with stiff opposition – especially from Alex, the kid they portrayed as being in danger with us. Jason was frightened and utterly confused: one minute watching TV and the next, this. When I came in, Alex was kicking and punching at the social worker who was trying to lead him along the hallway. When he saw me he seemed to muster extra strength and broke free. Both he and Jason ran to me. Had the boys willingly co-operated, or I arrived a little later, I wouldn't have witnessed such a horrible sight.

With the children about me, and trying desperately hard to keep a lid on my emotions and maintain my dignity, I endeavoured to choose words that weren't directly abusive to the social workers yet would convey my disgust at their behaviour. Inside I hated them for what they were doing. The police officers stood by impassively. I kept shaking my head in disbelief.

Finally, I lost some control. 'You can't do this! You can't do this!' I shouted in a loud but measured voice. 'If only you had gone down to the school before, you would've known how difficult Alex is, and how long we've been trying to get help with him.' That was typical me, trying to reason and getting nowhere, even when instincts tell me I'm wasting my time.

They may have been relieved that I only shouted. There wasn't anyone there worth hitting, and what satisfaction could I get from ending up in jail? That wouldn't help my sons. The police behaved impeccably on this occasion. The social workers spoke in moderately raised voices, not quite shouting but enough to irritate and anger me further. They seemed emboldened by my apparent reasonableness and the police presence – almost teasing.

In defeat I went over to the policeman nearest the door, who seemed to be in charge, and appealed to him: 'They can't do this, can they?' The officer stood helplessly with sympathy written all over his face, but his mouth refused to betray his feelings. He said with simple resignation, 'Yes, they can.'

Goodness knows what impression the court had been given about us to command such a considerable police presence, because the social workers had to obtain a Place of Safety order before they could legally remove the kids. We were simply ordinary folk, living ordinary lives in an ordinary street. The officers had now seen enough to know that their services were not needed. Certainly Sharon went spare with fury – what mother wouldn't? – and she shouted at the social workers, but the police never rebuked her. Far from it. This was every parent's worst nightmare come true – happening to us. And it felt particularly vindictive because we had been given no hint of the social workers' intentions on their visits the previous evening. The family had been knocked for six and we were powerless before them, other than to offer the resistance we did.

The stars of this drama were the children. By struggling with the social workers, and being impervious to all their professional coaxing, Alex and Jason demonstrated that their particular kind of 'help' was neither wanted, needed nor welcomed in our family. The four of us bitterly resented this new development and each in our own way spontaneously – but unitedly – reacted against it. It was obvious from the way the children cried and hung on to us that they were not the victims of abuse.

At last I added my voice to Sharon's and reluctantly told the boys to go with the social workers. I gathered them together, calmed them down, and gave reassurances and promises that we'd collect them as soon as possible. They complied but sobbed and were deeply distressed. I vowed to be in touch with my solicitors first thing in the morning. My sons were driven away, screaming, with the team leader in the police van. I spent most of that and subsequent evenings shaking my head and lamenting over and over again: 'They don't know what they've done.'

Events were moving faster than I could think about clearly, but from that moment I sensed that the trouble was only just beginning. Because I knew Alex so well, I feared that social services had opened a Pandora's box. Surely they had no right to take such drastic action, with the possibilities of long-term damage to a family, without irrefutable evidence or at least a thorough investigation. We had been coping with Alex for several years – all his life in fact; from our perspective several hours' effort by the social workers hardly constituted a proper investigation. The boys were well fed, well dressed and lived in a comfortable and clean house. I believed then, and still do, that the events of that day amounted to a flagrant abuse of social services' legal power. Before that Monday we hadn't even met, much less had dealings with, a social worker; we'd only gleaned bits and pieces about them from the media. Now here they were in real life because I'd dared physically to punish my child, whom I've always loved and cared for, in a manner that I felt appropriate to his wayward behaviour. And because Sharon, incensed by their attitude, had indicated they wouldn't find an ally in her, and that we reserved our right, as parents, to discipline our children how we saw fit. My greatest fear was that neither they, nor we, would be able to shut that Pandora's box again.

The crowds were gone. Next the silence. No Alex. No Jason. It is impossible to exaggerate the inner turmoil that I went through when my children were taken away. Every negative feeling imaginable floods the mind, and one is overwhelmed by anger and a sense of deep outrage. An uncontrollable urge takes over and you need someone to blame, but the social workers and police have gone home for the day. So you blame yourself, or the other parent, and tear into each other with bitter words. Then you cry incessantly, or pine and wilt away in silence until disorientation and numbness set in. Eventually you unburden yourself by chattering to everyone you know; they share your grief. But somehow their attempts to console seem way off target, for what can they say to begin to ease your inner pain? Our entire family seemed punch-drunk, and Sharon and I were left in a daze. Years later I still find it hard to believe the events of that day.

Eventually the anger resurfaces, coupled with the compelling need to do something. At the hospital, Alex was extensively examined by another doctor, the registrar, and the following day by the consultant himself. The consultant was annoyed that he had been called away, at the insistence of social services, to investigate 'a serious case of child abuse', since neither he nor the registrar concluded that any abuse had taken place. He told Sharon that he 'did not like the way the matter was being conducted' by social services but that he had a job to perform even though he was 'totally against it'. He also told her, as if knowing with foreboding what this type of investigation meant for us as a family, 'My sympathy goes out to you.' He and his colleague had concluded it was 'not necessary to take [your] kids away, had *they* done their homework correctly', and that a 'bruise on the arm', with reference to the small amount of redness he saw, did not require further investigation. The peeved doctor even bemoaned to Sharon that social services requested he carry out 'blood tests and X-rays'. He told her he did not see why this was necessary, but indicated he had no option but to do so.

The boys spent the next three days and nights on the children's ward. They were unwashed, teeth not brushed, slept in the same clothes, hair uncombed and matted, and in such a generally unkempt state as had *never* occurred at home. This was their introduction to care – social-services style. In a subsequent telephone conversation, our GP commented that he could see 'no justification for their action' in either his or the hospital's reports.

While the boys were in hospital, I busied myself with lawyers. Social services were doing the same. But they were used to it; we weren't. We'd entered into the strange and unfamiliar world of the professionals. In no time social services instigated wardship proceedings and the boys became wards of court, which meant that the court had, in effect, become the boys' legal guardian. Now any decision involving the children's welfare needed court approval. By Friday, a further court order had been obtained by social services to move the boys from hospital into a children's home, Stockport House, where they remained for the next two weeks.

The children were very upset when they arrived, and found it difficult to settle into that environment. Alex tried to run away on the first evening. Staff found him difficult to handle. He threw tantrums and was both verbally and physically abusive towards the other children and members of staff. He was so determined to get away he attempted to jump out of windows and generally behaved recklessly. Jason seemed to try to make up for this by attempting to be well behaved all the time. Sharon and I visited at least once a day, often twice, and brought other members of the family along. To begin with, we clashed with the staff, as we were very resentful and simply thought the children should be back home with us.

In truth, Sharon and I hated every visit to the home but felt we couldn't abandon the boys there. I was angry with Alex for putting us in this situation, and kept blaming myself for giving in to family pressure and taking him to the martial arts tournament that unfortunate day. Towards the end of the two weeks, however, our relationship with the staff had improved somewhat.

Affidavits were prepared and, following legal advice, Sharon and I agreed to the court that we would not physically chastise either child and would co-operate with any psychiatric assessment. This meant our willingness to submit to family therapy with the children, if required, and to allow an educational psychological assessment of Alex to take place (which was already being done, at our own suggestion, through the school). Without these agreements they would remain in care. Naturally we complied. Costs to us, a painful £600. Another condition attached was that social services would be granted a supervisory order, which meant we'd have to allow these people back into our homes periodically to see the boys.

The children's first brush with social services hadn't been a pleasant one. They'd already started to develop a strong dislike for the phrases 'social worker' and 'social services', but the problem went deeper than that. Emotional damage had been inflicted on both boys, and Alex's behaviour began to get worse.

Five

Two weeks went by before the boys were legally allowed to leave Stockport House. We were relieved and happy to have them back at home, but it soon became apparent that their relatively short stay in local authority care had seen a deterioration in their behaviour. Jason quickly readjusted to our routine, but Alex continued to act out new bad habits. He'd never used swear words at home before; now Jason complained that Alex swore at him not only when he was angry but also in normal conversation. We tried to nip it in the bud by sternly telling them both, 'Whatever you've picked up in Stockport House, leave in Stockport House!' For Alex, however, the message wasn't getting through.

One of the most frustrating aspects was his inability to learn from bad experiences. They were simply brushed aside almost as if they'd never happened – as if his mental slate had been wiped clean. Yet at the same time he would retain virtually all new bad habits to which he was exposed; these seemed to appeal most to his psyche. I found this puzzling, for either someone has a bad memory – full stop – or they don't. It didn't occur to me that this trait in Alex might be involuntary. Like everyone else, I was reacting to his behaviour as though it were deliberate. Alex acted: people reacted!

Alex had definitely changed. As well as swearing at other children too, he was showing an increased stubbornness towards his mother and other adults, a readiness to run from home when he couldn't get his own way, and he bragged to family members and close friends that no one was allowed to hit him.

According to the boys, social workers had told them prior to coming home that Mummy and Daddy were not allowed to discipline them physically in any way. They'd drummed this hard into Alex's head, though he didn't need telling twice. If we hit them they'd been instructed to tell the social worker. Some lessons Alex never learned; this one stuck! Pretty soon, Alex was boasting to his gran and aunts that if they raised a hand to him he would get them into trouble with social services, and that the same went for Mummy or Daddy.

If ever there was a child in this world that shouldn't have been given that message, it was Alex. Smacking either child had always been a last resort, but it had remained an option. Alex had been difficult enough to manage before, but now in their textbook wisdom social services unbolted the only door of possible restraint. To me this demonstrated how little they had taken on board about the intractability of Alex's behaviour, even though it had been well documented in reports from his school, the educational psychologist and the psychiatrist; and there'd been two weeks of sustained problems between Alex and staff and other children at Stockport House, not to mention the heightened tension in the hospital ward for the three days before that. Yet they'd given him a licence to cause chaos, and that's what he did.

How could social services have known the depth of my concern about Alex? How could they have known the extent to which he saw me as the ultimate authority, the only person he usually listened to without direct defiance? Alex had overexcitedly and publicly challenged this at the tournament, thus earning himself the punishment. Now social services had undermined me (and Sharon) to him. They had broken the only real link in Alex's mind to an idea of authority – his parents.

As the summer holidays approached, Mr Dixon must have been mightily relieved at the thought of six glorious weeks without Alex, who had by now achieved celebrity status at school. Staff were on the lookout for fresh signs of child abuse; and parents and children wanted the gossip about all that happened. His behaviour became even more outrageous, not only towards children but now also staff. Alex now ruled the roost – every roost.

I began to take social services' action even more personally than Sharon – and she was deeply offended. If my own child thought he had been given a licence blatantly to disobey me I was having no part of it and told Alex so. I was determined not to smack him, but made it clear that if he couldn't behave himself I would take him to social services and he could live with them if he wanted. This threat became my ultimate weapon. We knew he did not relish returning to a children's home.

The school summer holidays left us with a major problem. With relatives working, or distancing themselves from looking after Alex for any prolonged period, we had to look elsewhere for day care for the boys. When we learned there was to be a summer play scheme in the local park, we believed we'd found a possible solution.

From the first day there were complaints about Alex; the next six weeks were filled with more of the same. He was involved in numerous incidents: arguments, bullying, fights, verbal abuse of other park users, refusals to comply with instructions from the scheme's staff, including absconding from their sight without permission and sometimes leaving the park. Daytime incidents spilled over into the evening when complaints were made as we collected the boys, or when Jason related to us the events of the day. Sharon and I made warning noises but we never laid a finger on Alex. While not openly disobeying me to my face, he now took whatever we said with a pinch of salt. Jason, who could sustain play with friends or indeed anyone without trouble, frequently acted as a peacekeeper when conflict arose between Alex and others.

Having got himself into difficulties, Alex sometimes looked to Jason for support, expecting him to rush to his defence and fight. When Jason did, he was his big-brother hero; when he didn't, Alex would turn on him and argue or fight – often both. To say that Jason was under constant stress and often embarrassed by his brother's behaviour would be a gross understatement, but he had no means of escape. What sibling has? Of necessity they were thrust together. Jason is a forgiving soul, even to Alex, but because of the relentless daily problems there were times of sheer frustration, yet they could never do without each other for too long – a true love-hate relationship.

Incensed parents would on occasion knock on our front door to complain about injuries that their children had received earlier that day from Alex. One chap wanted to fight the boy on our doorstep. What can you do in such a situation? The father is shouting, threatening and swearing. You try to pacify him, giving assurances. Then just when he begins to accept that you don't encourage bad behaviour in your child, that you will deal with the matter appropriately, your son starts shouting abuse at him. I'd been trying to restrain Alex from going outside to confront the man by physically blocking the partly closed door and ordering him to step back inside. But from behind the safety of my shield he screamed insults at the father and his child, and I was forced to get angry to show the man that he could not push past me to beat up my son, who was, after all, only 8 years old. The perfect end after a hard day at work!

My threats to return Alex to the care of the social services began to have little effect. Sharon and I were having to live with the negative effects of their intervention. Each passing day brought increased problems. Then about eight or nine weeks after our first encounter with social services, matters came to a head. For no apparent reason Alex suddenly sprang up and viciously attacked Jason while I was in the house. He clawed at his brother's face like a wild tiger, inflicting terrible injuries. His brother screamed out in excruciating pain.

When I saw Jason's face I felt sickened and disgusted: it was a mess. I believed I had no alternative but to prove I did mean what I had threatened, though in my heart I didn't. Immediately, I took both the boys down to social services. My purpose was a dual one: to show them Jason's face and to register a strong protest at their involvement with my family. I was seething with fury.

Until this point I hadn't truly lost my temper with social services. Now I finally did. In a strong booming voice, I demanded to see whoever was in charge: I was livid and made a lot of noise. Then someone approached me with an air of superiority that made me see red; I cursed them bitterly. Profusely. In the midst of all this I thought I saw the female social worker with the smile scamper away. Others scurried away or sat in stunned silence in the open-plan public area of the office. I didn't want to deal with intermediaries. The team leader came out to speak to me. I told him what I thought of him and his department for turning my son into a wild animal and showed him the injuries on Jason's face, though I wasn't behaving much better at that time. He disapproved of my hostility towards Alex, but I ask: what did he expect? Alex had mauled his brother's face with a swift ferocity after no provocation. Was I supposed to cuddle him and tell him, 'Well done'?

I wanted to show them the increasing day-to-day problems of coping with Alex, especially for Jason, who was always suffering unjustly at Alex's hand. These people, however, could remain distant, in their offices, separated from the consequential reality of their decision-making. That day I was determined to interrupt their detached world and show them our reality, and they didn't like it one bit. I think they called the police but I had already left with the boys.

To test their response, on occasion I've asked social workers of varying ranks to take Alex into their home and live with him for a few days. Then they can attempt to apply all their textbook wisdom and tell me how those few days went. To date, not one of them has taken up the suggestion.

I wanted Jason's injuries to be treated and recorded by the hospital, and so asked a relative to escort him there while Alex and I went to see my solicitor. The solicitor listened but could offer no useful advice. Something snapped inside me as we drove towards the hospital to join Jason, and Alex suddenly burst into play with a smirk on his face while I was recounting what he'd done to his brother. It was his attitude that got me – he seemed insolent and indifferent, as if he'd already brushed aside the seriousness of his attack in spite of the freshness of the incident and my immediate and adverse reaction to it. I was incensed, changed direction, and headed again for the social services office. Alex immediately started to cry.

His tears were real enough; they always were. 'Don't give me to them,' he pleaded. When we reached the office I had to physically lift him out of the car, wrenching his grip away from whatever he had held on to, and bring him bawling loudly into the building. It was a pitiable sight.

'No, Daddy, no, Daddy, please don't leave, Daddy, Daddy, please don't leave me. I beg you, Daddy, I beg you, please let me come home.'

'No, Alex!' I shouted at him. 'This is what you want. I have been warning you and begging you to behave yourself. But everywhere you go you just cause trouble – you don't care.'

'Yes, I care, Daddy, I care, Daddy, I promise you I care, Daddy.' With tear-filled eyes and in a shaky voice hoarse from crying, he vowed: 'I'll be good at home, Daddy.'

That was what I wanted to hear but I couldn't be sure whether he meant it. I had seen so many convincing acts before. I searched his eyes and face, groping for reassurance, but when I spoke, what came out was: 'Look what you've done to your brother's face. You could have dug his eyes out. You could have blinded him!'

I felt I had to go through with it for him to get the point. He always seemed to escape from the effects of his behaviour and I could not allow him to continue like this. I also needed to show social services how wrong they had been to undermine our parental authority, and to impress upon them that they were not dealing with an example of a hypothetical, stereotypical black family gone adrift – that we were *real* people, with *real* feelings.

The staff and other parents in the waiting area were mesmerised as this drama unfolded before them. Alex gripped one of my legs tightly and refused to let go. I tried to break free and head for the main doors, but Alex still clung on; as I struggled to loosen his grip he grabbed nearby chairs and tables, with me dragging them along with us. They sent out a black social worker to try to pacify me, as if his colour would make a difference. Finally I managed to leave Alex in the building with other social workers while the black one followed me out. I went to my car and drove off, leaving him standing in the street.

Yes, I was a very bitter man. Yet the social workers didn't seem to care – as if the fuss I was causing was quite normal: we were just another case.

Needless to say, my confused and desperate action backfired. No sooner had I left the office than social services applied to the court on an emergency basis and took Alex back into care. Sharon was furious with me and we had a big row. She took grave exception to my explanation that I had returned home without one of her sons in order to 'teach him a lesson' and immediately drove off to social services to get him back, but to no avail.

It took another round at the High Court and another £600 before Alex was released back into our care for the second time. By then he had spent two damaging weeks in another children's home, the Bodley Road Centre. At least on this occasion they had decided not to tag Jason along into care too.

I suppose as a family we were a resilient bunch, though it wasn't easy for any of us, but the buck always seemed to stop with me. In spite of Alex's attack on Jason, the social services team leader saw me and Sharon as the problem in the family. He thought us unco-operative because we wanted Alex to see a psychiatrist of our choosing instead of theirs. I felt pressurised; I'd unwittingly played right into the hands of social services by handing them Alex on a silver platter and providing them with a public display of how apparently heartless I was towards him. I'd made it a mere formality for them to put him back into care. I was in the doghouse with Sharon and £1,200 out of pocket. Not bad for a guy trying to do the right thing!

We visited Alex regularly during the two weeks he was at Bodley Road. This home seemed rougher than Stockport House, mainly because younger children were not separated from teenagers. Some viewed this as poetic justice because Alex was now the one being bullied and attacked by older children, which I did not like one bit although I felt he'd put himself there. His complaints to me about other children were met coolly; I did nothing about them but continued visiting him just the same. On one occasion he was found pinned to the wall by four bigger boys with a chair leg squeezed up against his throat to force him to smoke. But, big as they were, none of this stopped Alex fighting back. Apparently he continued smoking from this point forward – on and off – though we were unaware of this at the time.

Back home I thought a change in tactics might yield better results. I knew Alex had always wanted a pet but feared he would not look after it. I had grown up with cats, and when I was about 9 I had had a pet mongrel dog called Sparky. They'd given me a lot of fun and companionship, plus responsibility. 'Maybe if I gave him the benefit of the doubt, a pet might give him something to love and look after,' I thought. Henry, our adopted stray, shabby garage cat, surprised us all one day when 'he' unexpectedly delivered a litter of kittens. I decided to give Alex one as his pet.

The joy on his face when presented with a beautiful, almost all-white fluffy kitten was wonderful to behold, and made the day he left Bodley Road complete. However, Alex failed to understand why Fluff would not follow and obey his instructions, despite our explaining that the kitten was an animal, and that animals do not understand what people say, though they do understand whether their owners are being kind or cruel. So we showed Alex how to be kind by gently stroking the kitten, telling him that the kitten liked that. Alex copied – whenever we were looking.

The kitten lasted two nights. I rescued it, half-dead, before daylight in the morning of the third day. I'd been woken by Alex creeping around the house and went to investigate. He'd put Fluff down the toilet bowl for a swim and had nearly drowned him. I plucked the kitten out of the loo, cleaned, dried and fed it, told Alex I would be taking it back to its mum in the garage later that day, and sent him back to his bed. Alex protested and pleaded that I allow the kitten to stay and made many promises about how he'd look after Fluff. The two budgerigars and goldfish were less fortunate.

A different social worker now started to visit us at home – Denzil Morgan, whom I'd left standing in the road as I drove away from social services a month or so earlier. I suspect Denzil was the department's idea of a peace offering. We supposed they felt that his colour would pacify Sharon and me.

Initially unwelcome, Denzil still came. In time we poured out some of our frustrations to him – not in a bad way, but as an outlet for our feelings. He was sympathetic but never said a word against his employers, though his face registered disappointment with them. However, after a few months he emigrated. We were then left without a social worker for almost a year. Bear in mind that we were the family who, just months previously, had been treated as if Alex and Jason were in constant mortal danger with us.

About the time Denzil came on the scene, we started family therapy with the court-approved consultant paediatric psychiatrist, appointed by social services: Dr Alan Thompson of the local children's hospital. He was the second psychiatrist to see Alex. The piercing look in Dr Thompson's eyes betrayed his dulcet voice and relaxed manner. He had been well briefed about us, we felt. It was almost as if I could see his brain ticking over. We didn't want to be there, and I'm sure he picked that up. In the main, we complied with his questioning and instructions. He interviewed us individually and collectively. Over the following year I updated him on events involving Alex at home and school. Because of work I wasn't always able to stick rigidly to the appointments but attended the majority.

As Dr Thompson began to grasp the true facts of our situation, his attitude to the family appeared to become increasingly sympathetic. I think he began to appreciate I was simply an ordinary father and husband trying to do my best under very difficult circumstances. As well as getting to know us better he was also able to experience Alex in person, and this might have influenced his growing air of commiseration. He appeared genuinely to want to help and sought to carry on from where Dr Singh had left off.

Perhaps Dr Thompson's conversations with Denzil and others within the department had had a bearing on why it took them nearly a year to assign a new social worker to Alex. Maybe social services could now see we were not the monsters they'd first thought us to be. Privately, some of the staff acknowledged that they had been appalled by the way our family had been treated. They thought the case had been insensitively handled, and that Sharon and I had every right to be angry.

Social services had all but disappeared, leaving a well and truly broken family in their wake.

Six

ALEX'S SCHOOL-RELATED problems continued and intensified when he began his second year at junior school in September 1988. Mr Dixon appeared to be at his wits' end. He invited us, yet again, to a meeting with the educational psychologist, Mr Rogers. They suggested that Alex be moved temporarily to a 'special' school to assess his educational needs. This decision might already have been taken by the local education authority, the area school psychologist, Mr Matthews (the headmaster of the intended special school), as well as Messrs Dixon and Rogers. Our later interpretation of the object of this meeting was that it was simply to sell this plan to us. It seemed a good idea.

Mr Dixon was extremely polite; he always was. But it was clear he looked forward to Alex's removal from the school until his needs had been properly assessed. Jason, however, fitted in well, was no trouble and was welcome to stay.

Before we finally gave permission for Alex to be moved, we had been invited to meet Mr Matthews and tour the school. 'Of course we can cope with children like Alex, we are all specially trained,' he assured us – or words to that effect. He proudly showed Sharon, Alex and me round the modern one-storey building. It seemed well equipped, and boasted an excellent staff-pupil ratio. Mr Matthews instilled a degree of confidence in us. I did try to explain that Alex was not like any kid I'd ever come across and indicated that it might prove to be the same for him. I emphasised the need for consistency and the necessity for us to work together. I gently suggested that he shouldn't be too confident, for if the school had a weakness Alex would soon find it. I also told him he could phone me at work if he needed to. Again he reassured us, this time a touch patronisingly. However, in the walkabout that followed our interview Mr Matthews got a taste of what was to come. In no time at all Alex was everywhere, excitedly touching everything. 'New things, new kids, equals more fun,' he might have been thinking.

Alex was still only 8½ years old. Many of his deeds, though very trying, were largely fuelled by a desire to play and have fun or were triggered by boredom. He was still almost entirely unable to foresee the consequences of his actions. In a classroom setting he had difficulty in coping with some of the work, so playing up became a convenient distraction. He was generally naive but this was successfully masked by his forward, sharp personality. His innocence and charm, however, took a nosedive the day he started at special school.

We'd gone along with the authorities' plans because we did not know of any better solution and wanted to help our son. So we entered unknown territory, and no one advised us of alternatives or explained to us how serious for Alex such a move was. We'd been swept along by the tide of daily events surrounding his behaviour. After all, the experts were claiming that this school was best for our child. Who were we to disagree?

We'd understood that Alex would attend for a two-term assessment lasting six months; after this period he would return to join his brother at junior school as a third-year pupil. Thus it came about that, early in 1989, Alex's educational assessment at special school began.

Before Denzil Morgan emigrated, he told me that meetings with Dr Thompson would be restarted since they did not duplicate the work of the school but addressed the dynamics within our family. Denzil had formed the opinion that I was more optimistic about social services' intervention than Sharon, who he thought interpreted their action as a way of punishing the family. I felt no such optimism but, like Sharon, was willing to co-operate with Dr Thompson – indeed, with anyone – if this would help my son.

★

Alex's behaviour deteriorated sharply at his new school, just as it had done after both the children's homes. That's when the penny finally dropped that these places were making Alex worse, not better. He became menacingly violent towards other children, his swearing was even more crude and obnoxious, while his behaviour towards Jason was outrageous.

The school itself had been experiencing a good deal of daily difficulty in coping with him. Initially they tried their best not to 'trouble us', but the envisaged settling-in period never ended. Alex began to abscond whenever the fancy took him, or when he was challenged. This was something he had never done at junior school, but had learned from his peers at the children's homes and special school. Fights were frequent – especially with Alan, the school's tough guy, whom Alex felt compelled to depose even though he was two or three years Alex's senior. They battled for top position in between their bouts of uneasy friendship, and weaker children got hurt in the process. When questioned as to why he did certain things, Alex explained that 'so-and-so' showed him this or told him that, referring to particular children in the school. Other times he'd cry for ages for no apparent reason, sometimes refusing all attempts to console him, just as he'd done since he was a toddler.

At about 8.30 a.m. a school van would call to collect him from home. En route, other children had to be collected. Because of this, and traffic, the 15-minute journey might end up taking half an hour or more. As his time at special school wore on, these trips deteriorated into a daily nightmare for the escorts. Sometimes there were fights between Alex and other children while the vehicle was moving. Eventually, after he'd started making repeated attempts to jump out of the van, sometimes while it was still in motion, the van collection was stopped for safety reasons. Thereafter he was usually shuttled to and from school by a minicab with an escort. Of all the daily incidents at school involving Alex, the majority probably remained unknown to us.

Sometimes Sharon or I would collect him from school, and one such evening Sharon heard him screaming as she walked up the pathway to the school entrance. Not untypically, Alex was in the headmaster's office. Without knocking she burst through the door and found Mr Matthews slapping Alex about the face. So engrossed was he in his action, he had failed to notice Sharon through his office window as she came up the path. A fraction of a second after she burst in Mr Matthews looked up, saw her, and the blood rushed to his face in what seemed to be a mixture of fear and embarrassment.

Sharon only just managed to contain her fury and proceeded to tell him a few home truths. He was supposed to be helping Alex, and she was disappointed and surprised that he, a headmaster of a special school no less, should behave towards a pupil in that way. 'What sort of example do you think you are setting these children? Do you think you can earn their respect by behaving in this manner?'

Mr Matthews apologised profusely and admitted that he had lost his temper. He had no answer for Sharon but attempted to describe what Alex had supposedly done to make him lose control. However, Sharon was in no mood to listen; she took Alex and left. As far as she was concerned, whatever Alex had done, Mr Matthews had dealt with it the wrong way.

At home, when Alex infuriated me I would sometimes react by slapping him on his arms or bottom, but it made little overall difference to his behaviour, apart from briefly stopping the bad deed. I could empathise with Mr Matthews, and did, though I knew it was wrong of him to lose his temper, as much as it was wrong of me when I lost mine. The scene that had been enacted between Sharon and Mr Matthews, in front of Alex, reminded me of our arguments at home. I always wished for a way out, or hoped that one morning I'd wake up to discover I'd been beamed-up by Scottie and that it had all been a bad dream. The reality, however, was that I could see no way out of a situation worsening by the day.

Out of ignorance, Sharon and I had done our son the gravest of injustices by allowing him to attend that special school. We'd set him up to fail and hadn't realised it. Blabbermouth Cynthia turned out to be right when she'd criticised the school. I wished I'd listened to her – and to Sharon.

After Alex had been at the school for a couple of months, and we'd witnessed the behaviour of the other pupils and talked to various parents in the community, we came to the conclusion that it was not much more than a dumping ground for socially dysfunctional children in the area: the young educational refuse of the borough. We couldn't wait for the two terms to end, to free Alex of the stigma of being placed in a special school. We wanted him to return to junior school with whatever additional specialist help was deemed suitable, as had been originally promised.

Having lost his temper, Mr Matthews had unwittingly dug his own pit when it came to controlling Alex: that thin psychological line in my son's head, which, once crossed, removed any possibility of respect, had been breached. Mr Matthews was not Alex's parent and did not have this right, and in his own way Alex understood this. He instinctively knew that Mr Matthews, and all the other professionals, did not love him, but that his parents did. Like animals, young children can sense who their friends and enemies are. From then on, metaphorically, Alex was king of that school. I could, and did, sympathise with Mr Matthews, for how was it possible for a headmaster to function when his authority was constantly undermined by an 8-year-old boy? But it must have been equally frustrating for Alex to be in a school setting that wasn't helping him.

The summer holidays arrived and Alex turned 9. He'd completed two terms at special school, but there was neither a new plan for the autumn nor any suggestion he could return to junior school. Denzil had been gone for several months and still no new social worker had been assigned, so Alex went back to special school. By the end of September, both a medical and an educational assessment had been completed. The medical assessment reported that Alex was a healthy, lively boy, who had a tendency to stammer and become hoarse when excitable or angry, and so a speech therapy report had been made. His long history of behavioural problems was remarked upon, finally that Alex's needs were being met at his current school. One wonders how long the medical examiner spent with Alex or with his teachers to reach this conclusion.

The educational assessment, signed by Mr Matthews, was thorough and thoughtful. It paid detailed attention to Alex's range of difficult behaviour, and noted that the only way to provide sufficient motivation was to give him one-to-one adult attention. Sometimes Alex would accept reprimands, but at others he would shout and scream and lash out, then cry as though he were inconsolable. On the whole, he seemed to relate better to adults than children. However, despite these problems and his lack of concentration, the standard of Alex's spoken language and vocabulary were considered to be reasonable, and it was thought he had the ability to produce a standard of written work expected of his age group if he didn't continually misbehave. While Alex could be capable when he tried, he would not carry out simple tasks unless absolutely sure he could complete them. He enjoyed science: he could rationalise information and took an active part in oral sessions.

Overall, while Alex appeared to be bright and articulate, he seemed unable to use his intelligence to learn from his mistakes, no matter how often the teachers discussed with him the events that led up to conflicts and suggested avoidance strategies. His emotional disturbances led to conflicts that seemed to be unnecessarily repetitive, and while he was sometimes potentially dangerous to others, albeit unintentionally, in fact he sometimes displayed a great deal of consideration and strong protective feelings for others. The assessment concluded that Alex was a little boy in a continual state of turmoil, in whom a battle between his emotions and his rational thoughts raged, and who was confused about his personal relationships. In order to try to overcome all this and give him a happier life, it was felt he should be in a structured, consistent environment that combined his schooling and living arrangements, and was staffed by those experienced in dealing with children with such severe difficulties.

Three months later, Dr Thompson, whom we had been seeing throughout the year, also strongly recommended that a therapeutic residential boarding school be found for Alex. In the meantime he was continuing to attend a school that admitted it did not meet his educational needs and could not cope with him. Ironically, I later learned that my local education authority warns professional advisers against discussing educational placements with parents, where their child might receive appropriate specialist education, emphasising that any final decision would rest with the local Director of Education. Was it our local department of education's policy never to discuss such a crucial matter with those who cared most? That this most important decision, with the potential to affect beneficially or adversely a child's entire future, should be made solely by the Director of Education, who was the least likely to have personal knowledge of the case, and whom the child and parents would probably never meet, seems extraordinary.

Interestingly, Alex complained of Mr Matthews's poking him in the chest, twisting his arm, shaking him, grabbing him by the clothes, and shouting and swearing at him. According to Alex these became the daily norm, mostly behind closed doors. I suspected Alex wasn't always lying or exaggerating, that some of it was true, but I also knew he wanted me to challenge Mr Matthews and spring to his defence, and I wasn't prepared to do that. I didn't want to fall into the trap of undermining any remnant of the headmaster's authority over Alex because I appreciated how difficult he was to cope with and that it would only have made things worse. So I bit my lip and said nothing, but it was eating me up inside – especially when Mr Matthews complained to me about Alex, unaware that my son had detailed his behaviour to me. When I'd get messages at work from the school and go to collect Alex, I saw the same frustration engraved all over Mr Matthews's face that I'd seen many times on Mr Dixon's – though I'd never heard of his losing his temper and striking a child. Mr Matthews's predicament was unenviable. There he was, lumbered with the responsibility of educating Alex after he'd recommended that he be moved to a more appropriate educational environment.

I'd try to encourage Alex to behave himself; he'd always promise me he would but rarely did. I've often agonised over what another father in my position might have done. Would he have continued to turn a blind eye as I did; or would he have supported his son's accusations, comforted him and therefore give him licence to cause even more chaos?

One day the school phoned the garage and left a message for me to collect Alex immediately. He had absconded earlier in the day and had returned with a large Alsatian dog. Terrifying or endangering fellow pupils with a stray dog appeared to be the last straw as far as Mr Matthews was concerned. He ordered me to remove Alex from his school. I did not argue. Naturally I was upset, but simply looked at Mr Matthews, took my son and left. I understood him to mean that he was expelling Alex, so I never took him back. He later claimed I had removed Alex from the school of my own accord. Alex had won again: he'd successfully dispensed with Mr Matthews and his special school.

Alex came to the garage with me every day, and for some months, to the best of my knowledge, no one from the school or the education department enquired as to why he was absent. Finally a new social worker, Mavis Pollard, was allocated to him. She made it a priority to get up to date on events since Denzil's departure. She'd been told I had removed Alex from school; I corrected this misconception. Sharon, she noted, thought that Alex had been suspended and that he was a sad, disturbed child in urgent need of specialist help. As far as Mavis was concerned, Alex needed to be in a therapeutic boarding school.

Mavis knew she wasn't welcome in our family; I don't recall ever once offering her a cup of tea, which was very unusual for us since we are normally very hospitable people. She seemed to dismiss past social-service decisions in which she hadn't been involved as if they didn't matter and bore no relationship to the current difficulties. Wary of our continued anger at the way Alex had been messed around, she began to watch us with her textbook-trained eyes and take meticulous notes.

Seven

Alex urgently needed to be taken in hand, and I seemed to be the only candidate remotely capable of doing so. At the time, no one else appeared willing to admit to that. His eight months at special school had been an unmitigated disaster – a period of Alex's life that had, to put it kindly, seen him move from being difficult to being – extremely difficult! Could I do better? I wasn't sure but I didn't have any choice: he's my son.

Alex was, of course, already familiar with the garage and knew all the staff. Everybody liked Jason, but the majority didn't much care for Alex's behaviour. I was none too keen to take him in with me every day – a garage is no place for a schoolboy – and I had visions of his ruining the business by driving customers away. I couldn't let that happen. Now I was going to be stressed not only at home and at weekends – a situation to which I'd become accustomed – but also at work. The only time I'd get peace from now on would be when I was sleeping.

From day one I decided that Alex must be educated and told him so. I couldn't allow him, after wrecking his school placement, to come to the garage and simply have fun, mucking around all day while driving everyone insane in the process. I hoped the absence of other kids would have a calming effect on him, and that my presence would offer stability. It was a temporary arrangement. The education authority had been informed of the situation, both by me and Mavis Pollard.

Knowing Alex as I did, I had to start things off on the right footing. This meant that each day I would set him work, help him with it, and check and mark the exercises when they had been completed, just as if he were at school – in effect, I became his teacher. But I couldn't set him too much, or devote as much time to him as a school would, because I was supposed to be at work myself. I thought that about an hour's worth each day would be sufficient. In reality this was about five minutes' work for an adult, half an hour for a capable child of Alex's age, and about an hour and a half for Alex at his worst.

After instructing my staff and dealing with the early-morning customers and telephone calls, I'd turn my attention to tutoring Alex by about 10 o'clock. He did not like this arrangement, though he was fascinated by being at the garage surrounded by adults and he quickly found ways to avoid sitting down to work. He'd suddenly discover an irresistible need to go to the toilet, or he might unexpectedly realise how hungry or thirsty he was. Sometimes a part of his anatomy would inexplicably begin to hurt him. All this was often to the accompaniment of protracted moaning, whining or tears, until someone in the garage would be moved to comment. Other times he claimed that he felt sick or was too tired.

I knew most of Alex's complaints were utter hogwash but dealt with them as tactfully as I could.

'Which part of your belly is hurting you, son?'

'Right here, Dad,' he'd say, lifting up his shirt.

'What happened to it, son; you seemed all right this morning?'

'I don't know, Dad, but I feel sick.'

'Do you think if you rest up a bit, you'll be all right later?'

In the early days, he'd answer, 'Yes.' After a few occasions he realised that this meant he'd be well enough to do the work later, so he then began to answer, 'No!' or, 'I don't know.' When I enquired whether he needed to go to the doctor or hospital, the answer was usually negative.

When Alex insisted that there was still a problem I'd say something like: 'This means you won't be able to come with me when I go over to so-and-so's later. I was going there after you'd finished your sums, but it looks like I'll have to leave you here till I get back.'

Some of my regular customers knew him and liked him – they'd only ever see him for five or ten minutes at a time, often months apart – and would give him money or small gifts, and generally fuss over him. It was difficult to keep him motivated, but I'd try to create a high point for him to look forward to, something that could tie in with whatever I had to do that day and which always came after his school work was done.

I'd be at my desk and settle down to do some paperwork or make phone calls. Alex would sit at his adopted desk, a lower work surface which abutted mine in an L-shape. Then the most amazing transformation would begin to take place. After a few minutes Alex would quietly, and without fuss, begin to do the sums I'd neatly prepared for him that morning. Then he'd get stuck, and with no mention of the pain that had disabled him minutes ago, would in a studious tone perhaps ask: 'Dad, where do I put the seven?' I'd answer in a matter-of-fact way, 'Do you remember, son, where you put the five? Shall I help you with another one? Look at your four-times table and see if you can spot which one is the correct answer,' and didn't dare make mention of his erstwhile pain. I'd then make up a new sum, just to make sure he'd got the hang of that particular stage, after which, in next to no time at all, he'd whiz through the pages and do all the sums. Usually he'd get all or nearly all of them right. I'd tell him, 'Well done. See, you *can* do it. My son isn't stupid, is he?' He'd smile proudly. Then I'd give him a cuddle, and talk about whatever he wanted to for a bit. Later, I'd fulfil whatever promise I had made. But it didn't always go that smoothly; these were the occasions when the day started well.

Sometimes I would see to it that all Alex's needs were met. If he felt 'tired' I'd allow him a rest period before starting work. If he said he was 'hungry' I gave him food. Then I would let him use the toilet, perhaps tend to his 'sick' finger or arm or leg, and repeatedly reassure him that I was there to help, thus giving him no excuse not to do the work. This was a one-to-one situation! I'd always patiently demonstrate the subject matter, and invent imaginative examples until Alex got the point. However, I never did his work for him; he was always required to do that for himself, no matter how long he took. We both found these teaching sessions taxing and mentally draining, but it was in this manner, at home and at the garage, that Alex learned the alphabet, how to count, how to read and write, and, later, how to do simple mathematics.

Eventually he began to appreciate that the quicker he did his work, the quicker he could 'help' me with mine. Like his former headmistress I resorted to giving him little tasks to pad out the day and make him feel useful, or allowed him to play with spanners and other safe hand-tools so that he believed he was fixing things like the mechanics. But it was at the garage that I first came to realise the most bewildering and terribly frustrating thing about teaching Alex: the next day he'd usually forgotten virtually everything new he'd learned the day before. At first I thought he was taking the mickey, but soon realised he was genuine. It was as if his memory had been wiped clean, like an unsaved computer disk file.

It was the first inkling I had that there might be an explanation as to why Alex was so difficult at school. It began to dawn on me that maybe he simply couldn't cope with learning. Look at the palaver he caused religiously every morning just because he couldn't face school work. It certainly wasn't easy to pinpoint. I never set out intentionally to analyse his behaviour in order to 'see' what was happening, but that's what it boiled down to: during those few minutes each day, when I tried to steer him into learning mode, he seemed overwhelmingly compelled to avoid all lessons at all costs. Is it any wonder the schools had been failing: they weren't giving him the sort of skilled one-to-one attention and environment he needed.

At first I didn't fully realise the significance of what I'd stumbled on in my tiny office as I systematically removed all Alex's apparent impediments to work, pitched his assignments in such a way that he could understand, and gave him the help, motivation and space he needed to do the task comfortably. And still, by no stretch of the imagination, did things always go smoothly.

His habit of running away, which had started at the children's homes and continued at the special school, was now firmly entrenched and proving to be a real nuisance as well as potentially very dangerous.

He appeared to assume that if absconding had obtained him the desired attention at school, then it would do so at home. And guess what – it did!

From the very first time Alex ran away from home, I adopted an unpopular stance and further isolated myself: I refused to search for him. As far as I was concerned I hadn't sent or chased him away and so I would not go looking. I saw it as another Alex ploy to get his own way and I would not be lured into any hunt. Some fairly harsh criticisms were levelled against me for this. Everyone else would react quickly and turn searching for him into a melodrama. They felt, not surprisingly, that the young child should be found immediately for he might be in danger. Naturally I also had the same fears; I could see how stupid his behaviour was, but on principle refused to allow myself to be manipulated.

Very soon a pattern began to establish itself. After running away, Alex would always return when he was hungry, or when it became dark, or after he had engaged in a fight and lost. If he'd stormed off and the weather was hostile, he certainly didn't stay out too long.

Social services (we spoke only to Mavis at this time) made no attempt to address this new problem. On several occasions, after a reasonable period of time had elapsed, I informed the police Alex was missing – that much I was prepared to do. Sharon, by herself or with others, would scour the neighbourhood. At times the situation verged on the ludicrous because, as we later discovered, Alex would hide at a vantage point and watch them. He would return home when he was good and ready. Mostly when he was missing he went to play with friends or got up to boyish mischief.

To begin with, he never ran away if I was at home. If I was out he'd use virtually any excuse to scarper when it suited him. Typically this would happen following an argument or struggle either when visiting relatives or at home with his brother and mother. Sometimes he simply wanted to go out to play, had been refused, and so was forced to find an excuse to justify his leaving. If a situation did not exist to fulfil Alex's own criteria for running away, he'd simply engineer one, then run. His misdeeds always had to be someone else's fault, never his.

I was not alone in recognising this pattern, but only I refused to be drawn into it. As time went by, even the social workers joined police and relatives in the searches. Later Alex would boast, mainly to Jason, about where he'd been and how he'd hidden behind garden bushes or walls when he saw them coming. On occasions, sensing he'd gone overboard or stayed out too long, he'd turn up at a relative's house or at a family friend's, or even call on one of my staff if he recognised where they lived, and draw them into the situation. Finally we'd get a telephone call informing us where our son was.

Wherever he ended up, he was usually shown hospitality while waiting to be collected, and his concerned hosts would ask him what had happened. Alex would use the opportunity to tell a story that was conveniently distorted in his favour. In those early days, nobody shut their door to him; he was always greeted with love and genuine concern. And wherever he ran, he went by foot.

Was there any length to which Alex would not go to get his own way? He was acting out, on a grander scale, techniques he'd long mastered at home and at school. Essentially this was to play one party off against the other for his own ends, but his game was becoming more dangerous for sure. It was the day he set off on what was to him the long journey on foot to my parents' house that Alex first toyed with the notion of suicide.

There'd been a sibling quarrel at home and impulsive Alex decided to go to his grandma's. He would have to cross several busy main roads and negotiate over two miles of six-lane motorway because he followed the route the family normally took in the car. When only halfway there, and overwrought with sadness, he caught sight of the canal which runs near the junction of the motorway intersection he was about to join. A terrible idea came into his head. He'd slid down the road sidings and gone to the edge of the canal when, from out of nowhere, another little boy appeared. This young lad of about 11, and unknown to us to this day, approached Alex and managed to talk him out of his idea just as he was apparently about to jump. As they were climbing up from the embankment back to the pavement a passing police car saw them. The boy handed Alex over to them and they duly returned him home.

Whether he would have made a serious attempt on his life, or whether he was feeling a little sorry of himself, no one will ever know. Many times before, Alex had inadvertently diced with death through his antics, but wanting to die was in an entirely different league. The idea that a 9-year-old child might deliberately endanger his own life was pretty shocking for Sharon and me, and vividly demonstrates the miserable depths to which my son's life had sunk. His whole predicament tore me apart. It compounded our bitterness towards social services and the education authority even further.

Alex's first instinct at the garage when school work was set was to run, but he didn't as he was with Daddy. He never looked forward to his studies, and even when he surprised himself and got his tasks right he'd still do all in his power to avert the prospect of a repetition. The environment provided him with many opportunities for distraction. There were far more interesting and mischievous things he'd rather be doing, he would think wistfully, as he looked down through my office window at the mechanics working below. Then the telephone would ring, or a customer would want my attention, or a vehicle had to be tested, or a mechanic needed my assistance. Each such occasion provided Alex with a perfect opportunity.

As soon as my back was turned he'd get into some sort of trouble. The mechanics he liked were treated by him as if they were kids – his buddies. To the others, he gave a lot of cheek and was often rude, interfering with their tools and other equipment. It was impossible to keep him in my sight: he was as slippery as a bar of soap in wet hands.

In no time at all the same old pattern began to emerge: adults would respond to him on his level. Sometimes I wished I could shout warnings from the rooftops or simply carry a large placard around with me: 'Alex never gives up, so if you respond to him he will wind you up more. Tell me and I will deal with it.' But there would always be at least one who was unable to see that and would fall right into the trap.

Some of the staff and customers hated Alex but he didn't care.

The wiser ones kept their distance and the truly clever ones mostly tried to humour him. He veered from being slightly cheeky to downright insulting, hurling abuse when my attention was elsewhere. When angered he'd swear and order them to get out of his dad's garage. Complaints came from left, right and centre. Needless to say I lost some customers – they did as Alex ordered, never to return. But even here he had his champions: those who succumbed to his charm, saw the funny side and had good belly laughs with him. Unwittingly they provided unnecessary encouragement.

When he started up the engine of a customer's car, a mechanic got to him just in the nick of time. Then he released the handbrake of a customer's parked car, causing it to roll backwards down the road and crash into the car behind. One time he flooded the garage with a freshly consignment of oil as staff enjoyed a morning tea break; the rest of the morning was spent cleaning up the mess. He was absolutely fascinated by the hoists – like a kitten bobbing its head up and down to the rhythm of a moving object. As with my old music centre he was burning to touch it. One day he got his chance and started to lower one while an unsuspecting mechanic worked beneath. Alex thought that quite funny, but the man was definitely not amused. When the disgruntled, angry mechanic swore at him and reported him to me, Alex was most upset. Later that day he got even: he set fire to the man's vehicle. The fire brigade was called, and Alex caused some excitement as disbelieving staff and a small crowd gathered to view the spectacle. The van was completely burned out.

Two very different incidents provide an insight into how Alex's mind was working at that time. He had been allowed to go to a nearby park to play with his brother, who came to the garage unescorted most afternoons after school. Minutes later a frantic Jason came running back, crying: 'Alex is in the middle of the road!' This was the main road to which ours was joined. Half the garage immediately stopped work and went to rescue him. The boys usually took the back way to the park, with no roads to cross. But for reasons best known to themselves, this time they'd decided to take the longer route via the six-lane dual carriageway. The traffic lights had apparently failed, and Alex decided to intervene. He later explained that he was only trying to help. I believed him, for *that's how he saw it*. (In principle, this is what often happened at school. For instance, when he saw two children who he thought were fighting but who were in fact playing, he'd go to the assistance of the one he felt needed it but would be shocked when both turned on him.) Alex had done what he'd seen the police do on so many occasions when the lights are out of order: step into the road and direct the traffic. He could have been killed. The motorists did not appreciate his efforts either as they tooted their horns and shouted angrily while swerving to avoid him.

The other incident occurred when he was with a kindly relative, who would take Alex occasionally to relieve the pressure on me. On one such afternoon, without warning or provocation, he burst into tears and climbed on to the balcony of her second-floor maisonette about 30 feet above the ground. He said he was going to jump. The shock turned her stomach, but she somehow managed to stay composed and after about ten minutes was able to persuade him to come in. What was the reason for that incident? It transpired that Alex had seen her daughter cuddle her lovingly in a moment of mother-daughter closeness shortly after her return home from school. That spontaneous display of tenderness affected him somehow; he felt nobody loved him and acted without thinking. Not surprisingly, that relative never again volunteered to accept responsibility for him.

Both acts were triggered by an unthinking impulse. It was therefore quite an achievement to have been able to modify Alex's behaviour sufficiently to allow some school work to take place, even if it was only for an hour or two each day, and to have been able to detect that he might have a serious learning difficulty.

Meanwhile the education authority appeared quite happy to let things drift along. It seemed as if they'd chosen to take a subservient position to social services, who likewise had done little to help us at this point. Sharon and I could not help but be amazed at the contrast. About a year before, they'd been so keen to save Alex from us;

now they'd opened Pandora's box they were nowhere to be found, in practical terms.

By April 1990 the social services hierarchy were presumably aware that Mr Matthews had struck Alex on at least two separate occasions at his school, but they were apparently more interested in pursuing me because a school escort had reported me for being angry with Alex and slapping him on the arm in front of them one morning as he misbehaved. They acknowledged that Mr Matthews's action prevented them from taking action against me.

It had been four months since Dr Thompson's report, and they knew that we didn't agree with the idea of a boarding school for Alex because we felt it might make him even worse. They decided that Alex should return to the special school. He did so at Easter, and immediately problems of the old order began to recur. But greater troubles of a different sort were looming. The stress of work, ongoing problems with Alex, the involvement of social services and our heated arguments had all taken a drastic toll on the family. Sharon returned to live with her parents, taking Jason, leaving me with Alex. Our marriage was over.

We were all devastated. The boys took it hard and I nearly cracked under the strain. Like a sealed cooking pot with nowhere to let off steam, it wasn't that surprising that something eventually blew. The break-up of our marriage further destabilised Alex. He blamed himself for the split, and an unhappy Jason began to fail miserably at school.

Because of her involvement with the family, Mavis knew that our fears for Alex's safety lay behind our objections to boarding school. She'd got to know Alex a bit better (though he didn't like her because he saw Mavis as social services) and discovered that he wished to do well at school, was keen on maths (probably because of his success at the garage) and was very worried about being sent to a residential school.

A troubled summer holiday passed, with Alex's days divided between the garage and the play scheme in the park. A month into the autumn term, the conflicts at school crescendoed, and the headmaster returned to what I considered to be his previously failed bully-boy tactics. One afternoon the school phoned and asked me to take Alex home after a series of incidents. In an almost carbon copy of what had happened about a year previously with Sharon, I arrived just after he had hit Alex.

A very heated verbal exchange followed. I lost my temper for the first and only time at that school, and told the headmaster exactly what I thought of him. I was a hair's breadth away from striking him. Apparently he could hit my child with impunity in the likely knowledge that he would be supported by his colleagues: without threat of legal action or a band of social workers and police descending on him. I encouraged him to admit that he and his school had achieved nothing, and pleaded with him to stop torturing the boy by allowing him to remain in his school and so setting him up to fail, then punishing him for that failure. I was also very angry with Alex for placing me in this situation. At that point everything got to me and I broke down in tears, cursing Alex for being a pain, the headmaster and just about everyone else who I believed had messed up the boy's 10-year-old life. I was also angry with myself for allowing it to happen. I asked Mr Matthews to have the guts to expel him – we both knew he didn't want Alex there – and this time requested he put it in writing. I hoped that this would force the education authority to do something constructive.

I lodged a formal complaint about Mr Matthews with the education authority. They in turn did nothing and sought to protect their man by commenting that he was 'a very good headmaster'. I was later to discover that they believed he acted properly, which I interpreted as a licence to strike children in his charge any time he felt the situation warranted it.

Mr Matthews did expel Alex. He complained that Alex's behaviour was becoming increasingly violent and that staff were worried for the safety of the other children. A case conference had been held a month earlier, attended by Mr Matthews, Mavis, a senior educational psychologist who had assessed Alex, a special education assistant, Sharon and myself. Sharon and I wanted him returned to mainstream education for the moment, while the rest kept on about boarding school. For the time being, however, it was back to the garage for Alex. After all the havoc he had caused last time round, I was despondent: the business was doing badly, and the word 'recession' was on everyone's lips. I couldn't cope any more and was rapidly losing my will to try.

Perhaps because of social-service pressure, and my angrier appeals for help, the education people now felt that Alex met the criteria for some home tuition. They recommended he receive three hours a week, split in two one-and-a-half-hour sessions, either at the garage or a nearby school. Three hours – such madness! Most kids get that in half a day. I found it difficult to follow or understand this logic and expressed my consternation, but they made me feel as though I should have been grateful for their magnanimity.

The day he was to have had his first session at the garage, there had been a morning of extreme provocation of staff by Alex. After several warnings I finally snapped, grabbed him and gave him a good smacking with a nearby piece of light plastic hose. He immediately ran to the police, who took him to the local hospital. They also came to see me and informed social services. My smacking him resulted in Alex's being placed on the 'At Risk' register for the second time, though Mavis confirmed that the hospital doctor was confused as to why Alex was there because the smacks could not in any way be said to have been hard or injured him. Some lessons are extremely easy for Alex to learn.

So once again I was cast in the role of the bad guy and repeatedly asked myself: 'Why me? Why me? What have I done to deserve this?' (Sharon asked herself the same question many times too.) I felt I had no alternative but to detach myself and let Alex do whatever he wanted. It seemed I was damned if I acted and damned if I didn't. Alex was never happy when he knew he'd succeeded in hurting me; he could always tell because those were the occasions I'd simply ignore him. Unfortunately he'd usually do something even more outrageous to recapture my attention. He continued to trifle with his own safety, and was often found wandering aimlessly around the local shopping centre and main roads, looking very dejected. Sometimes he ran or walked precariously between traffic. Many a time he was seen by local social workers, who did nothing. I'd simply wait for him to return. This he always did and would calmly apologise.

A draft statement of Alex's special educational needs was produced — neither Sharon nor I recollect seeing a copy of it at the time — which recommended that he be sent to a residential school for disturbed children. Through the efforts of Mavis a temporary special school facility, the Dudley Scheme, was located. This became the second special school that Alex attended. It was small with a low pupil-teacher ratio, and a 'rough' clientele of teenage young men aged 14 upwards. Some were very disturbed, though I didn't fully appreciate that at the time.

Sharon was dead against Alex's going there. On her initial visit she was appalled. She saw these young men openly smoke and swear in normal conversation with their teachers. There was no respect. She was disgusted and became convinced that this place would corrupt Alex further. She could see that whereas his actions were on the whole immature and childish, these young men were more calculating and deliberate.

Nevertheless, I felt so pressured by Alex's presence at work that I was willing to agree to anything, even though I felt the same way about Dudley as Sharon. I reasoned that some education was better than no education at all, and getting Alex away from the dangerous environment of the garage had now become my top priority. Dudley, I reasoned, was the lesser of two evils. But this proved to be yet another of the errors that everyone connected with Alex seemed to have been making.

I met the headmaster, David Burke, and briefed him and two of his colleagues in detail on what it would be like to interact with Alex. They were very grateful and were sure they'd be able to cope. I explained all the difficulties experienced at his last school. Alex was quite placid that afternoon and displayed few of his worrisome traits, even though the meeting lasted about three hours. They commented that it was very unusual for a parent to conduct these discussions in such a forthright and comprehensive manner, indicating that most they encountered weren't as devoted to their children. I asked that they would under no circumstances allow Alex to smoke, and we agreed to work together closely. Mr Burke would discuss the day's events with me after school by phone, and I'd try to address any problems during my evenings with Alex. I was dubious to say the least, but hoped for the best. They assured me there'd be no repetition of unprofessional outbursts of the type displayed by Mr Matthews – it was not their style. To be truthful, I don't believe it was Mr Matthews's style either – maybe not until he encountered Alex.

True to their word, they did contact me every day and we enjoyed a communicative two-way relationship. This partnership was maintained cordially almost throughout this temporary period, and in this way we did manage to avert a few problems or prevent them from escalating. However, their 'style' was far too laid back for my liking, and the other boys did not have a mind to treat the little kid with any special care, reacting with predictable hostility to his cheek and immature behaviour. It was here that Sharon and I first knew for sure that Alex occasionally smoked, got some exposure to pornographic literature and received man-sized blows from his teenage peers. I was forced to wonder why they couldn't come up with something better than Dudley. No matter how 'bad' he was, Alex was still only a 10-year-old boy! Sometimes the staff arrived on the scene too late to prevent him receiving a vicious beating from a teenager. He always failed to appreciate that they might not be as patient as adults usually were and could quickly lash out at him. Though he frequently got hurt and they towered over him, Alex always tried to fight back and rarely showed any fear.

However, it wasn't all bad – even at this time. I fervently believed myself to be the only one who was able to see the *whole* picture. After school, when work was no longer an issue and there was no stress in the household, Alex seemed momentarily at peace and was impeccably behaved. I would detach myself from whatever he'd been involved in during the day and we would start afresh in the evening.

Talk about Jekyll and Hyde: it would have been hard for anyone to recognise that he was the same child who had caused such turmoil during the day. We spent many wonderful, peaceful evenings and weekends together, times which undoubtedly drew us closer. Alex would be totally calm, and he'd happily help me with the household chores. We'd share in preparing and cooking our evening meal, cleaning the house, packing away the shopping. I used such occasions as we talked to try to instil good thoughts into Alex's mind, just as I had always tried since he and his brother were babes.

He'd tell me about Dudley, which boy did what to him, and what he'd do to them tomorrow. My blood sizzled at the injustices but I tried not to show it as he told me of fights with lads who were as big as or bigger than me. Again, he wasn't always lying, as I knew from Mr Burke's outline of the day's incidents, and Alex's bruises proved it. Because I was a black-belt martial artist and instructor, he believed I could physically overcome any of his tormentors with ease and wanted me to fight these lads for him. I spent many hours reasoning as tactfully as possible until he appeared to understand, but the next day he'd get himself into conflicts again. To be fair to him, a good deal of the time it wasn't his fault. He simply had no idea how to side-step trouble, even when the odds were heavily stacked against him.

We played together too, and from time to time he'd even surprise me by asking me to set him some maths questions. Ironically we both enjoyed playing the board game 'Frustration', as if I didn't have enough of that in real life. Sometimes we'd wrestle and fool around. He especially loved his neck being tickled. When I least expected it I'd get a cuddle and an 'I love you, Dad!' But no matter how much enjoyment Alex shared with me, he always wanted more and easily became bored. He pined for his mother, though they saw and spoke to each other several times a week.

All this was exhausting, so I gladly accepted my mother's invitation for Alex to spend some Saturday evenings with her. This gave me a little respite, but was never without problems. In particular, Alex took great pleasure in tormenting my elderly father who was terminally ill, stone deaf and able to walk only short distances with the aid of a Zimmer frame. When no one was looking, Alex found it terribly funny to tap the old man on his back or shoulder, and then run round to his grandad's other side so that he rarely ever saw who had tapped him though he knew it was Alex. (Jason desisted from antics when told to.) Eventually he'd get very angry and start to shout and swear at him – it was this that Alex found so amusing – and if his walking stick was near by he'd try to strike Alex with it, but Alex was too swift. Despite my mother and other relatives explaining to Alex that his grandad was a very sick man who could die at any time, Alex continued his game. Threatening to tell me made no difference: it was a case of out of sight and hence out of Alex's mind. The game continued for several weeks, after which an angry relative eventually told me what had been going on. I was very upset.

While I did not physically chastise him, I pointed out to Alex the seriousness of the situation. I explained that if Grandad fell over and hurt himself, or worse, he would get the blame; if he did it again I would smack him. Alex knew I meant it, and promised me he wouldn't annoy Grandad any more. On the very next visit he could not resist the temptation and again played the prank. My precious few hours each weekend while Alex was with my mother, the only leisure-time reprieve I got from my son, were now in jeopardy. On learning I was to collect him after he had upset Grandad and the family, Alex immediately ran away, walking the several miles to his mother's. On arrival he declared: 'I don't want to live with Dad any more, I want to live with you, Mum.' And he did. I was in no mood to argue and was glad of the break.

Alex had won again! He'd now succeeded in getting rid of Daddy.

Apart from acknowledging that he was an extremely emotionally disturbed boy, none of the professionals offered any explanation for the *cause* of Alex's bizarre behaviour. This included Dr Thompson, who had organised a full medical examination with a brain scan as part of his assessment, and had kindly offered to continue to see Alex on a regular basis long after his report had been made. This impressed me. All tests, educational and medical, proclaimed Alex normal: mentally and physically of 'average' abilities. But could any of the above be described as 'normal' behaviour for a 10-year-old, or indeed any child?

So Alex got me out of the way and I stayed there. Now it was

Sharon's turn. Would she fare any better? The difficulties at Dudley during the day now spilled over into her evenings and Alex gave her a terrible time. She received the same amount of practical assistance with Alex's day-to-day care: none! Within about two months she found it impossible to cope with him. On one occasion, she saw him dangling from a parapet which ran along a live railway line next to her home. Using great presence of mind, like my relative had when she saw him perched on her balcony, Sharon gently talked Alex down from the ledge; thoughts of suicide were not motivating him on this occasion.

She asked me to take him back but I said no. Alex then started to pine for me just as he had done for his mum, but I was still adamant. He could not return unless his behaviour improved. In one of my by now regular tête-à-têtes with myself – I really didn't have anyone else to talk to – I concluded: 'If I let Alex stew for a while longer without me, maybe he'll start appreciating my efforts a little bit more.' I thought that unless something changed in him we were all wasting our time. I was now prepared to stay out on a limb and wait for this change, but I was reasoning wrongly. I was still taking it all personally and in a sense punishing Alex by keeping my distance. Because I was mentally exhausted, I was applying an inappropriate adult logic to the situation. Mavis told me Alex found it difficult to judge whether his behaviour was right or wrong, or to appreciate how what he did affected other people.

Because of my obstinacy, Sharon felt she had no alternative but to hand Alex back to social services. They performed the necessary legalities and in no time at all he was placed in the care of Bodley Road, where he'd been over two years before. By then, Sharon and I had both accepted the education department's recommendation of boarding school though privately neither of us liked the idea. But we could offer nothing better and waited for a place to become available. We begged them to let Alex leave Dudley and in the meantime return to junior school with additional teaching support, but social services did not want this. We wanted to lower his profile, for he was without doubt acting up to his 'special' status. To us this seemed a far better option, even though with his education and entire life in such a mess it probably wouldn't have worked – but a drowning man clutches at straws. We were in no way against professional help for Alex; we merely wished to understand what that help entailed so we could make informed decisions, and sought respectfully to point out that, thus far, every placement had made him worse – not better – which was crystal clear for all to see. Yet no one could answer the one burning question we longed to have answered: 'What is wrong with Alex?' Sharon's and my position was as simple as it was logical: 'Unless we find out what is wrong with Alex, nothing will work,' – a conclusion the local authority could not sensibly argue with.

It was now April 1991. We understood that Alex was due to start boarding school in May, so Sharon thought he'd be in care for only a few weeks, after which the great panacea would come into effect. He would receive expert help on a daily basis to remedy his destructive, antisocial behaviour and to reverse his downward educational trend. Maybe they would even achieve what Mavis had told me was Alex's confessed inner hope: someone to help him be 'good enough at reading and writing to study science properly'.

Eight

W E CANNOT ALWAYS do justice in words to our thoughts and ideas. One may instinctively know something to be true but if challenged to express it – ah, that's another matter. I cannot offer concrete proof that Alex saw me as the ultimate authority, in the manner I've suggested earlier, but that's how his actions consistently came across to me. This doesn't mean that he never submitted to the authority of others; he did – if he was in a mood to listen. But when push came to shove, he listened to me more than to anyone else. Mentally I appeared to be able to connect with or influence Alex in ways others could not. That might simply have been because I am his father. From Alex's perspective I was the only other person worth listening to – a concept I'd never tried to cultivate in his mind or encourage.

The idea I find most difficult to express, and the one which troubled me most, was that Alex also saw me as the ultimate challenge. That thought has been with me since he was about 3 or 4 years old. It's how I've interpreted many of his actions. He seemed to want to get his own way with me as he could with everyone else, and I wasn't going to let that happen. I could never allow myself to be dominated by a child – any child. It was as if a psychic power struggle were going on between my son and me, of which he was not consciously aware.

I sensed that to submit to his extremes of behaviour might open the emotional floodgates. He was becoming increasingly frustrated and developing a wildness that, if unleashed, could do serious harm to others as well as himself. I don't think many understood that, but

I did. I knew that Alex was unable to see how much damage he would do to himself (indeed, had already done) by not listening to me. I knew he was limited in his ability to control his actions, but I desperately wanted to protect him from himself and others.

My knowledge of Alex, though incomplete, morally compelled me to do my best despite any inconveniences and pressures: he was *my* son. Social services had thrown a massive spanner in the works and opened those floodgates. Nevertheless, my input and presence still carried a substantial degree of weight and influence, even though, in our unspoken mental chess game, he was still driven to seek to gain mastery over me. Can you see the contradiction? It's not natural to want to defeat your own champion, especially if it is a parent, and I was such to Alex. It bugged me terribly that something might be happening to my son that he could not control, and that I did not know what that was. My fear was that if I allowed myself to give up or caved in under the pressure, anarchy would result. He might be unable to cope with this and be overtaken by events. Disaster might then be imminent. That's why, for Alex's sake, I had to maintain a degree of firmness, otherwise he would triumph, causing greater turmoil to himself.

Feeling cornered by events when Alex left of his own volition to live with his mother, under the circumstances there was not much I could do. Alex *could* manipulate me to a certain extent, because, as his parent I would always, together with Sharon, be dragged into any aftermath, but with so many exerting what I considered to be negative, unhelpful, even unhealthy influences on Alex, however well meaning their intentions, his life was now well and truly a mess. I had lost control of the situation and nobody was listening to me any more. Frustrated, I concentrated on my rapidly failing business.

I've always been conscious of a part of Alex that needs me which goes beyond the father-son relationship. This is another example of those thoughts I find difficult to put into words. It could never be, and never was, easy for me to cut myself off and abandon him. But when he ran away and decided he did not want to live with me any more, he created the circumstances that allowed me to distance myself. I felt hurt and betrayed; I thought him ungrateful. When

Sharon accepted him, I slipped into the background. When social services accepted him, I said to myself, 'Good! Now they will see what coping with Alex without me is really like.'

Alex was in a foul mood on 29 April, the day Sharon deposited him at social services. It must have seemed as if both his mum and his dad were deserting him. Mavis took charge of him, and he attacked her viciously: verbally and physically. When they were later driven to Bodley Road, after she thought he had calmed down, he kicked and thumped her and pulled her hair. As far as Alex was concerned, Mavis *was* social services – for which he'd developed his own hatred – and he vented his fury on her.

Within days it became abundantly clear to the staff at Bodley Road that this new Alex was infinitely more difficult than the one they'd encountered over two years before. After a few months of contending with teenagers at the Dudley Scheme, his peers now seemed a tame bunch. There were also much younger children there who were no match for Alex. He was a couple of months away from his eleventh birthday and thought himself quite grown-up. What made matters worse was that relations had deteriorated considerably at Dudley between Alex and the other pupils. He simply did not want to go there any more. It couldn't have been much fun knowing daily that he was almost bound to get involved in acts of physical violence with people nearly twice his size.

The long journey to Dudley had provided many opportunities for dangerous behaviour. While in transit, Alex had opened doors, struggled – including with the driver – and even escaped and run into oncoming traffic. He had been absolutely determined he would not be taken to that school. Enough was enough. Very soon the Scheme's involvement with Alex was abruptly terminated – at our suggestion – because there appeared to be no safe way of getting him there. Alex had won yet again, his short-term goal fulfilled. Now Bodley Road would have to cope with him 24 hours a day.

Sharon visited Alex regularly at the home, but though I phoned, at first I refused to go, even though she tried her best to change my mind. She explained that Alex couldn't understand why I stayed away. In fact, on one occasion he told her that he didn't want her to come, but said firmly: 'I want Daddy to visit me.' She felt I was punishing him, which in a sense I was. I was angry with everyone, and distancing myself was my strategy for protecting my own sanity, the only thing I could think of that might bring the professionals to their senses. Perhaps, I thought, they might start acting in Alex's favour by trying to discover the true nature of his disturbances, rather than simply blaming his parents, which to us seemed the easiest thing for them to do. The only responsibility I was willing to shoulder for Alex's predicament was that Sharon and I had made it worse for him than it would have been if we'd been more united.

Distancing myself from Alex was a huge error on my part, a gross miscalculation. It deprived him of a reason for trying – maybe even living – and instilled in him a sense of hopelessness. Instinctively, he knew I was the one person who came the closest to understanding him, and that I fought for him – in a special sense – with that understanding, even though we didn't always get on. Sensing this support had been withdrawn, Alex must have felt completely alone. He had become a rudderless vessel.

Bodley was under pressure. To discuss Alex's situation a meeting was convened which was chaired by Julia Warren, a social worker senior to Mavis. The education department sent their apologies: their non-attendance was not an infrequent event at such conferences. Alex was not receiving any education, and the talk was now that no boarding school would be available until September. Bodley was concerned that Alex demanded constant one-to-one attention which the centre was unable to give. Through her regular visits, and my regular telephone conversations with them, Sharon and I learned that the Bodley staff thought that Alex was frustrated, which resulted in his frequently becoming violent and destructive; that he was disruptive and unpredictable and so needed to be closely watched; and that he would run away on the slightest grounds. Interestingly they noted his concentration span was very short and that he desperately needed schooling. They felt unequipped to meet his needs and criticised social services for their lack of support and the education authority for not doing enough to educate Alex: the selfsame criticisms Sharon and I had been making all along.

★

After two months, Rachel Palmer, Alex's keyworker, told Sharon that she had submitted a long report to social services that spanned six pages and listed over a hundred incidents in which he had been involved. She emphasised to her that not all incidents could be remembered because they were so many: punching other residents, throwing furniture at staff, threatening himself with a knife, receiving stitches to his hand after punching his fist through a window, then pulling them out a few days later with a fork, absconding at will – to name but a few. She thought his needs were not being met and lamented how Alex had an awareness of this – and that he needed but was not getting an education – and that he had not even formed any relationships with staff or peers. Her report highlighted the extent of Alex's inner suffering as well as painting a grim picture of the relentless daily crises the staff had to deal with.

My son was behaving badly! But I could cope with only so much. It was as if for the past few years I'd been taking on the world, and the world had eventually won – the day Alex voluntarily went away. I hadn't seen Alex for several months, but there was never a question of my washing my hands of the whole affair. Otherwise I would have refused to speak to Alex or anyone connected with social services or education, whereas many hours were devoted to speaking to all three. I knew it was not right for others to be saddled with Alex when they were ill-informed and ill-equipped to cope with him. When I was told he had started to walk around nearly naked to attract the attention of a young female member of staff to whom he'd taken a shine, I felt I had to step in. I went to the home and rebuked him verbally.

Dr Thompson was still involved with our family, although the turbulence of the preceding year caused our appointments to become more irregular. I'd grown to respect Dr Thompson; he genuinely wanted to help Alex and demonstrated this by making the effort to see him at Bodley Road. However, his connection with Alex's case had all but run its course, and he could do little to help in a practical way. I suspect he hoped that the boarding-school placement would work. Unfortunately, in time, he formed the opinion that Alex would respond to secure boundaries, and that there was no organic or clinical mental cause for his behaviour.

Mavis wrote to Sharon on 17 June to say that she and a colleague had visited Viewmount School outside London, for emotionally difficult boys with behavioural and learning problems, to see whether it might be suitable for Alex. They had been impressed, and she emphasised it was a school, not a children's home, and that many of its students took GCSEs. She had arranged separate appointments for Sharon and me to go to the school with Alex in early July. The headmaster had stressed to her the necessity of working closely with parents, and that it should be clear which parent Alex would go to at weekends.

In the meantime Sharon came across an article about dyslexia in a magazine and could hardly contain her excitement when she realised how many of its symptoms could be identified with Alex. She'd seen articles about hyperactivity before, and when we'd discussed them with family and friends everyone, be it seriously or not, had thought it a foregone conclusion that Alex was hyperactive since he rarely sat still for five minutes. However, no social worker, teacher, doctor or any other professional had ever mentioned this condition to us. I'd seen snippets of TV documentaries and heard friends talk about the supposed effects of certain foods and additives in them. I'd even tried to cut out sweet things from Alex's diet when we were living alone, after one of my customers told me there'd been a dramatic improvement in his 7-year-old's behaviour since he'd stopped eating chocolate.

My response to Sharon's enthusiasm was cool. 'Yeah, yeah, I've heard it all before,' I thought, as she chattered over the phone about the article. Up to this point, I don't think I'd ever heard the word 'dyslexia'. At her insistence we met so that I could read the piece, and I realised that Sharon had been right, though Alex had other symptoms that dyslexia clearly did not cause. I was flabbergasted and immediately swung into action. This was the closest explanation for at least some of his behaviour that I'd come across that made sense. Was my son dyslexic?

We contacted social services and the education office, requesting that Alex be assessed for dyslexia; when they declined, I assured them we'd have him assessed ourselves, but they objected strongly, indicating they would prevent us because Alex was a ward of court. We didn't at that time understand the reason for their opposition, but there was no way we were going to be put off, and we made our own enquiries. Without telling them, we made an appointment with the Dyslexia Institute for 26 June, and on that day collected Alex from Bodley before the authorities had time to stop us. The institute was near Russell Square, Bloomsbury, and by the time we eventually found it I was not in a good mood. En route, Sharon and I fell into arguing about Alex's behaviour and blaming each other. So I escorted them into the building, met briefly with Dr Patricia Rouse, a consultant chartered psychologist, and left.

When Dr Rouse's report came through she said that, despite Alex's being of average intelligence, in tests he functioned about three years below his age. He had a poor short-term memory capacity, she said, and could not easily apply sequencing skills to material held in short-term memory. He found it difficult to assess knowledge of everyday objects and events and to solve verbal problems by applying working memory skills.

Because decoding print was such an effort for Alex, she explained that he tended to miss the significance of what he read and had a reading comprehension age of a 7½-year-old. The problems he had with auditory and visual memory meant that he found it difficult to recognise words by sight or sound. She agreed with Dr Thompson that Alex would need an intensive and caring specialist setting within which he could learn and develop internalised self-control and build on positive strengths. In the light of Alex's specific learning difficulties, she recommended that he receive individual, structured and specialist remedial teaching.

At Dr Rouse's recommendation, copies of her report were sent to the education department and social services.

On 3 July, Sharon took Alex to see Viewmount School. Fearing she might get lost, she decided not to drive but to go by train. Her sister Marva went too. Months before, Alex had told everyone that he did not want to and would not go to a boarding school. He'd developed a fixation against it, rather as he had with Mavis, seeing her as the personification of social services. He became distressed on the journey, even attempting to pull the emergency lever to stop the train. Neither his mother nor his aunt could console him.

When they reached the station he became frantic, ran on to a track with a live rail and refused to budge. Sharon and Marva froze with fright, then pleaded in vain with him to come away from the danger. A crowd of astonished onlookers quickly gathered. Two station guards similarly tried to persuade him to come off the track, to no avail. The atmosphere was unbearably tense: one wrong step and Alex could have been electrocuted. The police were called and, as soon as the power had been switched off, the guards escorted Alex back to the platform and a nearby room where the police helped to calm him down. Not untypically of Alex, when it was all over he seemed surprised by the fuss and attention his impulsiveness had caused. Having released his pent-up frustrations at being made to go on this journey, he calmly accompanied his mother and aunt to the interview as if nothing had happened.

When they arrived at the school, the headmaster Laurence Delfont, plus Mavis and a colleague, were waiting for them. As Sharon and Marva began to describe the events of the previous hour, together with other information about Alex and social services' involvement with him, Mavis became visibly embarrassed. It transpired that Mr Delfont had not been adequately briefed about the sort of behaviour Viewmount could realistically expect from Alex. At this point an angry Marva blew her top. Directing her attention to the headmaster, she blasted social services' whole involvement with our family. 'It's not good enough! It's just not good enough!' she protested. He listened attentively and appeared none too pleased that he'd not been properly informed. He'd had no idea that Alex was so difficult and began to express doubts as to whether Viewmount was the right place for him.

The headmaster showed them around the school, then Mavis and her escort drove back to London. He kindly offered to drive Sharon, Marva and Alex to the station, and during the short journey expressed his sympathy for the long history of difficulties the family had had to endure. He encouraged Sharon not to allow social services and the education department to bully us into accepting educational provisions for Alex that did not meet his needs.

The next day, Gordon Giles, social services' acting team leader involved with Alex's case, decided after consultation that as Alex was no longer confinable at Bodley Road he should be moved to Grange Court Manor in another county. He was taken there the following day, 5 July.

When Sharon and I were informed he was to be moved we didn't object. This proved to be another major blunder on our part. We thought Grange Court was a children's home like Stockport House or Bodley Road, but we were grossly mistaken. It was, in fact, a place where children aged 14 and over were sent to serve sentences for criminal activities. It had two separate parts: a large open unit for less serious offenders and a smaller secure unit for the more dangerous or persistent ones. No one had explained any of this to either Sharon or me. Alex was placed in the open unit.

Mavis advised Grange Court that Alex had physically abused her and that it had been decided she should no longer be his social worker. She claimed Alex had asked her for help so that he could become better. Rather strangely, her interpretation, and that of her superiors, seemed to be that my son had appealed to her to be controlled and locked up, but Mavis herself told me that Alex had in fact asked for help to make him *better*. From this point forward my son's life was never to be the same again.

Social services must have been aware that Alex was too young for residence in Grange Court, but they still decided to send him there. Mavis it seemed had finally succeeded in enlightening her colleagues as to the true extent of Alex's emotional and behavioural difficulties, and Grange Court was their answer.

On 10 July I was due to go to Viewmount with Alex. Having heard all about Sharon's journey the previous week and his subsequent removal from Bodley, I was far from pleased with him and had been determined not to go, but on the day I changed my mind and collected him in a taxi. I was still taking his behaviour personally, so I lectured him until we were midway between Grange Court and Viewmount. He was sitting on cushions next to me on the floor in the front of the taxi. He listened, looking dejected, and hardly spoke a word in his defence.

I could see unhappiness written all over his bleak, pathetic face, and I knew he could feel the pain in my heart. I'd given him these lectures a thousand times before. His grief pierced me, yet something was missing – I couldn't reach him. He seemed so hopeless and desperate, as if somewhere inside he knew he couldn't prevent these problems from recurring. Before, on optimistic days, he'd always offer many promises and genuinely wish that he could do better. Now he seemed resigned. To see a 10-year-old child so irretrievably withdrawn, like a wounded animal waiting to die . . . It's hard to put into words, but the pain we both felt that day was simply too much to bear.

Midway through the journey I stopped the cab and tried to chat to Alex. He revealed he'd been in fights with the young men at Grange Court. I wanted to hug him and will him out of his misery somehow, but couldn't bring myself to cuddle him. The whole situation made me feel incapable of helping him; besides, I knew something had to come from Alex too, but that wasn't happening. I realise now he simply wasn't capable of giving it. I never did reach out as I had wanted, as if a huge invisible brick wall separated us and I couldn't bring myself to climb it. I sighed, continued our journey, and went on with my lecture as we headed for Viewmount.

At the school, Alex behaved well and there were no scenes. Mr Delfont was sympathetic. The meeting was mainly concerned with my substantiating all he'd heard from Sharon the week before and adding more detail. He indicated that Viewmount needed to work closely with at least one parent, and Alex would need to spend weekends and holidays at home since that was an integral part of their approach. He expressed doubt as to whether this was the right place for him and I agreed. No firm decision was reached, though Alex's enrolment now looked extremely doubtful.

Staff at Grange Court expressed serious concerns to social services about Alex's safety. They thought he was too young, at risk, and wanted him moved (though not insisting on it). Other boys had offered to have sex with him. By the next day, 11 July, Gordon Giles and key staff from Bodley met with staff at Grange Court. All acknowledged Alex was too young and in danger. Another meeting was planned for the following week; a decision on Alex would be deferred till then, though they agreed it was only a matter of time before Alex would get hurt physically or sexually. Some Grange Court staff were also concerned about incidents of violence, not only from Alex's peers but also from unscrupulous staff-members – a phenomenon new to him. The first incident of this type happened the very next day on 12 July – not even a fortnight after his arrival. According to Alex, Philip Charles, a staff member, assaulted him; the matter was reported to the local police.

The first hint I got as to the depth of these fears for his safety was at the 17 July case conference held at the social services office. There for the first time I met Ralph Peters, the principal of Grange Court Manor. He seemed determined to convey to the meeting, firmly but politely, the simple fact that Alex was too young to be in Grange Court and was in danger. It was not the right place for him and Mr Peters wanted him moved.

As indicated before, during this period I poured my heart out to the authorities at such meetings, impromptu visits, and in numerous phone calls, always trying to keep the relevant people up to date on events. I implored them to change direction and seek out the causes of Alex's disturbances, as the judge had ordered several years before. Both Sharon and I wanted further tests to establish whether dyslexia, hyperactivity or food additives had any identifiable effect on his behaviour. Yet the professionals seemed to shoot down any suggestions we made as unworkable, as if agreeing to anything we might suggest would legitimise our old grievances.

By this stage, however, the idea of contending with the authorities was furthest from my mind. Having already seen their immense power in action, I was frightened to anger them further. All I wanted was for my son to get the help that he needed. His life had degenerated into an appalling mess because I'd chosen to take a back-seat. I now wanted to make amends – somebody had to. I knew I didn't have all the answers, but enough was enough. I concluded things had been better when Alex was with me at the garage – at least I loved him – so I suggested having him back and asked for care and tutorial assistance until a proper solution was found. But that idea was shot down too.

Alex was now in such danger at Grange Court that on Saturday 20 July he was moved from its open unit into a three-bedroomed local authority house. Here he was to be overseen, exclusively, by three agency staff during the day and two others at night. When I saw his face I was horrified: he'd received a vicious black eye from a youth. That had happened on 16 July, and I was now able to make sense of Mr Peters's guarded, uneasy apprehension at the case conference the day after.

Moreover, the three-bedroomed house abutted a larger care unit inhabited by about a dozen teenage girls with problems, and was close to a very busy road. Where was the sense in this? Grange Court had only just finished reporting that Alex had nearly been knocked over on such a main road, and a few weeks before there had been concerns about his fixation on a young woman at Bodley.

Agency staff at the house could not cope with Alex. They felt they had not been given enough information about his behaviour. By 22 July they found him uncontainable and without boundaries. Alex desperately wanted to escape his prison and absconded when he could. The girls next door and even passers-by came to his defence when he called for help as staff chased him about and tried to restrain him. This proved too much for them.

Lack of communication within and between departments often frustrated Sharon and me. Half the time, the right hand had no idea what the left hand was doing. We were fortunate to speak to the same person twice on any specific matter. If such an absence of continuity, which at times disintegrated into downright confusion, could exist within the same department, then what hope was there of liaison between them?

On 23 July Gordon Giles telephoned Sharon (confirming by letter the following day) to say that they were going to put Alex into the secure unit at Grange Court because he could not be contained in the community. This was later agreed to by the duty High Court judge, who granted the order. Mr Giles also telephoned me at the garage. I felt desperate for Alex. When he realised that he couldn't break out of the secure unit, I wondered if he would turn in on himself. I became haunted by the idea that he was going to die.

Secure, but not Safe

Nine

To get an 11-year-old child locked up in a secure unit in England and Wales, unless he or she has committed a murder, is not the easiest thing to accomplish, yet it seemed to be done in Alex's case with relative ease. To achieve it, a hierarchy of authorities had to be in agreement. In ascending order of importance, these were: the local Director of Social Services, a High Court judge and the Secretary of State for Health – in this case, the Right Honourable Mrs Virginia Bottomley.

Children may be locked up because they have committed a very serious criminal offence, or because they may endanger their own safety. It was for this latter reason that Alex was finally incarcerated. Things get a little fuzzy for me here as I try to disentangle the motives for deciding that this was the best course of action.

Were the decision-makers ignorant of what life would be like for Alex? That hardly seems likely when fears for his safety had already been voiced by Grange Court's principal. If there had been genuine concern for his safety and care, why was he placed in a criminal institution with hardened teenagers who tended towards violence and lawlessness? Before endorsing such drastic measures, should not great care have been taken to try to distinguish between children who are criminally inclined, and those who might have specialist educational or medical needs? Given Alex's history, did they contemplate what the outcome for Alex could be, or did they simply want him out of the way? Apart from putting him out of commission, what benefit could there possibly be in sending him to such a place? Especially when one considers that, in Mavis's opinion, Alex was unable to distinguish between his good and bad behaviour, or appreciate the effects that either might have. Might not a more fruitful way to deal with the situation be to make determined efforts to uncover the cause of Alex's behaviour and, at the very least, find the right boarding school or medical provision? Surely that would have been more appropriate than locking him up in a place which was of no therapeutic value whatsoever. Social services knew that, as did the education people and Grange Court's staff. So why was my son sent there?

Some might think me naive to ask these questions – after all, Alex was wildly out of control. Yet any child whose actions seriously threaten his own life is usually regarded as being desperately in need of help – medical or otherwise. Gordon Giles's comments to the courts, when seeking the secure order, indicate he and his department had my son's best interests at heart. Yet I couldn't help pondering: if every person who attempted suicide was locked up, would there not be a social uproar?

The secure unit was designed to house a maximum of six youths at any one time, and Alex may very well have been one of the youngest ever to enter it. At a mere six stone in weight and four and a half feet in height, no wonder he gave Ralph Peters cause to be concerned for his safety. Nevertheless, Mr Peters seemed obliged to accept Alex since Grange Court was a resource unit under the control of social services, which meant, I was later given to understand, that the department's director had the final say. In time, I came to regard Grange Court as their ultimate sanction for wayward youths; only the worst, or those who needed to be taught a sharp lesson, were sent there.

At first, Sharon and I had no idea that it housed some menacingly dangerous characters, sentenced to go there from different parts of the country. Was Alex unrealistically expected to avoid trouble simply because he was in a secure unit? That certainly did not fit his previous pattern of behaviour. It was like putting a bowlful of tasty food before a hungry cat or dog and expecting them not to eat it.

Right from the start, differences developed between Alex and other boys (referred to as 'clients') that would escalate into violent confrontations. The secure staff observed Alex. In August a member of staff told us that they had formed the opinion that his behaviour was erratic: he attacked others boys and staff without reason, had no self-control and showed no interest in school. An urgent psychiatric assessment was needed. They sought to control his behaviour by locking him in his bedroom, and initially thought that was working – after all but one youth had been moved from the unit. On a positive note, he did respond better to adult one-to-one situations.

Remember, only a few days before, things had got so bad that he had been moved from the open unit. Now it was as though he'd entered a war zone, being trapped with the worst aspects of Dudley. Boys much bigger than him were willing to hurt him; now he had no escape at the end of each day. He was well and truly out of his league.

During his stint at the open unit, staff had become increasingly amazed at this pint-sized boy's apparent bravery/stupidity and they repeatedly voiced concerns for his safety to the management. It certainly wasn't a question of bravery: Alex lacked any real understanding of the situation he was now in. Had he not found certain 'big brother' types who took him under their wing, and had there not been swift action by some alert staff, he would have been badly harmed for sure. As it was, he had already received that awful black eye. I later learned that Mr Peters had repeatedly suggested, requested, then urged the decision-makers to have Alex moved.

Ignorance can be a dangerous thing. And that's what Sharon and I were guilty of the day we did not challenge the decision to move Alex to Grange Court. What had we done to our son?

Many times I've wondered if anyone can understand what it feels like to have to bottle up a great anger. This was the state I was now reduced to: permanently angry. So I wasn't in a good mood on the evening of my first visit to Alex in the secure unit. I'd never been into that smaller building which lay to the left of the open unit as I approached from the road. I went first to the main entrance, as I had before, and staff directed me. It was dullish-bright summer's evening, without the sun. I was instructed to go to the visitors' entrance at the far end of the building. As I approached, I heard the sound of rowdy voices inside as I walked past the windows set into bleak, brown walls. I saw a bell, rang it, and waited for what seemed like ages before someone came to let me in. I was in for a rude awakening and shall never forget that night.

The first thing that struck me was the size of the keys that hung on the bunch manipulated by the warder. They were the largest I'd ever seen. The ominous sound of the huge key turning behind me as I stood in the small lobby made my heart sink. I was now locked in. A different key was used to unlock the door into the visitors' room: clunk. As the warder relocked it behind us: clunk. I could just see Alex's face through the heavy security glass in the upper portion of the door leading to the clients' quarters. He smiled excitedly and shouted, 'Daddy!' The warder went to that door and unlocked it: clunk. Alex rushed straight into my arms. The warder left us: clunk. We were locked in together. In an instant of time reality caught up with me with a vengeance: Alex, my son, was in prison! I berated myself, repeatedly, with the thought: 'What have you done, Chester? Chester, what have you done?'

Access to the rest of the building was impossible, unless by invitation and escorted by a member of staff possessing the appropriate key. This was for safety reasons. The volatility of some clients was such that, without this safeguard, protection from attack could not be guaranteed. It also prevented any disgruntled or angry visitors from launching their own attacks on a client or staff member. In the waiting room there was an alarm buzzer, a table and a built-in L-shaped bench along the windowed corner of the room. The windows were vertically panelled in reinforced glass, and could open only to the width of about an adult male fist – so no chance of escape here. Another locked door led to what I was later to discover was the school: a large, single room with some books.

I was devastated, and overwhelmed by a consuming sense of powerlessness and shock! I'd never been near the inside of a prison before: how could they do this to my son? When I saw the battered condition of Alex's face, his eye still bruised, I was mad. My feelings went from bitter anger to disbelief, to resignation and futility, but I didn't dare let them show. This was a time for me to be strong; Alex needed my support.

While I was caged in that room, what resulted was a two-tiered conversation: a tumultuous one within me and an almost absurdly matter-of-fact one with Alex. 'Hello, son. Are you all right? Look what you've let them do to you; they could have blinded you.' Inside, my mind ballooned with fury. The sight of my son's messed-up face was an outrage. My heart was no longer in my boots but rocketed firmly into my chest, and I was filled with an overwhelming sense of injustice and all-consuming bitterness. So while I was talking to Alex, my mind was actually saying: 'How dare they! How dare they! He's barely turned 11, he doesn't deserve this. Who the heck do they think they are?' Poor Alex!

His eye had discoloured horribly since I last saw him. 'Look what you've let them do to you,' I repeated as I instinctively blamed Alex for his predicament. In this I was no better than social services. But no sooner had the words left my mouth than I wanted to retract them. In my heart of hearts, I'd suspected Alex's inability to have much control over what he was doing. Thus for me at least, at long last, this part of the mystery was over. The impact of seeing my son incarcerated, with his face in a sickening state, convinced me that Alex could not help himself. And if he was not responsible for his actions, how could he be blamed for them? Imprisoning him was therefore morally, and possibly legally, wrong – particularly since he'd never been charged with a criminal act.

A veil suddenly lifted from my mind and it became crystal clear what action I should take: to get Alex away from this terrible place – fast – and look after him myself.

We sat on the bench and talked. I looked at his face and felt ill. His bloodshot, blacked-up eye was nearly closed. The area around his eye socket and brow was swollen, bruised to a mixture of red and bluish-black. I was reminded of the time when I'd entered a martial-arts competition in the early days without realising it was for black belts only. When I learned of the distinguished achievement of some of the other top competitors, and saw the punishment being meted out by them, I wanted to back out. However, to do so would have been to lose face so I bravely/foolishly stayed. As my misfortune would have it, I was drawn to fight against a very seasoned British champion. Had I known who he was, I probably *would* have backed out, but his name and face meant nothing to me. We 'danced' around for about half a minute as we weighed each other up, then my opponent clouted me very hard, with lighting speed, with the most vicious blow to my head I'd ever received in my life. His fist felt like a steel club wrapped in soft cloth. Immediately I saw a galaxy of bright flashing stars. He'd struck me in the bony area of my face, around the socket of my right eye. My vision went temporarily; I thought I was blinded. I wanted to cry. Never had I felt pain like that before in my life and I distinctly remember wanting to call for my mother. Macho pride prevented me from crying in an auditorium full of competitors and spectactors. Because I, too, had been out of my league and paid the price, I imagined how Alex might have felt and was doubly hurt for him. And my face hadn't swollen up the way his had, so goodness knows what pain he must have gone through. This fate was simply too harsh for a little boy.

The truth of the matter was there was not much I could do to help Alex, so I climbed that brick wall – the one I hadn't been able to the day we drove to Viewmount in the cab – and gave him a big cuddle. I tried to give him sorely needed comfort and let him know that from now on I was going to be there for him. I told him that I loved him, and I promised to do my best to get him out of there quickly.

I urged him as gently as I could to try not to annoy the bigger boys, and wanted him to realise that I was powerless to help if they hurt him. I was particularly careful not to transmit the 'I'm your father, and I can do anything' message that he so often sought from me. As I spoke to him consolingly and pledged my full support, the frostiness that had struck my heart the day he ran from me to live with his mother melted, and Alex's whole being perked up. He'd got Daddy back, and was sure he'd soon be going home with him.

I didn't want to crush his new-found hope, but the truth was:

getting him home would not be a simple matter. Reversing the decision of the Director of Social Services, the order of a High Court judge, and the approval of the Secretary of State for Health was going to need every ounce of tact I possessed. I decided then and there not to be in any way confrontational; I knew I had to co-operate to spare Alex more suffering. I was now certain that his situation couldn't improve without the best specialist diagnosis and help, and he wasn't going to get it in Grange Court. I feared for his future.

A year and a half earlier, Dr Thompson had recognised that putting Alex in a setting defined by forced co-operation would make him worse, and dismissed the idea that any professional would think of recommending such a course of action. If only his remarks had been heeded.

Alex had no idea of the inner turmoil with which I was battling, but he did know, without any shadow of a doubt, that his daddy was now firmly on his side. I encouraged him as best as I could and, after about half an hour, told him I was going. I was too upset to stay for two or three hours as I'd intended; I wanted to get out and scream loudly at the top of my voice. I'd never been locked up in a cell-sized room before, unable to get out at will, and I felt very uncomfortable. I rang the buzzer for the warder, who was surprised at the shortness of my visit. Alex was let back into the clients' area first; he ran to a window in the lounge. As I walked by, both of us visibly sad, he said, 'Bye, Dad! Can you come and see me tomorrow?' with that cute, dinky half-smile on his face. That's why a part of me admires Alex: even in a situation like this he tries to exhibit a happy spirit. I told him, 'Yes', even though I never wanted to set foot in that place again.

From that time onwards I visited him at least twice a week so he would be sure that I would never again abandon him, and we spoke regularly on the phone. Sharon and I mostly alternated our visits, and we would sometimes bring along other family members and friends. Thus between us, Alex had visits about five days a week. The black eye took several weeks to disappear.

★

That weekend, guilt racked my conscience and I hardly slept. 'Why should my son be locked up in that prison while I'm out here? It should be me, the social services, the education people and Sharon in there,' I thought, 'not Alex!' We were the ones who had collectively let him down so badly. I could see that, and was willing to admit it even if nobody else could or would. From then on, all I wanted was to do whatever I could to obtain support for my son. If that meant going back to court, then so be it.

Incensed, I wrote to Gordon Giles on 1 August requesting copies of all correspondence relating to Alex since social services and the education department had become involved. I also asked them to detail what help they had provided. No information was forthcoming, though they acknowledged receipt of my letter. Eventually, I requested to see Alex's files. However, it took a further two and a half years before I got sight of them – but that is to rush ahead.

Still numb from disbelief, I wondered if the people who locked my boy away were conscienceless aliens from some distant galaxy. I felt impotent and useless in the face of their despicable entrapment of my son. From Sharon's parents and my mother, down through all our relatives and friends, our whole circle was outraged. Some said: 'What's the matter with these people?' Others said: 'It's unbelievable; it's worse than watching a film!' 'Go to your lawyers; don't let them get away with it!' 'Go to the newspapers!'

Although Sharon and I didn't see eye to eye at this time, she was going through the same torment as I was at our son's prolonged suffering. We were strongly united in our support for him – especially when we discovered the extent of this new outrage. The vision of that prison, and of my son locked within it, have stayed with me to this day. I was so confused that I could hardly think straight or act sensibly. I felt a deep sense of failure that, as Alex's father, I'd let myself get my priorities so crossed, what with the mundane things, that I'd allowed him to suffer so much because I didn't give him the time that he needed. I felt terribly ashamed and hoped that one day he would forgive me. In the meantime, however, I had to get him out of Grange Court. I now hated the garage, which was struggling badly; it didn't seem to matter any more. How could I concentrate on running a business when my son was mentally falling apart at the seams and being physically battered about at that dreadful institution?

From what I could gather during discussions with the staff in the secure unit, they seemed a fairly self-confident bunch, convinced that the difficulties they were experiencing with Alex were teething problems. Their attitude appeared to be that he would, and *must*, change – it was his only way out. They expressed the view that he'd got away with everything thus far, but now he would be taken in hand – or, as Gordon Giles had put it, social services would control the situation.

After the first two weeks, which were fraught with daily incidents, it appeared that Mr Giles believed that Alex was beginning to settle down at the unit. What nonsense! It was Sharon and me supporting and encouraging him, and the fact that other boys were moved out of the unit because there was so much trouble, that made Alex appear more containable. We were constantly telling him that if he behaved, they'd soon let him out. In the meantime I frantically appealed to the authorities, spelling out to them all the reasons why he should not be there. Sharon was so disgusted that she saw any such efforts as an utter waste of time. She even caught staff teasing him – 'You gonna tell your mummy then?' – and complained in strong terms. As far as she was concerned, their minds were closed to anything we had to say – which were my sentiments too, but I still had to try.

After about a month, even I had to admit that reasoning with the authorities was a pointless exercise. What more could I do? I was offering to give up work and stay at home to look after Alex, but they didn't want to know.

In making a case to the local authority members to keep Alex in the secure unit, Mr Giles argued that the financial cost was the same (£192 daily) whether he was in the secure or open unit. After hinting that the secure unit was benefiting Alex, he then went on to paint a none-too-pleasant picture of him: intolerant, impatient, doesn't care, abusive, violent, assaults staff, and only just beginning to respond to secure accommodation. No mention was made of getting help for Alex, or the ill-treatment meted out to him. Alex came across as a wild animal that needed to be locked up, rather than a very emotionally ill child in need of help. Money also entered the equation: since the financial outlay was the same, did they believe they were getting good value for all that money? The department accomplished another remarkable legal feat: they could keep him there as long as *they* judged he met the legal criteria. Poor Alex!

The only way I could think of to break this deadlock was go right over everyone's head and complain, in writing, to the boss herself: Bertha Higgins, Director of Social Services. I was convinced she was too far up the chain to have personal knowledge of Alex and naively believed that as soon as she knew the facts she would look into my son's case and everything would be all right.

I wasn't very good at letter writing, but recognised the need to produce a good one in view of the seniority of the addressee. It took me days to draft and was littered with grammatical errors. I asked a friend to type it for me to make sure it was properly presented and posted it on 23 September. I was angry and didn't mince my words throughout its five pages. I pleaded with Ms Higgins for a common-sense approach in which, for Alex's sake, we would put the past behind us and start working together. I begged her and her department to listen to what I was saying, and put forward the following proposals:

1. That Alex be removed from the secure unit at Grange Court Manor as soon as possible and that a house or flat be provided which would also double as his school during the daytime. This accommodation should provide sufficient room for Jason and myself so as to re-create a family environment for him. The reasons for this are simple.

    All the evidence to date shows that Alex has great difficulty in interacting with his peers. This problem would be gone at a stroke because he would be the only child in the class. Once again the evidence shows that the best results are obtained when Alex is in a one-to-one child-adult relationship.

    I propose that two carefully selected teachers be made

available to Alex who between them can not only cover the National Curriculum but who also possess the necessary skills to teach children with learning difficulties such as his. These teachers would not have any problem with him because I would be near by. It would not be difficult for me to make the necessary arrangements so that I could work from home. I also propose that his school day be just the same as that of a normal school – i.e., 9 a.m. to 3.30 p.m. – and that his classroom resemble that of any school – i.e., he has a desk, chair and his teacher has a blackboard, etc. Part of his lessons could include techniques or suggestions made by his psychiatrist in order to readjust his behavioural and emotional problems.

All of this would be a temporary arrangement with the aim of calming him down mentally, physically and emotionally and would serve to get all distractions out of his way and thus prepare him for reintroduction to mainstream education. He would then have been able to discover the real excitement of learning and would hopefully see it as a better alternative that brings better reward than the path he has already chosen in life.

2. I further propose that Alex get the best psychiatric help available. I hasten to add that my son is not mad but suggest that there is something disturbing him and until we get to the root of that disturbance, Alex may never take his place in society. I undertake to take Alex wherever for as long as necessary as directed by the court if there is the slightest chance of it genuinely helping him.

3. That I have the full backing and support of the social services and that this wardship be lifted from both my children immediately so that his parents and not some faceless department become his real parents; and that Alex can regain the boundaries, and the security that those boundaries represented, which disappeared the day social services entered our lives.

I positively welcome your department to supervise the whole of this process and take part in repairing the damage it has caused. I also welcome any suggestions for respite care periodically, not for myself but for my two sons – i.e., local trips and outings as a reward if meaningful progress is made.

I know that what I have suggested might sound unorthodox but this is an extreme case. It needs an extreme solution. Read carefully all the reports on Alex and you will see that you are not dealing with the average overactive child, or someone who is unwanted or unloved. Some of his behaviour can be most disturbing. If these warnings go unheeded and he reaches adulthood, then mark my words, anything can happen.

Finally as to the matter of costs, I am in no position to calculate what they might be. Perhaps as an exercise you might wish to work out [the council's] costs since social services first entered our home over three years ago until now: the court cases, special schools, internment in various homes, transportation, etc. Someone must be paying for Alex's stay at Grange Court Manor, and the cost of the recent court hearing. Pretty expensive, I suppose. All of this could have been cheaper if your department's approach were different.

My proposal will work and I am sure will save [you] money too. The alternative is to enter into what I can only imagine as greater expense by sending Alex to yet another institution to fail yet again. I do not know how many more failures he can stand.

Meanwhile, what was daily life in Grange Court like for Alex? Well, as any child who has lived there, or in a similar place, will testify: you'd better learn to swim fast or you'll drown for sure. It didn't take Sharon or me too long to figure out that there was an unspoken, unwritten code of violence, where the staff repaid assaults with interest if provoked. I believe this to have been the source of their confidence when Alex first arrived. However, whatever success this unofficial regime may have boasted with others in its past, I knew it wouldn't work with him. And we were not prepared to stand idly by and allow him to be put through it. Yet despite our frequent presence in the unit, Alex regularly complained to us about brutality at the hands of other boys and some staff members. They, in turn, complained about Alex. It was impossible for us to be there 24 hours a day to protect him.

Sharon responded by robustly warning staff off. She made her presence felt by trying to investigate the complaints Alex made, getting his side of the story rather than listening only to theirs. As a consequence she spent many hours with him at the unit, to support him and reduce conflicts. Learning of these incidents, I spent most of my visits with Alex talking things through, trying to stop him getting into trouble in the first place. When he told me about being attacked by boys who were on average five years older than he, and about being pushed around by staff, I tried not to show how incensed I was. 'Then don't play with so-and-so; you know you can't get on . . . If he does it again, tell the staff; let them sort it out. Tell your social worker; tell the manager . . . Do you like it when they lock you up in your bedroom? Then don't . . .' etc., etc. I passed on much of what Alex told me to Grange Court's management and social services, but still his complaints kept coming.

The idea that my son was being bullied or abused by certain members of staff was a bitter pill for me to swallow. Secure-unit staff are trained to carry out physical restraints according to legal guidelines if clients are being violent. In such cases, this might require the application of controlled joint-locking techniques, such as 'wrist and arm locks'. Once subdued, the boys are escorted to their cell (bedroom) where they are locked up for a period of time to cool off – some establishments refer to this as 'time out'.

Alex told me that assaults by staff, if they were to occur, would usually happen during such attempts to restrain because the abuse would then be virtually impossible to prove. 'There would be no marks, Dad.' It seems that the boys were aware they could get hurt and this kept most of them in check, but not so Alex. He was less able to control his actions, which resulted in a disproportionate number of restraints for him. The more moderate staff refused to talk about their tougher colleagues. I observed that some were apprehensive and guarded. 'It's more than my job's worth,' quipped one; another indicated that he (and others) sometimes looked away so that they did not witness what was happening. He couldn't report on what he didn't see, if asked. This made sense, for sometimes boys did complain about their treatment – as Alex had on many occasions – insisting that so-and-so 'saw' what happened.

A client's complaints seldom resulted in action being taken against staff – even when police were called – through lack of evidence. According to Alex, some boys were conditioned into thinking that no one would believe them and thus it was pointless complaining. Sharon and I were determined to take this matter back to court. Alex's so-called 'settling in' seemed to have been brought about by too many of these almost daily dubious restraints and 'time out' periods. And there was absolutely nothing Sharon or I could do about it.

I began to notice that certain names kept recurring in Alex's complaints of staff abuse. According to him, two particular people had taken to winding him up and teasing him whenever they were on duty and felt like doing so. He, in turn, could not fail to respond, usually in some abusive or violent way. Then sometimes, he said, between two and six staff would descend and frogmarch him to his cell while he was still struggling, kicking and swearing. They would make a dash for the door, while another would be on hand to quickly slam and lock it. The animal was put back in its cage! Alex would then be locked up for anything from minutes to hours. Sometimes this happened more than once during the same day.

Once Alex saw another boy flung into his room with such force that he struck the opposite wall, badly damaging his arm. The boy refused to complain; he rarely had visitors, so Alex complained for him. Alex told me and his mother that the staff had taken no notice. We passed the complaint back to the staff, but to my knowledge nothing was ever done about it. I warned them that there would be trouble if anything similar happened to my son.

Those who empathised with Alex would spend ages reasoning with him, trying to prevent him becoming prey for colleagues who could easily make things unpleasant. Frustratingly for them – as it has been for Sharon, and me and anyone else who tried to help Alex – he didn't always get the point even when he appeared to, and had such a low tolerance level that he would soon get into more trouble, even with the very members of staff who had been trying to help him keep his nose clean.

Of course, Alex didn't need the more insensitive staff to cause him to make trouble – he could manage that all by himself, and did most days. But even if he had known how to try to break free from his own negative cycle, some of the other boys would have prevented him in much the same pattern that had occurred from as far back as infant school. They too wound him up and teased him, called his parents and family names, and started fights, yet Alex usually copped most of the blame and punishment. Some of these other kids even swore at me and spoiled for fights as I walked away silently past the lounge window. Alex would spring to my defence and accordingly pay the price – more restraints – while I drove dispiritedly home.

Even though there were hardly ever any completely trouble-free days for Alex, most days would have pockets of relative peace. These were mainly achieved by a series of 'bribes', part of a so-called behaviour-modification programme, comprising access to computer games and videos (most of which were unsuitable for an 11-year-old), access to the pool and table-tennis tables, pocket money, small gifts and sweets. Some members of staff, those who liked him and those who were indifferent, found they could maintain longer periods of peace simply by giving in to him and allowing excessive access to all these treats – especially computer games. Also unofficially on offer were cigarettes, videos that featured horror, sex and violence, and pornographic material. According to Alex one member of staff regularly titillated the boys in his favour with boastful talk of his supposed sexual adventures with his girlfriend; details of which – via the boys – unfortunately filtered back to Alex. By the time Alex eventually left Grange Court, there was hardly a current 15- or 18-rated video that he had not seen. But, as far as I could ascertain, the biggest official carrot was a morning or afternoon away from the unit, spent swimming or doing some other sport activity.

The longer Alex stayed at Grange Court, the more angry we became. It was absolutely preposterous that our son should be exposed to this sort of disgusting, lewd corruption – not to mention violence and sexual propositions – right under our noses. But there was nothing we could do about it. Complaining proved to be a total waste of time; this was 'normal' life at Grange Court. The day-to-day grind was beginning to get to some of the staff who had begun to accept that Alex was not getting better but much worse, and who supported his swift removal. His key-teacher, Janice Galloway, after complaining that Alex destroyed books, had bad mood swings and generally refused any school work that represented the slightest challenge to him, despaired that efforts to educate and discipline him in the classroom met with hysterical tantrums of one description or another. If he didn't calm down quickly, then he'd be 'timed out'. Still social services wouldn't budge from their stance.

In a funny sort of way, as certain members of staff got to know us better, we became allied to them in trying to effect Alex's release. In the privacy of the visitors' room, several openly expressed to us their concerns for his safety. They commented on the fact that they thought we loved our son, that he loved us, that Grange was not the right place for Alex, and they asked if we were doing anything to get him out. They urged us not to abandon him to the system and encouraged us not to give up our fight. Some of them grew to like Alex, despite all the problems, and watched over him as best they could. He sometimes cried when one of his favourites had to go off duty to be replaced by a less sympathetic individual. Having failed to break his will, some of them began to spread the rumour that Alex was mad and was going to be placed in a 'madhouse'. Soon the clients joined in, calling him 'nutcase', 'sicko' and other cruel names, and tormenting him about being sent to 'the funny farm'.

It transpired that the rumour had spread to Grange Court's staff that 'the department' was trying to get Alex certified so that he could be moved, and elements within Grange Court actively backed this view. We had already been told that they were trying to get a fresh assessment from a top psychiatrist and that Alex would remain at the unit until it was carried out. We didn't object to the assessment because we, too, wanted to know what was wrong with our son.

In fact, another psychological assessment had already been carried out at the secure unit by Jean Davies, a chartered psychologist, on the orders of the Official Solicitor as Alex's guardian *ad litem*. Mrs Davies, we were later told, had decided that Alex needed to live in a small therapeutic unit where he could get regular psychotherapy and attend lessons that were able to meet his emotional and educational needs. He would benefit from experiencing academic achievement, while his leisure time should allow him to burn up physical energy constructively. She concluded that Sharon and I needed to be happy with any future placement and emphasised that our regular contact with Alex should be maintained. Her report, however, was not considered weighty enough by social services, who held out for a top child psychiatrist, with the apparent ulterior hope of getting him certified. When the rumours eventually reached our ears we tried to reassure Alex that he was not mad and would not be sent to a madhouse.

His portfolio was becoming extensive and was heavily weighted against him. The social worker popped in to see him only 'when passing in the area', except when required to respond to an emergency or attend a scheduled meeting. Sharon and I between us visited him almost daily. Thus we usually heard both sides of most incidents by being able to speak to Alex, the staff and sometimes to other boys, whereas social services mainly got the official version.

On 3 October, Sharon and I challenged their handling of Alex's case in the High Court, but we were bitterly disappointed when we learned that the full wardship hearing would not take place until 13 January 1992, over three months later. How would we face Alex with this heartbreaking news? After ten weeks' imprisonment at Grange Court he was beginning to show signs of serious mental deterioration. The strain showed on his face and in his voice. Our efforts to keep his spirit alive had now begun to wane: we sounded like worn-out records. All our pleading for good behaviour made little difference. Alex's attention was usually fixed on whichever boy or member of staff had most recently hurt him and he'd be full of talk about getting even.

It was painful to watch his decline at the hands of this regime, whether it was through abuse or over-indulgence in their stick-and-carrot approach. They expected him to play ball, but Alex did not know how: he did not comprehend the rules. I found it impossible to respect an organisation that pandered to its clients' every whim, but if that didn't work thumped them when no one was looking – according to Alex. On our visits he would beg us to take him home. It was truly harrowing to disappoint him repeatedly and to abandon him with that desperation in his eyes; an almost knowing look that blamed us for his cruel plight. How long could his spirit last out?

On 6 October, Bertha Higgins's reply to my letter arrived via her Head of Division, Keith Bradshaw. The gist of it was that I could make a formal complaint if I wished. He wrote: 'As yet, we and other experts consulted have been unable to establish the cause of Alex's behaviour for the past six years and I understand how distressing this must be for you.' He went on to confirm that their plan of action was that 'a further psychiatric assessment should be undertaken to complete a full assessment of Alex's needs'. While paying lip-service to wishing for Alex's eventual return home to me, he went on: 'We do believe that the lifting of wardship and a return to your care would be premature.' He hoped I'd be reassured by the letter, and felt that Alex was making progress at Grange Court. I wondered if Keith Bradshaw was talking about the same child.

On the whole the staff didn't have any problems with me and found me co-operative. I tried to be respectful to all and to register complaints through the proper channels. Perhaps because I was too quiet, some paid little respect to the fact that I was Alex's father and had attendant feelings for him. Vince Brown, one of the two members of staff who regularly tormented Alex, became quite bold in his disregard. He knew that Alex was complaining to me about him but that I hadn't taken any action. Little did he know, or perhaps he didn't care, that my blood boiled each time Alex would protest.

On the evening of Saturday 2 November, about 20 minutes before I was due to visit, he assaulted my son during a restraint. When I arrived I could hear Alex crying and shouting abuse that implicated him. I saw red. When they let Alex into the visitors' room he was obviously in a good deal of pain. I asked him what had happened. He was still crying as he told me that the man had knocked him about, wrenching his arm and one of his fingers beyond the point required to subdue him, thus virtually rendering his arm dead with pain.

Had that door not been locked, it would have been Vince and me. In that moment I threw away all my martial-arts reserve and demanded to see him. My temper was fully aroused. I cared nothing for the etiquette of self-defence; all I wanted to do was to sort him out once and for all. The unit came to a standstill. Staff and clients ran from every direction, jostling each other to peer through the glass panel. Among them the culprit himself eventually appeared, safely on the other side of the locked door. I demanded that he face me. 'What you did to Alex just now, please come and do it to me!' I shouted. 'Come on, I beg you. You're pretty good at beating up 11-year-old boys, why don't you try it on me? Come on, unlock the door; come on, you coward. You are bigger than me, aren't you?' Everyone was transfixed. For about 20 minutes I did my best to lure him out, but he wouldn't rise to the bait.

At last Alex could see that his daddy cared. For the moment, I didn't mind what signals I was giving him – even if they were wrong ones. I wanted to show them – all of them – that Alex had a father, so they'd better stop taking liberties with my boy. In the end, all that came of my display was a temporary ban on visiting Alex, which was lifted only when I gave assurances a few days later that I'd behave properly towards staff. I didn't want to get in trouble with the police, and if I was banned from seeing Alex I wouldn't have been able to keep tabs on what was going on. Meanwhile Alex boasted to everyone about what his daddy would do to them if they hurt him. In my anger at Alex's treatment I'd fallen into the very trap that I'd so meticulously tried to avoid with Mr Matthews and all the other professionals by undermining their institution's authority. I later got an official ticking-off from the social services department.

Two days after the incident, a concerned Ralph Peters complained to social services' management that Alex's placement was inappropriate and that the unit was not being properly supported by the department. Timothy Booth, the divisional manager of yet another sector that would shortly be assuming responsibility for Alex, was disappointed by the complaint and claimed that Gordon Giles and Pauline Dutton (Alex's new social worker) had maintained a considerable amount of contact with Alex in an attempt to support him, us and the unit. Well, that was certainly news to both Sharon and me: we'd only seen Gordon once or twice, and Pauline not much more than that. As for the times Alex saw them, these were probably few.

After four months at Grange Court, even those who didn't particularly like Alex felt he couldn't cope any longer with the secure-unit system. They knew he'd been there too long. Even boys sentenced for criminal activities were seldom locked up there for more than three months, we were told privately by disgusted staff.

The unit's team leader, David Brookes, commented in a review of 20 November that the Director of Social Services had obtained permission from the High Court to place Alex in a secure unit *without* time limit. A week later they returned and procured leave to keep him until he was assessed by a psychiatrist or other expert approved by the Official Solicitor. David Brookes summed up Alex's extremes in behaviour as ranging from well behaved to violent, and pleasant to abusive. He observed Alex sometimes sought cuddles and requested bedtime stories from certain staff. He also acknowledged that Alex had learning difficulties (he had seen Dr Rouse's report) and that Alex's being in the secure unit *did not* meet with the spirit of Dr Thompson's recommendations, but that another psychiatrist had been commissioned for a second opinion. The hope was that he would be moved to a therapeutic community.

That same month we learned that an eminent child psychiatrist, Dr Gerald Heath from a leading children's hospital, was to see Alex. Sharon and I welcomed this. 'Soon we'll find out what's wrong with Alex, and this nightmare will be over,' we thought. Dr Heath started his assessment of Alex at Grange Court on 25 November. He then arranged interviews at the hospital for me on 12 December and for Sharon the following day.

In the interim, Vince again assaulted Alex in an incident which I later understood Vince had provoked. Alex alleged that during this restraint the man was 'strangling' him around his neck and that he wouldn't let go. Struggling, Alex eventually managed to bite his finger, breaking the skin, whereupon Vince attacked him viciously. Another member of staff had to pull Vince off Alex. It's of interest to note that this man weighed about fourteen stone compared to Alex's approximate seven. To add insult to injury, Vince was then encouraged by one of his superiors to press assault charges against the child and the police were called – a new tactic. Shortly thereafter, Alex was arrested, handcuffed and frogmarched from his bedroom, in front of all present in the unit, into a waiting police car.

I was informed later that my son was being detained at the local police station. When I went to see him he was locked in a cell. He heard my voice, stood on tiptoe and pressed against the locked cell door to see me. His sad eyes were barely visible from the slot in the door as he called out to me, 'Daddy!' Grange Court finally appeared to have declared legal war on Alex. He had to remain in the cell for several hours before a local solicitor arrived to represent him and he was later released back to Grange Court.

Following the rumours about him, Alex was keen to declare emphatically to Dr Heath that he was not mad, but it wasn't until his interview with Sharon that Dr Heath became really excited, when, in passing, she commented that years before someone had expressed the view that Alex had the devil in him. Their conversation changed direction as Sharon told him about Alex jumping out of the window, burning his face with the curling-tongs, hearing the bones in his head, and other disturbing incidents. She revealed that a few weeks before, Alex had told her how a 'voice' had ordered him to hit another lad in the unit. Dr Heath was intrigued. He wanted to see Alex again before completing his report. He considered the matter urgent enough to make arrangements to see him the next day – a Saturday – and requested that both Sharon and I be there. He wanted to know more about the voices in Alex's head.

We met in the visitors' room at Grange Court Manor. What followed was truly remarkable. For almost two hours, Alex spoke openly and lucidly, in a fascinating, spellbinding interview, about what was going on inside him.

He claimed that he was not mad, but that he was possessed by two spirits who spoke in a strange language when talking together, but who would address him in English. He said one was good and the other bad. The bad one gave him precise instructions as to the bad things he should do. They specifically centred on hurting other people. A bell would ring, and then the voices would call him and tell him what to do. If he did not carry out these instructions he'd be punished, mostly by terrifyingly monstrous dreams and visions. When asked about the small electrical items that he mysteriously fixed at home, he claimed he had only to touch them with his hand in a certain way, and added that he'd even fixed things since being in the secure unit. He was fascinated by his power and frightened by it. As a reward for obedience the voices were granting him 'gifts' which made him more powerful. He expressed a fear of upsetting them, as they both protected him with a shield and punished him with nightmares. He claimed they threatened him with the removal of the shield, whereupon he'd become as vulnerable as ordinary people and as such could easily be killed. He concluded by asking his mum how he could get rid of them.

The psychiatrist, Sharon and I questioned him at appropriate openings throughout the conversation. Alex, for the most part, gave clear, co-ordinated answers. Sharon and I spoke comfortably to him and enquired as to why he hadn't told us these things before. He said he thought that no one would believe him. We gave him our reassurances and pledged our continued support.

Dr Heath said he didn't think Alex was lying. He did, however, believe he displayed some of the characteristics of schizophrenia. This contradicted Dr Thompson's findings: no proof of mental illness. Furthermore, the onset of schizophrenia is thought not normally to occur before the early to mid-twenties and seldom in the late teens, whereas Alex's disturbances had been lifelong. Dr Heath felt further investigation was required and would, in due course, seek the second opinion of another distinguished consultant, Dr Frederick Marley, of a renowned mental hospital. Ironically, a couple of years later I saw from a TV documentary that Dr Marley was engaged in research with children who bore characteristics strikingly similar to Alex's own. The main difference was that the children being treated were still under 5 years old.

The idea of possession seemed a little far-fetched, and was too much for Sharon to swallow; she wanted further investigations into dyslexia and hyperactivity. I must admit I wasn't comfortable with the notion that ghouls and malevolent spirits might somehow plague my son's life. My cousin's comment had come flooding back. I kept an open mind and, remembering the oddities I had observed with him over the years, couldn't dismiss everything that Alex had said. Dr Heath could offer no explanations for any of these phenomena. So, in the end, I accepted Sharon's wish to pursue Alex's dyslexia and hyperactivity, and the doctor's proposals for clinical medical investigations; and I decided to reserve judgement on the spirits.

There was a ray of hope at last, and Sharon and I were greatly relieved that something positive was happening. Alex, too, seemed at greater ease, in much the same way as he did in the aftermath of the 'bones' incident, for sharing his innermost feelings.

Midway during the interview, Dr Heath had kindly intervened on Alex's behalf when police arrived at the unit to arrest him in connection with yet another incident earlier that afternoon. He assured us that Alex should in no way be at Grange Court and promised to take immediate action to try to secure his release. That same day, I believe he spoke to the Director of Social Services and, insofar as I could ascertain, suggested that Alex be moved, sooner rather than later, to a place where he could receive appropriate *medical* treatment.

From that day forward, Grange Court seemed to relax its approach towards Alex, and after observing the marked improvement in the unit when Alex was afforded some freedom, staff began to see this as a better option for all concerned. They then began to recommend to social services that Alex be allowed to spend days out with his parents. Social services allowed this to take place but, for reasons best known to themselves, initially ruled out overnight stays and insisted he be returned by 9 p.m.

Alex had spent nearly five months in the secure unit. The big court hearing, due in January, was set aside pending the further psychiatric assessment from Dr Marley. About this time a new social worker, Wendy Chowdri, and her team manager, Judith Daniels, were allocated to Alex. Eventually social services agreed to his spending weekends at home, but not before they returned to court to extend the secure order for a further six weeks. Sharon and I challenged this but to no avail. The weekends at home appeared to have been a minor compromise, perhaps to keep us quiet and ensure our co-operation.

I was unclear whether it was fears for Alex's safety, or for children he'd be staying with (probably mainly the latter) that led Dr Marley and his team to deny Alex admission to his hospital after they'd spoken further with Grange Court's staff. Initially they had seemed keen to take him. This meant that Alex had to remain longer in Grange Court. Dr Heath then made several requests to other colleagues to see if any could accommodate him. Finally arrangements were made for Alex to be assessed at Dr Heath's own hospital's Morgana Stanfield Foundation, under consultant child psychiatrist Professor Cedric Richardson. Finally, 222 days after going into the secure unit, Alex was released.

Ten

ALEX WAS ELATED by his freedom, albeit limited, and Sharon and I were cautiously optimistic. We were no match for the system, but we were heartened by the intervention of Dr Heath and the advent of the two new social workers. Social services may have thought that we would relate better to other black people, or perhaps it was their official policy at the time to match clients with their social workers, but it didn't matter to me what colour they were; my only interest was that for the first time in four years social services appeared to have started listening.

Wendy was a sympathetic, gentle Asian woman with grown-up children. She didn't talk as though she were reading the latest Children's Act, or a chapter from a social-services manual. She sounded like an ordinary human being. I can't overemphasise how refreshing that was. Judith was also a mother, and a fellow Jamaican. In time we got to know them both quite well and I privately nicknamed them Pinky and Perky, for we rarely saw one without the other, and if we did, the other would shortly appear.

Both gave the impression of genuinely wanting to help, though they conspicuously avoided any criticism of the department. They wanted to let bygones be bygones, and move the situation on — under the circumstances quite sensibly, I thought. We were glad of the welcome relief, especially for Alex. Yet despite their sympathy and understanding, Wendy and Judith did not appear to grasp that the idea of placing him in a mental institution would be another futile exercise unless the causes of his problems were identified and treated. Nevertheless, without their help and co-operation Alex might have been left indefinitely to decline at Grange Court, and I was grateful for their help.

The animosity between our family and social services began to subside as soon as it became clear that Alex's release was imminent, though we had to go back to court before he was finally freed. It wasn't that Sharon and I became bosom buddies with Wendy and Judith – far from it – but they did treat us with respect and tried to accommodate our feelings, instead of subjecting us to ever-increasing doses of infuriating departmentalese. We couldn't have been that difficult to please: despite everything the department had put us through, this new social services/client relationship got off to a good start.

The terms of Alex's release didn't work out the way we were all hoping, however. While he had been in the secure unit, our marital home had been repossessed and my business had succumbed to the recession. I was out of work and homeless. Having to say goodbye to my staff was painful. And having to face that initial ignominious dole queue, and being spoken to as if I were dirt, was humiliating and hurtful for a self-made man who thrived on boundless enthusiasm. I felt a complete failure. Now I had been reduced to claiming state benefit. Jason had returned to live with me several months before the repossession, and he and I stayed with various relatives and friends. Though Jason missed his old home he refused to leave his dad and appeared to take the situation in his stride. He was still able to attend his same school, but the poor chap, hardly surprisingly, couldn't concentrate and slipped way behind.

For the moment my homelessness need not have been of any significance to Alex as the short-term plan was to move him straight into the Morgana Stanfield Foundation (MSF) at the children's hospital. There he would be an in-patient, possibly for up to six months. We were pleased to go along with this arrangement, convinced that all our concerns about Alex's behaviour and personality would be investigated fully. Any major decision involving him at this time had to be sanctioned by the High Court, and because I was receiving an appropriate state benefit I was able to fight for Alex's interests with the help of legal aid.

At some stage before committing themselves to the plan the MSF decided that a phased introduction would be preferable: a sort of trial period to see whether Alex fitted in and to give him time to adjust. They reserved the right to refuse him admission if they wished. This was after all a hospital with an entirely different regime and atmosphere from Grange Court. During this introductory period, which would last a fortnight, either Sharon or I, or both of us, would take him for his daytime appointments. However, after only two visits we were informed that they had decided not to admit Alex as an in-patient, but were happy to treat him on an out-patient basis for the duration of their assessment.

We were upset by this decision and remonstrated with them, but to no avail. But, we asked, how would they be able to observe Alex's sometimes highly disturbed sleep patterns if he did not stay at the unit overnight? To be seen in all his moods, Alex needed to be observed around the clock, which initially had seemed to be the basis upon which the MSF wished to be involved. What about the examination of his brain, and the tests that had been ordered by the High Court? What about monitoring Alex's blood, diet, dyslexia, hyperactivity, vision, hearing, speech – anything – to see if they might reveal something new? All had been rejected as being unnecessary by the MSF.

Sharon and I had thought Dr Heath's and then the unit's involvement a godsend; we couldn't have asked for better. We assumed they had taken on board the full import of Alex's sad and troubled life. So high were our expectations that we'd imagined them carrying out all conceivable tests, hooking our son up to state-of-the-art machines if necessary, until they found out what was wrong. So we were very disappointed when they would not admit him. Maybe we were being unrealistic. Neither of us had ever worked with a hospital at this level before and perhaps we failed to understand how they operated.

We felt the MSF were backing out of the challenge before they'd set about tackling it. We couldn't understand what could have altered so much, in so short a space of time, to make them change their minds. But from our first visit, Sharon and I could tell that the children there were not at all like Alex. One sat and rocked repetitively; another sat motionless; another seemed to cry incessantly; some hardly uttered a word; the majority looked retarded; all seemed totally innocent and inoffensive. There was no escaping the fact this unit was for the mentally ill, but after nearly seven months at Grange Court we were more than happy to allow Alex to go there, not only because there was no one there to beat him up, but also because it was in one of the country's top children's hospitals – here he was bound to get the best specialist treatment, so we thought. What did it matter as long as he got the help he needed? In a few months everything would be all right and Alex would come home . . . Then they burst our bubble.

Sharon stepped in and agreed to let Alex live with her, though everyone had reservations. I couldn't imagine her being able to cope with him for very long but I knew she'd try her best. This made my own housing situation more urgent. My hope had been that I would have been rehoused and thus be ready to care for Alex by the time his treatment at the MSF had been completed.

I wanted my anxiety and frustration at the MSF's decision to be recorded and made a huge effort to write a dispassionate letter to the medical head of the unit, Professor Richardson, setting down my considered thoughts as to which aspects of Alex's health, personality and intelligence might fruitfully be subjected to tests. I quote the letter in full, warts and all, for it mirrors exactly the extent of my speculation about Alex's condition at the time.

26 March 1992

Dear Professor Richardson

I refer to our meeting on Wednesday 4 March. This was prompted at our request following the then recent contact with various members of your team, whilst Alex was in attendance at the unit. After being shown the MSF timetable, Sharon and I were most concerned, as on visual inspection it was difficult to identify what treatment was being made available to Alex.

As none of your team (whom we spoke to) could clarify this for us, we wanted to see if you could, and at the same time make you aware of our view that whilst Alex was here to be observed, simultaneously we thought some serious testing would also be part of that programme, if for nothing else than to eliminate some of the possible causes of his disturbances.

To that end, we discussed with you nine separate items on which we wanted reassurance at the end of your four-to-six-week period of assessment. They were as follows:

1. Your own dyslexia assessment
2. Test for hyperactiveness
3. Diet testing
4. Brain scan
5. Eye test
6. Hearing test
7. Respiratory test
8. Speech-impediment test
9. Special-gift test

The Reasons

The following comments are ours. They are formed from our layman's point of view and a lifetime's experience of Alex and are not intended to cause offence or to tell you how to do your job.

Dyslexia assessment
Alex clearly has learning difficulties as any of the schools he has attended will testify. They will also tell you that Alex is an extremely bright child. Dyslexia might explain this anomaly.

Test for hyperactiveness
Under observation you will find it very difficult to keep Alex still for even five minutes unless he wants to – i.e., when he is watching a favourite television programme or playing a computer game. During his 'bored' periods, he is a 'hive' of activity and frequently goes 'over the top' and gets himself into trouble.

Diet testing
There could be something biologically wrong causing an imbalance in his brain. Perhaps an innocent everyday food, which could have the effect of keeping Alex on a permanent 'high'. Although we have juggled about with Alex's diet, cutting out 'E' products and fizzy drinks, etc., and replacing them with natural products where possible, we did this without advice or skilled supervision and any real consistency. Alex certainly has some worrying eating habits – i.e., his abnormal craving for sweet things. If left alone Alex would consume enormous quantities of chocolate, biscuits, sweets, fizzy drinks, etc. Maybe sugar could be causing this imbalance resulting in some sort of pressure on his brain.

Brain scan
I think it was in 1989 that Alex had a brain scan at your hospital with no adverse results. Though he is now a few years older I equally expect this test (which, as I understand, the court has ordered) once again to be OK. Although Alex's physical brain might be OK it does not necessarily mean that it is working correctly. I am a mechanic by trade and the closest analogy I can make is to that of an engine. Sometimes a customer will complain and say 'my engine is no good'. Very often, the fault lies not with the engine but with one of its peripheral components. Cleaning and fine tuning of the carburettor has resulted in many a condemned engine running like a dream.

Eyes, hearing, respiratory and speech-impediment test
I see these as symptoms of what is wrong but not the cause of Alex's problems. Alex complains about his vision. He was admitted to [our local] general hospital (approx. 1989–90) when struck by a mystery illness affecting his ears and nose, and we have received no explanation of the cause to date. His speech has also deteriorated as Dr Heath will readily testify. (Alex also indicates a rise in body temperature prior to most of his outbursts.)

Special-gift test
This is where Sharon and I can best equate ourselves with the proverbial 'drowning man clutching at straws'. We are exasperated

and don't know what is causing Alex's behaviour and all we want is a logical answer for Alex's unusual personality. No professional so far has been able to furnish us with an answer, so why should this be ruled out? According to Alex he is a psychic and has powers. Sharon and I claim no such abilities, yet Alex has been able to do some remarkable things which no one can explain to date. He also has a passion for computers. Although not academically gifted, Alex may have some hidden talent which he is too young to control or develop, causing him great frustration. On the other side of the coin, it may be purely an undiscovered medical condition. Maybe a blood disorder, an allergy or some other chemical disorder. If it is medical, then I am of the opinion that it has got to be something directly affecting his brain, a common denominator like blood, oxygen or water. For example, if his diet were the cause, it would readily explain all the points raised (except his special gifts). Once the offending compound has been identified, then it could be removed from his diet or be treated.

At our meeting on 4 March you saw it as a foregone conclusion that Alex had to be admitted into the MS Foundation: why should Alex be 'short-changed' yet again, which has been his experience to date? I would like to recount to you a conversation Alex had with his mother following yet another setback at Grange Court. Alex said, 'Mummy, I feel like I am at a bus stop and it is cold and raining and different buses come along and all the other people get on and I am the only one left waiting for my bus to come.' Needless to say, Sharon was overwhelmed and burst into tears.

Given all our above detailed concern as parents of a very unusual child, I fail to see how the points raised can be thoroughly investigated as an out-patient in only a few visits. Do you think that justice is being done to Alex? Going through the motions (for whatever the reason) is unlikely to be of any real benefit to Alex. I put it to you and Dr Heath, presumably parents yourself, if this were your child would you feel that the very best was being done?

Please forgive my ignorance, but I am also amazed at the stark difference in diagnosis by two eminent psychiatrists. Dr Heath on the one hand declared Alex to be suffering from a psychotic illness (after only two visits), and in an equally short time you conclude that he has no mental illness at all. May I respectfully remind you gentlemen that an 11-year old boy's entire future is at stake and the court's final decisions will be heavily influenced by whatever you say. The apparent disparity that exists between the two diagnoses in itself gives credence to the argument above for a full and thorough investigation of all Alex's problems.

Finally, Sharon and I were overjoyed when we found that a top psychiatrist from a world-renowned hospital would be involved with our son. We felt that now, at least, we would soon know the answers. Ultimately Alex is our charge, and as such Sharon and I will soldier along with our son and hope that social services will give us the backing we need to do so. However, I would still like a copy of any test result or therapy sessions carried out by yourselves and your reasons in writing for not accepting Alex as an in-patient as previously agreed.

In the meantime we accepted the out-patient treatment. Twice weekly, a combination of Sharon, Jason and me – often all three – accompanied Alex for his appointments until the assessment was finished.

Normally we would be greeted by Paul Johnson, the unit's social worker. Poor chap! He initially bore the brunt of our frustrations. We couldn't understand his role: why we had to leave one set of social workers in the East End only to see another in the West. His questions seemed to be prying and intrusive. However, it didn't take too long for me to accept that he was only doing his job. He already knew a good deal about how we felt from the wealth of information on file, and, mellowing, I soon formed the opinion that he was better at his job than the vast majority we'd formerly encountered.

If we were early for an appointment we'd go to the canteen for a cup of tea and a snack, and sometimes we lunched there. After each visit we'd take the boys to a nearby park, which was frequented by many children, parents and nurses from the hospital. They would look at a small collection of animals and then play around before we drove home.

While milling around the hospital, I was deeply touched when I saw children with horrific illnesses, deformities and injuries bravely struggling for survival. I looked at Alex and couldn't help but think how fortunate we were. Still, that didn't stop me wishing that he could arouse in others but a small part of the spontaneous affection and understanding those children were receiving. Then finally it clicked and I was able to understand what accounted for the difference and so get to the heart of the matter: their illnesses could be seen, Alex's could not. He looked a picture of boyish vigour and health, yet was bad-tempered and easily violent. I desperately wanted to know and understand, even more than before, the true nature of this strange illness that made people hate rather than love Alex; that caused people to be hostile and cruel, rather than helpful and kind. It had dominated my life for more than 11 years and had wrecked my family in its wake. What was this insidious puzzle that no one could unravel?

Like Dr Thompson, at first I think the MSF people were a little suspicious of Sharon and me – particularly me. However, like Dr Thompson, after a few doses of Alex they too appeared to show more compassion towards us. But Sharon and I were still not happy. When would the 'treatment' begin?

Much of the time we sat around in a waiting area. Alex had sessions with the unit's psychologist, psychotherapist, specialist teacher, social worker, and once or twice with Professor Richardson himself. After a couple of weeks it dawned on us that this *was* the treatment: talk, talk and more talk. Talk with Alex. Talk with us. Sometimes talk with all of us. But we'd been through that several times before and it had accomplished nothing. Where were the tests, the hooking-up to machines and everything else we'd expected? There weren't going to be any. Professor Richardson and his team concluded that Alex was not suffering from a formal mental illness, but a conduct disorder and was hyperactive. He blamed Alex's condition on his eccentric personality and our family – meaning

Sharon and me. He was adamant that no dysfunction or damage in Alex's brain accounted for his behaviour, and agreed with Dr Thompson that the best place for him would be a residential centre that specialised in emotionally and behaviourally disturbed children. Finally he stressed the need for ongoing individual psychotherapy for Alex.

As far as I could interpret his analysis, this meant that there was nothing wrong with Alex other than that he was an exceptionally naughty boy with unusual behaviour, an unusual temperament, and unusual parents whose differences of opinion he was smart enough to exploit. Two eminent child psychiatrists, Dr Heath and Professor Richardson, after seeing the same child, the same family and reading the same historical data, had indeed come up with conflicting diagnoses.

I didn't question for one moment the sincerity of either man, but I knew that my son's entire future lay in the balance. Such differing opinions confirmed for me the fact that there was something exceptionally odd about Alex. These medical supremos had succeeded only in underlining the dilemma that had for so long vexed us, our extended family and friends: *could Alex help himself or couldn't he?* If he could, then those who had chosen to judge him harshly could reason that he deserved much of what he got. If he couldn't, then we had all wronged him considerably and he deserved not only sympathy but also every bit of appropriate professional help that he could get, immediately, as the very least act of compensation.

Sharon and I concluded that what had happened at the MSF was a repeat of the pattern that had emerged nearly everywhere else. We felt that the practitioners were going through the motions, looking to confirm a preconceived textbook truth which was not necessarily *the* truth, followed by the inevitable recommendation of boarding school without ever identifying what was wrong with Alex in the first place. If his core problem was not understood, how could even the greatest therapeutic boarding institution in the world begin to help him? Our argument seemed rational to us, but we were made to feel that we lesser mortals weren't supposed to have such thoughts, let alone be audacious enough to voice them.

It felt as if our family was a set of square pegs which the professionals were assiduously trying to fit into round holes. We loved our children and they loved us. Jason was not a disturbed child, yet had come from the same background. Most puzzling of all was the bond of love that bound Alex and me together, since I seemed to come off worst in these evaluations. Yes, we were angry; yes, we were confused and could make things worse. What family wouldn't be? As each new set of experts looked for an explanation, preconceived or otherwise, they would meet with eventual disappointment. Then they'd want to move us on – quickly. The MSF, however, were a decent bunch. Following their initial report, they offered a further three months' assistance to Alex in lieu of anything else being readily available. We accepted. And by the end of March 1992, social services, in the shape of Wendy Chowdri, had begun to accept that the education department should be providing Alex with one-to-one tuition.

In the meantime, and not surprisingly, stresses began to develop between Sharon and Alex. He was slipping back into his old ways: throwing tantrums, absconding and returning at will, winding people up, fighting in the neighbourhood, even biting a local girl quite badly. He seemed to have learned not a single lesson from Grange Court other than how to be nastier and more vulgar than before. Nevertheless, we kept up our visits to the MSF, sometimes three times in one week. By 16 April, on one of her periodic visits to Sharon and Alex, Wendy acknowledged that the placement wasn't working and showed signs of imminent breakdown. Yet Sharon was given no help in real terms with Alex's daily care. Similarly, not even a minute's daily education was offered. Dismayed by this, I wrote to Stan Wilson, Director of Education, enclosing documents outlining Alex's history and pointing out that at 'nearly 12 years old, he has just four years left in the education system, and, with an average academic level of a 7–8-year-old he has eight years' worth of work to do within those four years – that's an awful lot of catching up to do.'

During this time the MSF people got to know us all better and saw for themselves how difficult Alex was. They also realised how crucial I was to any realistic plan for his future. They knew that my idea of looking after him myself, with input from the education department and social services, had been vetoed, but could now see the logic behind it. Like Wendy, they came to appreciate that all I was trying to do was to support my son. I wanted to calm him down and settle him sufficiently so that he would co-operate with, and thus benefit from, whatever appropriate specialist educational and medical help would eventually be offered. If I couldn't accomplish that, it seemed highly unlikely anyone else would. Because of the damage done, especially at Grange Court, even I now had only a slim chance, but it deserved to be looked at seriously. I'd also been making exhaustive attempts to find a private tutor who specialised in dyslexia. After some considerable effort, I eventually located one who was willing to help if invited by the education department or social services, since I could not afford his very reasonable fees.

By the time the MSF's second report was filed, on 19 June 1992, they'd modified their original recommendations slightly, having taken on board some of what we had been saying. This strengthened my position. Alex needed to be understood as an individual and to have a tailor-made package built up around him. He had, point-blank, ruled out any notion of going to boarding school. As a consequence, the MSF supported my plan to look after him, and in the short term for Alex to receive one-to-one tuition at home. They also strongly recommended that he receive regular psychotherapy at a reputable institution such as the Tavistock Clinic, which they had already approached on his behalf, for at least the next three years. They were quite specific: *ongoing, long-term psychotherapy* was to be an *integral part* of whatever future plan was to be decided for Alex. Up to the time of writing, social services have never complied with that recommendation and Alex has received no psychotherapy.

Just as there was a positive professional development, fortune was about to deal us another woeful blow. Alex was tremendously attracted to animals – cats and dogs in particular. They seemed to satisfy some inner instinct, perhaps the need to love something on his terms, his way. Cats were cuddly, though they could be boringly indifferent and independent. Dogs were fun, they did more and followed their owners around, and he always dreamed of having his own one day. The problem was, Alex did not know how to maintain his love for pets. I had learned that from the Fluff incident. He could end up hurting them, mostly accidentally or through playing too roughly, or quite deliberately because they would not obey his exacting instructions. For Sharon to give in and get him a cat, after much pleading on Alex's part, was perhaps not the most prudent thing to do – a mistake I repeated some months later with a dog. She was simply trying to make her son happy, but in the process she made a rod for her own back. They had the cat for about ten weeks. Tensions developed over it and she decided the cat must go. So Alex absconded with it and went to social services; the placement with his mother was abruptly over. However, Wendy came to the rescue. Alex had won again.

Try as she did, things could not be patched up that day between Sharon and Alex, and I'd not been rehoused as yet. Wendy was unsuccessful in finding a children's home that could accommodate him immediately other than Grange Court, and she was trying desperately to keep him out of there. Later that day, when she reached me by phone and explained what had happened, she mentioned that Alex might have to return to Grange Court. My disappointment was so deep that it turned to anger against him. I told her that if he wanted to go back there, then so be it. After all our efforts he'd let us down over a stupid cat (no offence to cat owners intended).

I knew Alex wasn't thinking straight – he seldom did when emotionally aroused – but metaphorically he'd kicked us right in the teeth by telling social services that he was willing to go back. After all he'd been through, I thought, didn't he have the sense to know that social services were not to be played around with? But I was applying adult logic, which he was far too naive to do. Then Wendy told me of an alternative: Stockport House. It had been earmarked as a contingency in case a breakdown in Sharon's and Alex's relationship occurred. (This was the very first children's home in which Alex and Jason had been placed four years before.) They were willing to accept Alex on condition that someone independent of their own staff had round-the-clock responsibility for him. Guess who Wendy thought would be the perfect candidate for the job: me.

Stockport House had a few three-bedroomed flats attached to their complex which served as emergency units for families in crisis, such as those displaced by fire. They were prepared to provide Alex with somewhere to stay – nothing else. With frustration and anger I told Wendy that there was no way I would move into any children's home to live, not even for Alex, and hung up the phone.

Shortly afterwards I bumped into my mother. Furious, I told her the latest happenings and how I felt. She sympathised, but then her mature wisdom stepped in and saved the day. 'Alex is your son,' she said. 'Swallow your pride and go with him. He won't survive another dose of Grange Court.' I agreed. I didn't relish the idea of moving into the home, but listened to my mother. If Alex were put back in Grange Court, I'd have monumental difficulties getting him out again. Swift action was needed.

On arriving at Stockport House, seething, I was met by an ever-calm Wendy. I looked at Alex with disdain and shouted at him. She led me to a grubby ground-floor apartment. It was very basic, but she doubted we'd be there two weeks. When I looked about the place, my spirits sank; it was nasty, bleak and depressing. I shook my head, felt humiliated and thought: 'The things you are expected to do for love.'

I know Alex didn't think me very loving that evening. I told him off for putting me in this situation and laid down the law. 'Since this is what you want, you are going to be with me 24 hours a day. But you'll have to do your school work, just like you had to at the garage. If you run away, I will not smack you; I don't want to get into trouble with the police, but when you return you will still have to do the work.' I also explained to him that we would go out and have fun like we did in the old days, but only if he co-operated. He didn't mind the bit about enjoying ourselves, but he didn't like the education part at all. And then I saw that look in his eye: the glint that always spelled trouble, though he never opened his mouth in defiance.

★

Thus it was I took up residence at Stockport House. Scornfully I scrubbed the bathroom, kitchen (including the kitchen sink and all the utensils) and changed the bed clothes – just in case. But the floors were too much for me; the more I swept, the more dirt and dust came from the carpets. A sleepless night ensued. Ironically, I never did meet that cat.

There was a prearranged planning meeting at the MSF on the following day, 14 May. Michele Saunders from the education department argued in favour of Alex's going to a boarding school. However, she was outgunned: both the MSF and social services favoured my alternative plan as a short-term precursor to any long-term arrangement. Talk about dragging the donkey to the well! A month later, on 17 June, the education people agreed to a seven-hours-a-week, home-tutorial package for Alex. Three tutors would be involved, including the one who specialised in dyslexia. Although I'd trained and sparred at a club that was littered with highly credited champions in the martial-arts world, I'd never had to fight like this before. I felt exonerated.

I'm getting ahead of myself: I still had to cope with Alex on my own. In the mornings, I'd prepare breakfast and set him school work. Eventually he'd settle down and do the work and I would help him as I used to before. Then he'd mix with children he'd befriended in the unit, visit their rooms or play pool. I'd tidy the flat, and sometimes Alex would help. He begged me to teach him martial arts in the spacious sitting room; I refused, but we'd have a little wrestle as a compromise. I'd schedule some fun activity for the afternoon, so he'd have the whole morning, if necessary, to complete his school work – though I never set him more than about an hour's worth. In addition, we all kept regular appointments at the MSF.

Ah, but those mornings! Alex tried every trick in the book to get out of his school work and I had to use every ounce of tact I possessed to make sure he didn't. At Stockport House I found another piece of the Alex jigsaw: he could not cope with being educated – full stop – but I wasn't any the wiser as to why. Here it was just me and him, and I had time to watch, digest and reflect. It became crystal clear: lick Alex's educational problem – whatever that was –

and at a stroke his behavioural problems would begin to sort themselves out. I reread Dr Rouse's year-old dyslexia report, took notes from it, and tried to apply its contents as best I could. I was now Alex's sole teacher.

Nevertheless, Alex is Alex. Even with all this one-to-one help, and no matter how patient I was, within a fortnight it became too much for him. He'd climb through one of the windows and be off like a whippet when I was in another room. I made no attempt to stop him and never ran after him. Doing his school work became a battle of wills: a power struggle. He became more daring as he realised that I meant what I'd said about not smacking him; I kept my word and never laid a finger on him. Minutes or hours later, in he'd come again, apologise, sit at the work I'd set and ask my help. He'd be especially prompt when a favourite activity had been planned for the afternoon. For the rest of that particular day there'd be no more problems. On his unauthorised excursions he'd roam the streets, sometimes end up in bad company and get into trouble. On occasions the police were involved. And even when a 16-year-old yob took a brick to his head and smashed it open, that didn't stop him running from his school work the very next day.

I didn't hang around for Alex to return from his escapades, especially if I had other things to do away from the unit. One day he came back when I was absent, decided to stay a while, but intended to depart again before my return. I came back earlier than he'd expected and when he caught sight of me he made a dash to escape. For reasons quite beyond me, I found myself chasing after him — something I'd vowed never to do.

He was swift and agile, but not enough. I caught up with him 50 or so yards beyond the unit's entrance. We grappled. He struggled like a wild person and was surprisingly strong for his size, but he could not overpower me. I dragged him back into the home. Children and staff came running out from every direction to view the excitement. The unit's manager, whom I shall call Bill Smart, a person I'd never seen before, appeared from nowhere and skilfully helped to defuse the situation. He escorted us away from the crowd as I hauled Alex back to our flat.

Bill had intended to remain only until the situation was calm. He asked what had happened. I punished Alex, who was still breathing fire, by ordering him to stand facing a corner in the room; he gave me that hate-filled look but promptly complied. There was something different about Bill: he seemed truly concerned. Then, for the second time that day, I found myself behaving uncharacteristically. I related Alex's life story to this total stranger, incoherently cramming it all into about 15 minutes.

Meanwhile, the wild child of minutes earlier had calmed himself down and lovingly apologised as if nothing had happened. Bill was fascinated by the transformation. When I mentioned that Alex claimed he was possessed by spirits, like Dr Heath Bill listened even more intently than before. Finally, when I allowed him to get a word in edgeways, he told me he knew a person he believed might be able to help, and he assured me that this person was in no way connected to the occult. I gave him permission to consult her and Bill seemed to vanish as mysteriously as he had appeared.

A few days passed and I could not find Bill anywhere. I dismissed him as yet another waste of time, but some days later, to my surprise, he did reappear. He explained that he hadn't wanted to talk to me again until he had contacted his colleague, and apparently it had taken a while before he caught up with her on the telephone. He now wanted to share with me the gist of their conversation. He did not know whether what she'd told him applied to Alex, but he invited me to his office to listen none the less.

Eleven

Alex's behaviour at Stockport House had certainly upset me. Why? Because I tried so hard not to give him the slightest reason for us to fall out. I was now working for him voluntarily, full-time, and unable to concentrate on anything else. Often I was torn mentally in two. When I thought of Alex as being ungrateful, I was the old Chester who took things personally. When I thought how confused and frightening the inside of his mind must be I felt great compassion for him, and even admired him at times, wondering where on earth he got his strength from; then I was the new Chester who realised that Alex couldn't improve his negatively charged behaviour without help. I tried to supply as much of that help as possible myself. I planned all his lessons meticulously, taking considerable care not to make them too hard or too easy. I gave him every conceivable help I could with his work to energise his mind. I tried to organise his days in an attempt to negate any potential trouble, but I couldn't do it all on my own. Social services weren't providing anything in the way of additional help or respite. The home-tuition arrangement was in hand but hadn't as yet come on stream.

Bill Smart escorted me to his office. He started to spout a load of scientific babble to do with the brain. He was using long and complicated words, the majority of which I'd never even heard let alone could pronounce, biology not having been my strongest subject at school. Then he simplified things for me. He used a board on his office wall and began to draw elementary diagrams, explaining them in terms of what might be happening in Alex's head. He was in fact demonstrating what his colleague and friend, Vivienne Gill, had explained to him over the phone. I soon realised that Bill was no ordinary social worker.

I could barely contain my excitement. What he said astounded me. Spontaneous outbursts followed: 'Yes, that's Alex all right! That's exactly what he does!' 'I've always wondered why he did this.' 'That makes sense!' 'So that's why he does that . . .'

Bill had given me a crash lesson in the workings of the brain, which provided me with my first insight into what might be happening scientifically inside Alex's head. As well as talking about the brain as two halves, which even I knew, among other things he spoke about a forebrain, a midbrain and a hindbrain. He explained what the left part did, and the right, and the other areas, and how vital it was that they all communicated. The essence of the diagnosis was that there might be something faulty in the way the parts of Alex's brain interacted.

This made sense. There was nothing obviously amiss with Alex's neurological physiology, otherwise the brain scan ordered by Dr Thompson a few years before, and the several physical examinations he had been given, would have revealed it. It now made greater sense why Professor Richardson was so reticent about ordering another scan: he didn't expect it to disclose anything new. I won't pretend to have understood half of what Bill explained, but my curiosity was roused and I wanted to know more.

His presentation particularly struck me because it focused on possible causes within Alex's brain and not on the state of his parents' relationship. I'm not too proud to acknowledge when blame lies with me, but admit to being hurt by the innuendoes of professionals who indicated that Alex's problems lay solely with Sharon and me. Bill's explanation chimed with much of my son's behaviour and that was good enough for me, though I still had many questions. I could barely contain myself, I was ecstatic. I wanted to meet this woman who could apparently diagnose my son so accurately even though she'd never met him, and only through second-hand information. I knew she must be special.

I couldn't explain to Sharon what had happened but asked her to come and meet Bill. She did so the following day, and once again Bill kindly obliged. Shortly after, I contacted Judith and shared with her this new development. Maybe it was because of my sheer excitement that she agreed to a meeting, but I don't think we shared the same degree of optimism. Nevertheless, she heard enough to be willing to explore this new lead and sanctioned the idea of a preliminary meeting with Vivienne Gill so that she could assess Alex.

The sessions at the hospital were almost at an end. Alex and I were rehoused and so moved out of Stockport House. The three home tutors had been agreed upon by the education department and ourselves, and the dyslexia teacher wasted no time in starting work with Alex. The school summer holidays were fast approaching, as was Alex's twelfth birthday, and the other two tutors would not become involved in earnest until September. Ms Gill agreed to assess Alex. Things were looking good: the best they'd been since the day social services crashed into our lives. But I did have one major worry. I was getting no rest from Alex, nor he from me, and our relationship was already strained.

Vivienne Gill was an unassuming middle-aged woman. A former deputy head teacher who had worked with children with learning difficulties for some 17 years, she now freelanced from home in her own enterprise, New Dimensions in Education. The walls of her consulting area were, like virtually all the others in her modest apartment, covered floor to ceiling with enough books for it to resemble a small library. She was an unusual lady with an equally unusual-looking home. What also struck me was the sizeable assortment of odd trinkets, ornaments and effigies about the place – presents and souvenirs she'd collected from her worldwide travels. When Alex and I arrived, Judith and Wendy had already begun to acquaint themselves with Ms Gill. Alex was fascinated: this place was exciting; it had lots of interesting things to see and touch. However, it was the long curved sword and the pair of matching Arabian daggers hanging on the wall that most caught his attention.

In her quest for answers as to why some children were able to learn while others with similar opportunities were not, Ms Gill had found herself challenging and increasingly moving away from traditional educational dogma. She found it difficult to accept ideas that were at odds with her experience of teaching hundreds of children and she wanted to understand the disparity. Her quest led her to study the works of many prominent educational and scientific researchers in this field, and this prompted her to investigate the make-up of the brain: its chemistry, the effects on it of various chemicals, plus many other areas I am not qualified to explain. Further, she wanted to learn all she could about human behaviour and to understand the disparate elements that make human beings behave the way they do. This in turn led her to consider the research of leading neurologists, psychiatrists, psychologists, psychotherapists and sociologists. She began to carry out her own research, comparing her findings with those of other similarly minded professionals, both in and out of the mainstream. She was able to implement her discoveries by starting her own practice, seeking to help disturbed and educationally retarded children and their parents.

When I first consulted her, Vivienne had already built up an established clientele of satisfied customers. She never advertised. Children were brought from all over the country to see her through personal recommendation. I saw people there of differing colour, nationality and social status; they arrived by car, foot, bus, taxi and Rolls-Royce. She was willing to try to help anyone.

I soon discovered a common denominator between us all. By the time Vivienne became known to parents of difficult or underachieving children, they had invariably seen a plethora of psychiatrists, psychologists and the like, had been dissatisfied with the outcome and were feeling let down by the system. Then, fortuitously, someone would recommend Vivienne to them. Because her work was not in the mainstream, some parents were sceptical but felt they had nothing to lose by seeing her. Typically, after a short while, they'd become pleased when they saw positive improvements in their children. Most of her clients were aged around 6, which meant they were getting help before their condition worsened.

At our first meeting, Vivienne continued the biology lesson that Bill had started. She made us think about routine daily actions in a way we'd never done before, and in terms of how they related to brain activity. She spoke about kinesiology, the science that deals with the mechanics of bodily movement, and about the importance of diet. She explained a little about a technique called muscle-testing and the concepts behind it, and about neuro-linguistics. She spoke with Alex to the extent he permitted. I think the social workers were as surprised as I was by what we were hearing, some of which was beyond our understanding. However, Judith and Wendy supported the idea of continued consultation to see if any good would come of it.

I'd brought along copies of Professor Richardson's and the MSF reports but, unlike any other experts we met, Vivienne was not at first in the least bit interested in reading other people's views of Alex, and she brushed them aside each time I tried to introduce them into the conversation. She wanted to assess the situation through fresh eyes and not allow her judgements to be coloured by what others had written about him. This impressed me, and in time she read extensively through Alex's file.

Over the next few months, many meetings took place between Vivienne, Alex and me as part of a treatment programme. Slowly but surely, a picture of how human beings function began to form in my mind as Vivienne explained how different segments of the brain are associated with the various functions of speech, vision, memory and movement, for example, and how they all work together. I learned that the two hemispheres of the brain send myriads of biochemical signals back and forth, and that Alex was somehow deficient in this aspect. It was here she felt the answer to his problems lay, though she could offer no proof of this, and no explanations as to why he should have this problem. He had simply been born that way, she indicated. She did, however, feel that poor diet was exacerbating chemical imbalances or deficiencies already present, resulting in his being hyperactive, muddled and aggressive. The fault lay in the intrinsic 'wiring' of his brain (how the messages are transmitted), and not in the 'hardware' (the brain itself). There was nothing biologically amiss, but some signals were not being correctly transmitted and others were not being stored effectively, resulting in poor memory. This made sense to me.

As a mechanic, I'd specialised in that part of the motor vehicle which mechanics fear the most and which puzzles even the most able technicians: the automatic transmission. Unlike its manual counterpart, it is incredibly difficult to grasp how this piece of equipment works without specialist training. The mechanic cannot actually 'see' first gear, second gear, etc. An invisible combination of internal events has to combine to create each gear, making automatic gearboxes a taboo to most mechanics. A capable non-specialist mechanic could take one apart and put it together, and might never get it to work correctly simply because he didn't understand the cause of the original fault. But there has to be a logical reason for every phenomenon – even when we don't yet understand it.

Thus Vivienne's résumé appealed to my sense of logic and my mechanical background. I'm not suggesting that the human brain can realistically be compared to a piece of mechanical equipment, but for analogical purposes there are similarities; in fact, the control unit in an automatic transmission is commonly referred to as the 'brain' by mechanics. But Vivienne's explanation made more sense to me than anything I'd heard from a professional thus far; from Dr Khan's 'Fine boy, fine boy' diagnosis of seven years ago, after my son's failed attempt at 'flying like Superman', right through to Professor Richardson's seemingly blaming Alex for his unusual personality and circumstances. I could see, even more clearly than when Bill had explained it, why the psychiatrists and other clinicians had declared Alex not to be suffering from any biological problem: there were no signs of hardware damage.

The ideas Vivienne put forward were also compatible with the findings of the Dyslexia Institute, whose report had concluded that Alex was suffering from visual and auditory short-term memory. In no way did she consider Alex's position hopeless or irreparable; he simply needed the right help. All this was extremely enlightening and made me realise that Sharon and I hadn't been so stupid after all in seeking out proper solutions for Alex, as the headmaster of

Viewmount had encouraged, and as I'd tried to do in my long letter to Professor Richardson four months previously.

Vivienne stressed the importance of knowing the effects of diet on brain activity, especially additives found in much of today's food. She embarked on the following three-pronged approach in her treatment programme: test for and eliminate from his diet the most harmful substances, which should dramatically reduce his hyperactivity and behaviour-related difficulties; try to stimulate Alex's brain with neuro-linguistic and kinesiological exercises and techniques which should help to reduce his immature baby-like responses; employ her own style of psychotherapy to make Alex face up to his learning and behavioural problems. Vivienne also identified to me a negative, cyclical pattern of behaviour that Alex had been using – ever so successfully, though to his own detriment – that had to be broken if he was to make any meaningful progress in life. She wanted the whole family to engage in joint therapy with her, but in the end most of her work was done with Alex and me only, and occasionally Jason. She never met Sharon, though they did have lengthy conversations by phone. Like all other professionals before her, Vivienne recognised that the marital difficulties between us contributed significantly to Alex's condition. She was dismayed by the obstinacy in our relationship and how this was still affecting Alex. But she saw this as one of many problems which were making Alex worse, and which obscured and exacerbated his underlying brain deficit.

From my association with Vivienne, I gained invaluable insight into Alex's tormented little world. In answer to any emotional arousal, his responses were still mostly those of a baby or young child. The outside world could tolerate this only while he was very young and became increasingly hostile to his immature responses as he grew older. Onlookers, including some professionals, saw only his real age and behaviour and reacted to that; they couldn't see the emotional baby inside, or, because of his extreme antisocial behaviour, did not care. What they saw were the actions of a maturish intelligent child behaving in an unacceptable manner. To the untrained eye, Alex exhibited no discernible evidence of any sort of affliction, mental or otherwise. His behaviour, therefore, was sometimes misinterpreted as being deliberate: from silly to wicked. Lack of understanding, and ignorance, prevailed. In time, Alex found his own ways to survive through satisfying his immediate, short-term desires. He never intended to be nasty and was mostly surprised by the negative reactions he earned from others. However, the deficiency in his brain prevented him learning from this, as other children would, because he quickly forgot about it. He thus repeated his errors in every new situation. He could not regulate or assess his own behaviour. This was the vicious cycle that Vivienne wanted to be broken as an absolute prerequisite before he could be helped. To accomplish that, a great deal of skill would be required; everyone had to co-operate.

This little boy had, through no fault of his own, found himself in a no-win situation. His brain was like a minefield of activity with explosions occurring faster than his ability to cope with them. The wonder is that he didn't in fact go mad. In his head, Alex was locked in his own world; his near-perfect body was trapped in ours. Neither of us understood each other's world; a classic 'catch-22' situation! No amount of shouting, threatening, punishment, swearing, hitting, advice and reprimands conveyed anything of lasting value to him. His brain could not retain the information long enough to do anything constructive with it.

Vivienne was apprehensive about the supposed paranormal incidents in Alex's life and could offer no clear explanations for these. She hoped her treatment would minimise the frightening pictures in his mind, and sensed an impenetrable energy about him which made her uneasy. This reminded me of Sharon's comment – 'It's as though he is in a glass cage looking out at all of us, we can't touch him' – and also of Alex's remark about being protected by a shield. It tied in with my long-held feelings that there was something about Alex which not even I could reach when he flipped into a particular mode. I wanted to understand it.

Vivienne's treatment programme was designed to activate the learning processes that were available to Alex and to boost them; to equip him with strategies to enable him to learn and remember. If it was to work, the co-operation of everyone connected with his care was essential. Sadly, this was not always forthcoming. The home-tutorial/medical programme that I'd vigorously fought for had just begun, except there was no longer a medical provision. Social services didn't pursue the MSF's recommendations for psychotherapy. Alex and I were seeing Vivienne, but we did expect it to come on stream at some time in the not too distant future. It never did. My dream was that the vicious cycle be broken; my plan seemed the only way to do it. Under existing circumstances, Vivienne agreed there was no other way to move the situation on, but she soon started to have reservations. With her involvement, I felt that at last I had an ally who, at least partially, understood the true nature of Alex's problems. We could join forces, as it were, to help him. But she saw him only two or three times a week for a few hours, and the bulk of helping Alex still remained squarely on my shoulders – everyone else would pop in for an hour or two and then disappear. I would report to her each time we met any new positive or calamitous events.

Vivienne was appalled by the extent to which Alex had been failed by all the various authorities, and by Sharon and myself. Even the home-tutorial arrangement was grossly inadequate, she felt. The dyslexia tutor came for three hours each Wednesday morning. The maths and science tutors each came for one hour every Tuesday and Thursday. Alex was receiving a total of seven hours' education a week, and the lessons were fraught with difficulties.

It soon became clear that none of the tutors was qualified to teach such a disturbed child, let alone cope with him. This in itself triggered Alex to frustrate their good intentions and doomed the arrangement, but it was the best deal I could get for Alex from the local education authority.

The set-up was that they would tutor Alex on a one-to-one basis in a 'school' room in our house. I was never to get involved or interfere with the teaching process. I'd hoped that my presence would be sufficient to ensure Alex's co-operation with his tutors, but I was wrong. The old pattern, familiar to me but not them, emerged: he tried everything he could to avoid doing his school work. The tutors, like all previous teachers before them and myself, used every tactic to persuade him.

On a good day he'd settle down at some stage and do maybe 20 minutes' work. But as soon as they tried to introduce a new topic, a wide range of antics effectively ensured that no further learning took place that day. Sometimes they would fail even to start a lesson. Within minutes of arriving, they'd sense they were going to get little by way of co-operation from Alex and he'd rarely disappoint them.

Each tutor had his or her own strategy when the lesson was in danger of breaking down. The dyslexia tutor, a strapping man with a booming voice, would call me to intervene, and sometimes this worked. I'd reprimand, coax or reason with Alex and he'd settle. Alex had an incredible skill of extracting the sympathy of a third party when he found himself in conflict – as when staff had tried to control him on the main road near the three-bedroomed house and he had appealed to passers-by. Hence the need would arise for me to show him in front of his tutors that I was serious about his education, but even this tactic began to fail towards the end of the tutorial arrangement. The maths teacher was always calm. She'd threaten to abort the lesson and leave if he didn't behave. Alex would then plead for her to remain because he didn't want me to find out that he'd been misbehaving. She'd agree and he'd settle down to work, but this too began to fail towards the end. I thought the science tutor experienced the fewest problems. His lessons were more practical and so were less threatening to Alex, but he also suffered an amount of grief when he introduced reading and writing exercises. However, he rarely called me or threatened to walk out, but stuck with each lesson.

All the tutors tried their best to reason with Alex, sometimes counselling him for most, if not all, of the lesson, and were often at a loss because they could see no cause for some of his actions. They all felt the tutorial arrangement at home was unnatural, even unhealthy, and that Alex needed to mix with other children in a school. I explained that the arrangement wasn't ideal, but it was the best under the circumstances and that their role was crucial in helping

Alex cope with any future school placement. To support the tutors, I'd insist Alex do as homework any classwork they set, that he, through misbehaviour, had successfully avoided – when they asked me. If Alex did not co-operate, then I might withhold privileges or cancel any fun activity we had planned. This undoubtedly caused the tension to rise between us. He was already upset with me because I made him go to see Vivienne, for whom he was developing a hatred.

As far as Alex was concerned, Vivienne was the reason why he could no longer have chocolates, sweets, junk food and fizzy drinks. Vivienne was the person who was telling Daddy what to do and Daddy was listening to her. She was the one who seemed able to get inside his brain and made him feel very uncomfortable by asking all sorts of questions that made him think and talk about things he didn't really want to. Soon not even his secret hope of one day being able to play with the Arabian daggers, perhaps without Vivienne or me knowing, held any fascination for him. He became increasingly critical of Vivienne and, in time, declared her sessions to be 'rubbish'. Although she was very gentle in her approach, he soon discovered her to be as tough as old boots – 'worse than Daddy', he complained to his mother. Unlike everyone else, he could not bend her to his will. In a short space of time he developed a fixation against her.

At the age of 12 Alex was about the same size as Vivienne and he knew she was no match for him physically. He had done battle with dragons and monsters in his mind; he had vanquished boys bigger than himself in fights; he had got rid of doctors, teachers, social workers and other adults whom he didn't like; he had made several professionals look stupid and incompetent. But this mite of a woman refused to get off his case. 'Why don't you leave me alone, you old witch?' he unceremoniously asked her.

Alex tested her boundaries to *beyond* the limit. He touched her possessions without permission. He sought to intimidate her by looking her in the eye and talking disparagingly an inch away from her face when I was in the next room. He sulked, was rude, crude, cried, laughed, acted like a baby. When all else failed, he took to insulting her by nicknaming her 'the Midget', and sometimes referred to her as such in false muted tones, knowing that she could overhear. But he nearly won the battle of wills – nearly reduced her to tears – by telling her she hadn't got any qualifications and then demanding to see them before continuing the session. Notwithstanding these insults, he found it impossible to shake her off. Vivienne skilfully dealt with each situation.

This was a new and uncomfortable experience for Alex but it was working. Vivienne and I acted as a team when he tried to wreck each session. Events never got out of hand because, at Vivienne's request, I was always there, either in the therapy room or somewhere near by when she wanted to see him on his own. She never held back in reprimanding me too when she felt I'd handled a situation badly. We'd later discuss everything on the telephone. She told me not to worry, in that Alex's testing of her never became too loud or vulgar, not only because I was there but also because, deep down, he had come to appreciate that she was genuinely trying to help him.

Eventually I noticed Vivienne had achieved something that seemed truly unique, which nobody else, not even I, had come near to accomplishing before: Alex appeared to begin to think and reason. He usually seemed unable to do so when emotionally aroused but she'd triggered something in his brain. Through her skill, and her skill alone, Alex began slowly but surely to co-operate. This good work needed to continue; it was only just the beginning. Vivienne and I couldn't do it all on our own.

Once Alex had ritually tested the limits at the start of each session, he'd accept the futility of it and settle down. He'd then comply fully with Vivienne's instructions until it was time to go. He always gave her a hug and kiss before leaving, sometimes adding an 'I love you' that made it all worthwhile for Vivienne. She later described him as the most disturbed child she'd ever worked with. Alex began to calm down and show faint signs of improvement with his tutors. The dietary restrictions seemed to be working and he appeared less hyperactive. Wendy acknowledged that our strategy was beginning to pay off. Some form of stability and structure was beginning to return to Alex's messed-up life.

Though I was enthusiastic, this positive development was too fragile to last. The lack of respite from each other for Alex and me was becoming a real problem, plus the tutors' frustration with his behaviour and my inability to replicate Vivienne's skill when trying to alleviate *their* problems, and especially Alex's inherent selfishness: all these conspired to threaten any progress in his condition. The tutors were becoming less effective by the day as Alex stubbornly found more ways to irritate and anger them. In the end, this is how it was: the good work at Vivienne's was undone each time Alex had to face his next tutorial lesson.

Around this time I learned of an organisation in West London called Sankofa. It helped children with learning difficulties and was reputed to get good results, using the techniques of the acclaimed educational guru Professor Rueven Feuerstein of Israel. Alex and I met with its Educational Director Gladstone Bennett, who later carried out an assessment. He criticised the current home-tuition programme: it significantly failed to meet Alex's needs.

The dyslexia tutor began to get angry with Alex, shouting and swearing, and telling him that he didn't have to be there and wasn't obliged to 'put up with this'. The message was clear: he was doing Alex a favour. According to Alex, the maths teacher would ask if he 'knew how lucky' he was, and then tell him, and once or twice aborted lessons when she could not cope or he showed no appreciation of her efforts. I got upset with Alex for wrecking his lessons, and became disappointed and frustrated with the tutors for not having skills like Vivienne's or enough patience to teach him, though – like her – they were very sorely tried. It frustrated me that they were key players in Alex's future but he didn't seem to realise. Any recommendations they were going to make might have profound implications for his future education and care. I needed them for him, but events showed that they, quite unintentionally, were making things worse. Alex began to abscond whenever that impulse overtook him. Only the science teacher kept his cool. The whole arrangement was in danger of imminent collapse. I became increasingly frustrated with Alex, social services and the education department, and was rapidly approaching the end of my tether. Alex didn't seem to care, and I wasn't receiving the respite or help I needed, despite urgent written pleas. I was out on a limb, usually with round-the-clock responsibility for Alex and very little support or rest.

One day I made a stupid error of judgement. I left Alex and Jason alone for three hours to attend a keep-fit training session at the gym. I'd sought the boys' permission first, asking whether I could trust them for a few hours. I chanced it because they'd been in a very good mood that morning. They insisted I go and virtually threw me out of the house. I wanted this break. On my return, however, Alex was nowhere to be found. Jason was alone in the house and the bathroom door was hanging off. They'd been fighting. I reported Alex missing to the police when he failed to show up at any friends' or relatives' houses. The following day he finally appeared at a relative's house around 10 o'clock at night. I was asked to collect him, and did, and gave him what I believed was a thoroughly deserved hiding. He told me he'd spent the night with a friend on a notorious estate several miles away, even though I'd forbidden him ever to go there again. Apparently the previous weekend he'd absconded from a visit to Sharon after boasting to his brother: 'I can do anything I want and get away with it.' That comment had upset me, and his return to that estate was a direct act of disobedience. It also revealed how unrealistically Alex still saw himself in relation to the rest of the world.

On the way home, I stopped to let Sharon know what I had done. She had been beside herself with worry and had, along with her family, spent much of that day searching the streets. I then went to the police and showed them that I had found Alex and had hit him, slapping hard on his arms, legs and bottom. They told him off for wasting police time. I had been filled with anxiety for Alex's safety and future, and was disgusted that he was putting us through all this pain yet again. My only motive was to try, for his own benefit, to bring my son back under some control. The next morning I took him to social services so that they too would know he'd been found, and I reported that I had hit him. I demanded more support and respite care from them and the education department, and later complained in writing to both departments' directors.

Some people criticise the law for its inconsistencies, calling it an ass; sometimes one hardly has to wonder why. Because I'd physically chastised Alex, a child-protection conference was convened with a representative from the police present. I had to give an undertaking, under the threat of criminal prosecution, never physically to discipline Alex again. I gave the undertaking, but felt very hurt that no one seemed to appreciate what I was trying to do. I felt like giving up. Now Alex had in effect been told not to listen to me, his mother, Vivienne or anyone else who was firm with him. He got the point and exploited it to the full. Part of me did give up at that stage – in much the same way as the time Alex ran from me to his mother – and from then on things started to go rapidly downhill for Alex.

I was still getting very little help in real terms. Social services did eventually provide an agency worker, Brad Samuels, who was supposed to take Alex out for a few hours a couple of times a week to give me a break. After four such outings he apologetically told me he could not cope and withdrew from the arrangement. A kind and compassionate man, Brad felt profoundly sorry for Alex and me because he understood our plight. Temporary respite was arranged at another children's home, but that was abruptly terminated after only two visits – they could not cope either.

Then Alex brought a knife into the maths teacher's lesson. He did not threaten her with it in any way, but claimed to be acting out a scene from the horror film trilogy, *Child's Play*, which he'd seen repeatedly in Grange Court Manor. He had memorised his favourite parts, frame by frame. This trilogy would later become infamous in connection with a widely publicised child-murder case. It is about a boy doll that comes to life, possessed by the spirit of an evil killer, and proceeds to murder a number of people with a long-bladed knife. Alex had been complaining to Vivienne that the maths teacher was horrible, that she didn't like him and the feeling was mutual and that he would get rid of her – but he didn't say how. He'd meant her no physical harm but sought to frighten her. He succeeded. She left. Now we were down to two tutors.

Vivienne had kick-started Alex's thinking all right. Insofar as I could deduce, this may have been the first time Alex had ever *consciously* planned an action, if indeed he did. However, I'm far from convinced. He later said he thought it would be funny – an impulsive act, similar to how he used to annoy Grandad. Apparently, like his teasing of his grandfather, he had no insight into how serious, and stupid, his actions were, or the repercussions they would have. It proved to be the undoing of his then relatively easy life, compared with Grange Court, and triggered an unfortunate sequence of events that were to have sad and far-reaching consequences.

The dyslexia tutor's attempts to educate Alex deteriorated into farce. When he finally seemed determined to leave, I shouted and slapped Alex in front of him out of frustration. He later reported me to the social and education authorities. He was as sincere in his attempts to help Alex as I was – passionately so. But Alex was too much for him and had won, yet again. Now we were down to one tutor.

Each time a science lesson was due, Alex started to abscond minutes before the teacher arrived. I made no attempt to stop him; I intended to go to prison for no one – not even Alex. Having found a formula that worked, he did the same shortly before we were due to go to Vivienne's therapy sessions. He disappeared for hours on end, mixed with bad company, fought and got into trouble. Sometimes he showed up at social services and gave them heaps of grief. 'Great,' I thought, 'they are the ones who deserve it.' Of course, Alex wasn't doing himself any favours. I couldn't let him win outright, and so set basic English and maths exercises for him. Some days he got down to it; other days he didn't. I made him understand that if he was going to live with me, school work and seeing Vivienne Gill were not up for negotiation. I would order him straight into the 'school' room to finish whatever had been set, no matter what time of the day or night he returned.

At 12½ years old, Alex was unequipped to cope with his new-found freedom. I neither disciplined nor argued with him when he absconded. When he showed up on their doorstep, social services began to tell him: 'Go back home to your father.' Talk about closing the stable doors after the horse has bolted! His mother and other relatives gave him the same message. His own friends' parents were becoming exasperated with him. It became heartbreaking for Sharon when he'd arrive at her door, dirty, smelly and hungry. She'd relent and let him in, see that he had a bath, and give him food and clean clothes. He'd sleep for the night, then promptly disappear the next day. On occasions, police plucked him off the street in the early hours of the morning and brought him back to his mother's home or mine. Whenever he ran out of alternatives he would phone me, crying and dejected, apologising profusely, and make all the promises under the sun before returning home. After bathing, eating and sleeping, the following day he'd be off as soon as the mood took him.

Both my own and Sharon's families were now well and truly fed up with the Alex saga. No one was immune. Some said the incidents in Alex's life were like a soap opera – never-ending. But this particular programme couldn't be switched off, the cast wasn't getting paid and no one looked forward to the next episode. Just about everyone had had enough of Alex's problems and was tired of being drawn into them yet again. However, there was one important person who had no means of escape from them: Jason. He held much silent resentment for his brother, whose problems had all but ruined the quality of his own life. Paradoxically, both boys dearly loved each other, though bitter enmity would often erupt between them.

Over the years, Jason had developed an almost adult restraint towards his brother, but by now he was becoming increasingly intolerant of him. If adults couldn't cope with Alex, what chance did he have? Although he was the elder brother, Jason lived in Alex's shadow. People mostly referred to 'Alex and Jason' in that order. This Jason could not stand. He took it personally when Alex's behaviour affected him. He couldn't understand why promised family trips and treats would have to be abandoned. Nor could he accept the fact that his playtime with his own friends often ended in arguments and fights when his brother pushed himself to centre stage. Jason's drawings and other possessions were frequently deliberately damaged or destroyed when the mood took Alex. Even at school, he couldn't find peace. When Alex ran away, he would often turn up at Jason's school, embarrass his brother and cause problems. Many of Jason's friends became wary of him, and some 'hard' kids at the school heard that he was tough and wanted to fight him. All this affected Jason's concentration and he fell behind with his studies.

I tried my best to explain to Jason that Alex couldn't always help his actions and that he should try to ignore them, but that was easier said than done, even for me, let alone Jason. In their sometimes bloodstained fights and wrangles, Jason usually held back and never used his full force. However, the Grange Court pattern of frequent unbridled tension, conflict and violence remained with Alex, and these were barely contained. He'd be perfectly calm for a time, then, without provocation, would spoil for a fight with whoever was available. This destructive sequence had been significantly modified after we moved into Stockport House, but without me there to defuse situations as they arose, they would easily escalate into violence. As they did on Wednesday 20 January 1993.

Following his disastrous weeks of 'freedom', it appeared that the penny might have dropped with Alex, for he decided to return to live with me and co-operate with his now defunct tutorial and therapy sessions. On 19 January he asked Wendy to take him to his mum so that he could spend a few days with her before coming back to me. She agreed. That evening went well.

The next day, Wednesday, Jason was harassed by a group of boys spoiling for a fight because, as I was later given to understand, they thought he was Alex. Apparently Alex had defeated a boy days before, and his friends were looking for revenge. Jason went to his mother's home considerably upset and he and Alex argued. It turned into a fight. On this occasion, Jason showed no restraint. When Sharon didn't intervene in Alex's favour, he got upset. When she reprimanded him and sided with Jason, he became distraught.

Sharon and Jason left the room, leaving Alex alone – another of his typical tantrums, they thought. Unfortunately it wasn't. It was then alleged that Alex tried to kill himself, in another impulsive act, by tying his brother's karate belt around his neck and dangling himself from it through a bedroom window. In reality he was supporting his feet on a ledge. Police and medics were called by onlookers. When Alex didn't get the desired attention from his mother and brother, it was alleged he let go. Somehow Sharon and Jason managed to pull him back through the window. Then he became wildly out of control and, in a frenzied state, started smashing up the room. Six police and ambulance men eventually subdued him. Thereafter he was taken to hospital, where he was sedated and spent the next three days. He never did come home to me. Instead he was returned to Grange Court Manor.

Twelve

I BLAMED MYSELF, the education department and social services for this tragic state of affairs. My patience wore out, and the authorities seemed uninterested in supporting me. My failure to handle difficult situations was interpreted by them as proof that Alex needed to be in a boarding school, but the arrangement had been designed to calm and prepare him for a school of some kind. This fact seemed, conveniently, to have escaped their notice. Of course, the alleged attempted suicide caused concern. It gave Alex the attention he craved but had been denied during his recent 'freedom'. In fact, it earned him far more attention than he could ever have imagined. By endangering his life he once again met the legal criteria for a secure unit, and unwittingly walked straight into social services' hands. A fresh psychiatric assessment was sought.

The first day at the local hospital, the furthest thing from my mind was the idea of Alex's returning to Grange Court Manor. The next day, when the sedatives began to wear off, he started to cause pandemonium on the ward. Staff were concerned – and rightly so – for the safety of the other children, some of whom were very sick.

While we were there, Sharon and I talked to Timothy Booth, Judith's boss, and a number of other people connected to the hospital and social services. The hospital wanted Alex removed from the ward; I wanted to take him home, but was not permitted to do so. Since being there, Alex had told everyone he wanted to go home with his dad. The hospital had no objection to this, but Mr Booth did. In view of the seriousness of Alex's alleged suicide attempt, social services believed that Alex should remain in hospital until the assessment had been carried out. I disagreed. The only reason the arrangement at home had broken down was because of his learning disability combined with a lack of support. I wanted them to understand that it was the process of education that Alex was running from, of which I'd become a symbol, and not me personally; that even at this late stage the arrangement was still salvageable, provided everyone acted appropriately and quickly. I was willing to continue to help, and so was Vivienne.

'Let him come home with me – even if it means putting bars on the doors and windows,' I pleaded. 'Let someone stay with me at the house; let them live there if necessary, but don't put my boy back in that prison.' I was referring to Grange Court, since it had become obvious that that's where they would send him if it were not possible to transfer him directly to another hospital for the psychiatric assessment. My suggestion was ridiculed by Judith as unreasonable, and she suggested even I was admitting that Alex needed to be in a secure unit. My words were not meant to advocate the use of bars in themselves, but were a desperate plea for help, as I'm sure she knew.

Sharon felt that Alex needed specialist help, but supported his return to me provided I was given home support. Deep down I couldn't see why they were insisting he remain in hospital, or why he needed another assessment when he'd been seen by at least four separate psychiatrists in less than 12 months. Nevertheless, neither Sharon nor I objected to their wanting another. When I'd suggested someone stay with me to help with Alex's care as a measure against future breakdown, Judith had laughed scornfully. Social services were adamant that Alex remain, and eventually the hospital relented on condition that someone else had responsibility for his round-the-clock supervision. No one laughed this time. On the contrary, an agency care worker was promptly provided later that day.

I was getting nowhere and I felt furious. If Alex were certified as suffering from a mental illness he would cease to be the responsibility of social services and would then come under the direct control of the Department of Health. As far as we understood the situation,

Alex could then be detained indefinitely under the Mental Health Act – admittedly a worst-case scenario. Mr Booth said that he'd spent hours talking to the Department of Health. They, in turn, approached the Fulchester Centre, a combined mental hospital and secure unit, with a view to accepting Alex.

'It's the best in the country!' Booth assured me when the Fulchester Centre eventually agreed to assess him. No mention was made of what certification by the Fulchester Centre might mean for Alex's future. Nor had we been informed that this unit accommodated only criminally insane youngsters, most of whom had committed very serious crimes. Yet none of the previous psychiatrists had diagnosed Alex as mentally ill.

Sharon and I spent most of that day, 22 January, with Alex. After we left he caused mayhem on the ward. He wanted to go home, and it became intolerable for the hospital. As I understand it, they insisted Alex be moved immediately even though it was very late. To secure his compliance, social workers told him he was being taken home to me; this was about 2 o'clock in the morning. On the journey, when Alex realised he was in fact being taken to Grange Court, he escaped from the car and tried to head for home. A search ensued. Finding him in the darkness was not easy. The police were called and eventually he was caught. At 5 o'clock on Saturday morning he was delivered, struggling and screaming, back to the secure unit at Grange Court. I was at home, fast asleep in bed, oblivious to what was going on. I visited him later that day.

That weekend at Grange Court Manor, Alex was still on a high from the hospital. In no time at all he had the secure unit in a spin. How little insight he had into the seriousness of his new situation was evident when, on Sunday, he wrapped a duvet cover around his neck, in front of the staff, to suggest that he was going to kill himself. I was led to believe by certain staff that this was never thought to be genuine, merely a prank, but nevertheless it was duly recorded as a second suicide attempt. The problem the unit had, however, was not a fear that Alex would kill himself, but a personality collision that exploded into a clash of the Titans between Alex and another inmate, Gary. They took an instant dislike to each other.

Becoming acquainted with Gary was a revelation. In all the years I'd known Alex, I'd never met anyone truly like him. Now here – as large as life – was another, bigger, version. I'd seen children who were considered bad or dangerous, but they were never like my son so far as I could detect. Gary, however, seemed to be a carbon copy, but much worse. There was no build-up period: he would flip his lid without warning. He was about three years older than Alex, and wild – really wild. The most vile, unprintable language spewed out of his mouth. On catching sight of me for the first time, as I passed quietly by the lounge window on my way to the visitors' room, he lunged at the glass and cursed me bitterly. Alex sprang to my defence and the staff grappled to separate the two. Throughout my visit, Gary rained down verbal abuse on Alex, Sharon, Jason and me from the other end of the unit. There would be no peace as long as those two remained together.

Gary's impact on me cannot be overstated; he filled me with trepidation for Alex's future. I wondered, 'Is this what Alex is going to be like when he is 15?' That thought scared the life out of me. From that moment on, I saw it as my absolute duty to do all I could to prevent my son turning out the same.

I couldn't get angry with the lad, however, even though what I saw of his character was pretty vile. On the contrary, I felt pity for him. I had no knowledge of his background, but thought that he must have been through the mill. He seemed to hate everyone, but at least Alex had us fighting on his side. I imagined Gary to be the product of the same sort of misunderstandings but without any form of support and so felt deeply sorry for him, though he never knew. I took some comfort from the fact that, despite my and Sharon's many failings, Alex always knew that we loved him.

Tensions mounted very quickly. The staff wanted one of the two boys to be moved from the unit, but the powers above them would not – or could not – agree to it, reducing staff to the role of bystanders and referees. Gary and Alex teased and cursed each other at the slightest opportunity. It acted as a precursor to fighting. Whoever had started a disturbance would be restrained and 'timed out'. Then, from the other side of the cell, the frenzied occupant could be heard kicking and thumping until he calmed himself down or wore himself out, while the 'free' boy enjoyed the other's solitary confinement, and laughed and mocked with relish. After a suitable period of time, which varied from incident to incident, the offending boy would be allowed to leave his cell. Later, the whole process might be repeated; neither seemed to learn anything from the experience. Their bitter animosity continued for the duration of Alex's second stint in Grange Court's secure unit.

On one occasion I arrived to visit Alex when the visitors' room was unavailable, so I was let through the unit's main entrance and offices. On catching sight of me Gary prepared to attack. Suddenly, at least half a dozen staff sprang on him from every direction. Judging by the sounds he made, it may have been beyond what was necessary to control him. This was Grange Court in action. They then virtually threw him into his cell and slammed it shut while he struggled and screamed abuse, loudly and in vain. It was all over in a couple of minutes. The staff then returned to their routine as if nothing had happened. All in a day's work.

I knew they had acted in my interest, which prevented me from getting into trouble for I would have had to defend myself. But they went way over the top: not even Gary should be treated that way. After what I had witnessed I saw no reason to doubt Alex's previous claims that they had treated him the same.

Once again, Alex's daily life revolved around close-quarter, high-tension verbal and physical violence. He played pool, table tennis and computer games, took part in degrading sexual talk, and watched highly suspect videos – anything except therapy or study. He received no education. It was in these surroundings that a quick report was made by consultant psychiatrist Dr Sonia Patel, as the Fulchester Centre requested a fresh local assessment before dispatching anyone to interview Alex. He treated this lady with his usual disdain and suspicion. She stated that Alex was unstable enough to harm himself, but she did not describe him as suffering from any form of mental illness.

A concerned Vivienne Gill had visited Alex the previous day. She submitted a report to Judith and Wendy in which she emphasised the need for him to revert to a restricted diet, and for our family's problems in parenting him to be addressed. Alex needed to be in a calm state or no useful work could take place: he was being stimulated by recent events (suicide attempt, hospital, police, return to Grange, Gary, etc.) and these were being exacerbated by the effects of chemical additives in his now unregulated eating habits. She panned the home-tutors arrangement as inadequate, criticised his environment for failing to meet his needs and acknowledged Alex's skill of pitting one parent against the other. She also drew attention to the intense stress both Alex and I were under (a precursor to the breakdown between Alex, the tutors and me), and thought I had been tested beyond my limits. Stressing the importance of regulating his biochemistry, she was willing to continue work with Alex in the hope that his environment would be more supportive.

The Fulchester Centre agreed to see Alex to determine whether he met their criteria for a full assessment. On 1 February, psychiatrist Dr Dennis Thomas and his social worker colleague Beverley Smith came down from the North. At Grange Court they interviewed Alex (to the extent he permitted), some of the staff and me. During the course of the day they spoke to Sharon by phone. They seemed sincere and this made it easier for me to speak to them. They had ample opportunity to observe Alex in action and, as usual, he rose to the occasion.

It was I who capitalised most on their time, not Alex, however. Recognising the seriousness of Alex's situation, that his entire future and liberty hung in the balance, I wanted to enlist their help, rather than provoke the kind of intransigent opposition that had hitherto so badly damaged my son. So for some two hours in the visitors' room I poured my heart out, detailing as much as I could of Alex's tragic history. I tried to describe his bizarre behaviour and personality. I admitted that Sharon's and my different approaches to parenting, and our numerous arguments, had made a bad situation worse, a plight compounded by the actions of social services and the education department. I told them of the dyslexia report, of the psychiatric input thus far, and of the enlightening work of Vivienne Gill and how it had begun to bear fruit, until the arrangement had failed through lack of support for me and my own lack of patience, leading finally to Alex's alleged suicide attempt.

I asked Dr Thomas and Ms Smith to learn from what had gone before, and, for Alex's sake, ensure similar mistakes weren't repeated. I urged them to formulate a rock-solid plan that addressed all the issues I'd raised, so that my son would not be failed again. If the Fulchester Centre, no matter how exclusive, had weaknesses, then Alex would very likely find and instinctively exploit them. I suggested that it was crucial that everyone work in unison to prevent this. Their colleagues needed to be fully briefed on how they should respond to Alex, especially those who would be involved at the sharp end of his day-to-day care.

They were grateful for my input and commented that they thought my understanding of the situation had been good. Given the information they now had, did they think that the Fulchester Centre could help Alex in the long term? They indicated yes, but said a formal 28-day assessment had to take place first and they could not predict how that might turn out. They agreed Grange Court was definitely not right for him and promised to do all they could to expedite a prompt transfer to their unit for an assessment. They also reassured me that Alex wouldn't be pumped full of drugs. At the time our family was most concerned about this. We'd often read or heard in the media of difficult-to-control schizophrenics in mental hospitals being turned into zombies, even accidentally dying on occasion. My fear might have seemed to them like paranoia, but on no account was I going to risk my son becoming one of those awful statistics. Dr Thomas and Ms Smith smiled and gave assurances. I extended my unreserved support, and offered to visit the centre and meet with staff before Alex went there if the proposal to assess him was successful. It was, and the date set for this transfer was 24 February.

In the meantime, Alex's daily battles continued with Gary, other boys and some staff, and during this period he was set upon by an agency social worker. Ever since the emergency meeting at the hospital, the arrangement to provide an agency care worker to supervise Alex had continued with shifts in the secure unit. One might reasonably ask: if he was in a secure unit, why go to this extra expense? It was one of these workers, a big man of about 16 stone, who assaulted Alex. Richard Evans, a staff member attached to Grange Court, formally complained on Alex's behalf, but with no effect. Then, recognising their error, the authorities promptly whisked the individual responsible away from the unit within the hour. I didn't find out about this assault till much later.

I never stopped trying to make sense of everything that happened with Alex. Even with Bill's and Vivienne's explanations, I still searched for answers. Vivienne had shown me how Alex saw life, and offered reasons for some of his behaviour. I was eternally grateful but longed to understand what was going on inside his head. Maybe it was the mechanic in me.

At that time the entire country was trying to come to terms with the tragic James Bulger case in which a toddler was horrifically killed by two 10-year-old boys. I was deeply distressed by it, especially when debates raged about possible explanations for the boys' abnormal behaviour. Several centred on the effects the horror movie *Child's Play* might have had on the impressionable youngsters who committed the crime – the film Alex had learned by heart. On 19 February, the day of my first visit to the Fulchester Centre, I was on a train speeding towards Manchester.

Maybe I was too absorbed in Alex's life, perhaps it was vice versa, but Alex was with me everywhere I went – day and night. When he wasn't there physically he was still a presence, even in my dreams. Then, somewhere in the Midlands, I started to find answers to what I did not yet understand. As I sat silently in the privacy of my own thoughts in the partly filled second-class compartment, from out of nowhere, it was as if layer after layer of fine gauze began to lift from my mind. Don't ask me to explain it – I can't! I found myself thinking about Bill, Vivienne, the social workers, the teachers, the psychiatrists, myself and Sharon – just about everyone who had contributed positively or negatively to Alex's eccentric life. As the train sped, so did my mind, much too fast for me to absorb everything. Pictures within pictures, flashbacks upon flashbacks, snippets from numerous events all mingled with diagrams and pictures of the brain, documentaries seen on television, news reports heard on the radio, poignant comments spoken or read somewhere, and, of course, the Bulger case. It connected with something in my here-and-now and delivered to me a weird sense of new understanding.

I was so wrapped up in these sensations that I didn't at first realise I'd reached my destination, and I got off the train more confused than ever. I couldn't articulate what seemed so clear in my head, but it was as if I had been handed a key piece of Alex's mental jigsaw and now the confusion was almost over. Over the next few months these feelings were to recur many times with decreasing clarity, mostly on long train journeys to and from visiting Alex. Finally they ceased. By the end of the period, something had undoubtedly clicked into place; I had my own vivid picture of what was going on inside Alex's head: scientifically, emotionally, educationally and parapsychologically. I could 'see' it all with my mind's eye, but could not explain it to a soul – and didn't try. Like Alex, I didn't want anyone to think that I was mad.

The Fulchester Centre formed part of a large Victorian-style hospital building. It looked like a newer and much larger version of Grange Court's secure unit, but its keys were just as big . . . It was officially a secure hospital for criminally disturbed adolescents. Alex would be receiving the best England had to offer. I was sad to learn that Dr Thomas was no longer in the centre's employ, and Beverley disappeared after a brief hello. I met a few of the staff and filled them in as well as I could about Alex. They seemed extremely confident about their ability to cope. They reassured me I had nothing to be concerned about and were very kind. I'd seen all this before. Their responses made me feel patronised – but only a little. On the positive front, they seemed seriously professional and I was cautiously optimistic. At least I'd tried. I took the train back to London.

The weekend slipped by. I spoke to Judith by phone on Monday 22 February, reported my views of the centre and discussed the matter of transport. I offered to drive Alex to minimise the risk of problems in getting him there. I was surprised and annoyed when she flatly refused. He had been responding to me well at the time and I saw myself as the best person to escort him. Apparently they'd been deliberating the same issue, but had decided that their staff would drive him. I protested, but the department was adamant. This made me feel as if Alex was not my son but their property and they could do with him as they wished. Nevertheless after much persistence from me they conceded that I could come with them *if* I wanted. The car would be leaving at 8 o'clock on Wednesday morning. Sharon and Wendy had already elected to go by train.

I arrived at Grange Court about 7.30 a.m. Alex was ready and waiting, as was the rest of the unit. He was in good spirits and noticeably pleased to be getting away from Gary, laughing and teasing that he'd be still stuck at Grange Court. Gary cursed him from his cell, but he was to enjoy himself immensely at Alex's expense much sooner than he could have imagined. We waited for the car to arrive. I found out that Gregory, the latest agency worker caring for Alex at Grange Court, had been booked to accompany him to the new unit. Then a police transit van pulled up: *this was the car that would be taking Alex up north*. It had heavy security grilles and was normally used to transport criminals. Nearly everyone present, including the Grange Court staff, stood open-mouthed in disbelief. No one had warned us about this decision. There was no time to react.

Two uniformed police officers stepped out. They looked as if they expected their cargo to be adult-sized. When they saw how small he was, they looked at me as if to say: 'Sorry, mate, we're just following orders.' On entering the unit, one handcuffed the 12-year-old's wrist to his and escorted him the few steps to the rear compartment of the van without a struggle, to the sound of a delighted Gary, who mocked his now caged opponent exuberantly from the safety of the lounge. The officers released the cuffs, even though Alex's hands were small enough to slip through them. The whole scene was absurd. Gregory and I climbed in, and the van departed.

This was the single time in my life when I felt most humiliated publicly. For the next five hours, through the outskirts of London and then along the motorway, people gawped at us. Each time we pulled up at traffic lights or slowed down, it seemed as if pedestrians and motorists alike became contortionists, determined to register our faces. We felt like criminals. For the first time colour became an issue. Gregory, like Alex and me, is black, and a lengthy discussion ensued about the way young blacks are treated in care; he giving me the benefit of his insider's knowledge. Poor Alex. He was as stunned as we were. Gregory, whom he seemed to like, was grossly disappointed with social services. He knew nothing of this odious plan, and felt it was unnecessary and unfair. I could not help but wonder of Judith: 'How could you be party to this?' Gregory started to talk about his concern over the way Alex was being treated at Grange Court, and how he watched out for him when he was on duty. He said he admired me and begged me not to give up on Alex or abandon him, for he knew at first-hand how tough it could be for a black boy caught up on the bad side of the care system. He did not think Alex would survive without our support. We got to know each other a little in the back of that van, and Alex eventually fell asleep while we talked and the police burned up the motorway.

We arrived at the Fulchester Centre around lunchtime. Sharon, Wendy and other staff were waiting for us. A meeting followed. I blasted social services for their insensitivity. Sharon, who had been in a relatively good mood that morning, became very angry, and Wendy turned red with embarrassment. They'd travelled the whole morning together without Wendy giving so much as a hint about the police escorting Alex.

Then we were shown around the place and Alex caught his first glimpse of his new peers. We saw that the centre was split into two sections, and learned that one was for short-term residents on 28-day assessments like Alex and the other for long-term clients. At about 4.30 the others left for the station, and a disgusted Sharon refused to sit with Wendy on the return journey. I stayed as long as I could to help Alex settle in and left with just enough time to catch the last train back to London. He did not want me to go and became quite sullen. I'd promised I would visit him every Sunday and Wednesday. This was a new experience for me which meant very long days. Sharon and Jason visited on Saturdays. All our expenses were paid by social services.

After a couple of visits, I could see why the team seemed so self-assured. I was very, very impressed – there *was* something special about this centre. The laxity I'd become so used to observing at Grange Court was not present here. Most of those I spoke to – doctors, nurses, management staff – seemed totally committed and diligent, and the night staff even reported Alex's sleep disturbances. But what impressed me more than anything was that they seemed to be applying firm but fair consistency and carried out a number of tests. No matter what tricks Alex tried, he couldn't get his own way or run off and slip through their net. I co-operated fully with the staff, giving them any information they requested. I'd stay with Alex in the TV room on the ward, or we'd find somewhere to be by ourselves. His table-tennis playing, developed at Grange Court, was by now getting really good – he nearly beat me, to his surprise.

On my third visit, on 7 March, Alex cried and begged me: 'Please get me out of here; they will drive me mad!' My first thoughts were he was attempting to manipulate me because he'd discovered he could neither get his own way nor escape from the situation. I wasn't going to fall for it – not that I could have got him out anyway. He even confessed that he could now see how easy he'd had it at home, wished he'd co-operated with Vivienne and the tutors, and promised to do so if he was allowed back.

I explained to him that he was in here because he'd tried to commit suicide and there was very little I could do to change it. 'You need to show them you are not mad by behaving yourself; then they will let you go home.' Alex told me that he hadn't tried to commit suicide; that his feet had been on the ledge all the time. I was unsure whether he was being truthful and urged him to repeat this to the centre's staff. He said that he could not stay there because *some* kids and *some* staff were driving him mad. He named names, but I'd heard it all before and took no action. He did look depressed, though. What saddened me was the prospect of more Grange

Court-style conflicts creating a deadlock: the same game but with different players. I perked him up until it was time to catch the last train.

On the way home I reflected: 'If this place really can help Alex, any progress they make could quickly be undermined if another Alex versus Gary pattern is allowed to develop.' Time and time again I'd consistently demonstrated that I understood my son better than anyone else. Maybe the staff did listen politely when I tried to warn them, but they didn't appear to take my message on board.

On my very next visit, complaints about male nursing care staff greeted my ears. According to Alex, one nurse had told him: 'When you grow up you are going to be a pimp.' Another nurse, he said, had deliberately twisted his wrist excessively during restraints, causing him much pain. I was incensed and complained to the Registrar. He flatly refused to believe that either nurse had said or done anything wrong.

But I knew my son. I knew he told lies. I mostly tended to give the other person the benefit of the doubt when Alex complained, choosing to take his comments coolly until I could determine the facts; but I knew he didn't lie all the time. This was when my relationship with the Fulchester Centre started to sour.

On my next visit, I was greeted by a complaining Alex who told me that two other nurses had earlier assaulted him during a restraint and that he was still in pain. One of the nurses was in the next room when Alex told me this, so I dealt with the situation myself and confronted him. Angrily, but with control, I told him clearly that I was not going to tolerate him or anyone else abusing my son and that I would be complaining formally. He gave me a self-confident look that suggested, 'I don't give a damn what you say or do' – though the words never came from his lips. Two days later, I was informed by the ward manager that the nurse I confronted had made a formal complaint about my 'abusive' behaviour. Her telephone call was to inform me that my future visits would be restricted to the visitors' room, so contact with others on the ward would be impossible. After a long discussion, in which I was able to explain my point of view, she persuaded me to make a formal complaint, assuring me it would be fully investigated. I told her I could foresee the outcome of any such investigation and was proved right: Alex's accusations were not upheld.

My next visit coincided with a scheduled case conference on Alex's assessment. Wendy Chowdri and Timothy Booth represented social services. A number of key participants from the Fulchester Centre were present. The meeting was chaired by Beverley Smith, the social worker who had accompanied Dr Thomas to interview Alex at Grange Court. Dr Margaret Stuart, consultant forensic psychiatrist, whom I later realised was an extremely eminent and respected adviser to the Department of Health and boss of the Fulchester Centre, sat inconspicuously in the group. I'd never met her before and thought that she was simply another doctor involved in part of the assessment process.

Social services and I had almost taken it as a foregone conclusion that the centre would accept Alex. I was still hoping that they would because, despite my recent complaint, this was the only mainstream institution I'd come across that seemed to be going in the right direction to help him. My only concern had been that the centre's good work should not be jeopardised.

It was a big shock when it soon became evident that the Fulchester Centre was *not*, under any circumstances, going to accept Alex. The doctor, who had seen Alex and me on several occasions, concluded that he was neither physically nor mentally ill. He also ruled out Professor Richardson's diagnosis of hyperactivity. He did not believe that Alex was suffering from a depressive illness, and dismissed any so-called paranormal experiences as of no importance.

If the Fulchester Centre was the top place in the country and they had decided not to help my son, then I was perfectly within my rights to know why. It soon became apparent, however, that their irrevocable decision had *already* been taken. The conference was simply to notify interested parties. I could see there was no point in arguing, but for my own satisfaction I was determined to establish that there was something *different* about Alex by relating a recent, somewhat out-of-the-norm experience involving him, for which

Dr Stuart could offer no rational explanation. Alex was more than just an exceptionally naughty or bad boy.

Then something clicked and I realised that Dr Stuart was in fact the nice lady I'd had a long telephone chat with several weeks before, and who had been very sympathetic and helpful – prior to Alex's arrival. I thought to myself, 'Now you've gone and done it, Chester. She's definitely not going to accept him now.' She was still polite, but insisted that the Fulchester Centre did not think Alex was suffering from a formal mental illness and therefore it was not the right place for him. He had problems with his behaviour, not his brain. She thought that I might not appreciate what a positive diagnosis that was for Alex, and what dividends it yielded in terms of his future care. I understood perfectly what she meant: Alex could not now be sent to a mental institution – theirs or anyone else's. I was delighted that it was now official and beyond doubt that Alex was *not* clinically mad, but I was disappointed because I felt that the centre could have helped him if they had really wanted to. Maybe I was wrong. Maybe Alex's stressful behaviour, his outspoken desire to leave the centre and my recent complaints influenced the decision-making process significantly.

I now wanted Alex returned to me, which had always been my objective. The centre advised against this in the short term, but agreed he could come home after his behaviour had been modified sufficiently in a residential environment. Timothy Booth sprang to life and was rather keen to ascertain what sort of unit they thought would be suitable. I think that's when I first heard the word Moorcroft, but it meant nothing to me. I saw disappointment in his face. This didn't seem to be the decision he'd hoped for or expected. Dr Stuart must have delivered a fatal body-blow to what I believe was social services' game plan. The ball – Alex – was firmly back in *their* court. Yet I feared that the centre's assessment would provide them with a different tactic. It recommended a residential unit with both secure and open units which permitted gradual progression from one to the other, and detailed various resources and treatments that such a place should offer. To me, it was simply a glorified way of recommending another version of Grange Court Manor. If

Timothy and I both left the Fulchester Centre bitterly disappointed that day, it was for very different reasons.

Three days later, on 20 March, Sharon filed a report on her visit. She claimed she saw Alex assaulted by two male staff as he excitedly rushed to embrace her. In the struggle one hit him then the other joined in. Both threw him to the floor, twisted his arm up his back and knelt on him. She was shocked and disgusted.

Alex was to leave the unit no later than 24 March, the formal end of the assessment period. Social services were in a spin as they'd found no alternative placement. According to them, all attempts to find a vacancy, anywhere in the country, in an institution with both open and secure units, had failed. I offered to have Alex back home with me.

On 22 March, following a lengthy telephone conversation with Judith, I thought they'd agreed to this but I must have misunderstood. She'd meant I could have Alex *until* a secure unit became available. Later that afternoon when I spoke on the phone to Timothy, he expressed pleasure at my co-operation with this arrangement. I was shocked. I'd agreed with Judith that Alex would come to me, with new tutorial support and renewed sessions with Vivienne Gill, who was still very willing to help, pending his being able to go to a school and come home in the evenings – nothing else.

Judith and I must have been speaking at cross purposes. My discussion with Timothy turned to argument. They wanted me to look after Alex for about six weeks, until a place in another secure unit became available. I refused and told him point-blank that it was cruel and I would not be a party to it. Then came the bombshell: 'Since that is your decision, Alex will be returned to Grange Court secure unit until another one becomes available', or words to that effect. Timothy expected me to go up to Manchester to fetch Alex by train, as had been previously agreed with Judith. I told him that if he wanted Alex to go to Grange Court he'd better take him there himself. I certainly wasn't going to.

With Timothy's decision to return my son to Grange Court, war was declared. Alex needed someone to fight for his rights so I sought legal advice. With the furore we'd caused over the police-van incident fresh in their minds, the department faced a new dilemma: how to get Alex back from the North to Grange Court. They knew there was no way he would walk willingly into Grange Court Manor and be reunited with Gary. And if Alex was not in a mood to co-operate, travelling by car could be very dangerous. The trick they'd previously used came to their rescue. Alex was told he was being returned to his dad, with escorts, by train. It worked.

Thirteen

So they managed to get Alex back to Grange Court under cover of darkness on the night of 23 March, but not before he'd absconded from his escorts' care when he realised he was not being brought home to me. This time he ended up in the police station near my home.

The secure unit was not overjoyed to be faced with Alex for round three of their mutually unwanted relationship, but once again neither had a choice in the matter. I visited him the following day.

After my conversation with Timothy Booth, I found this new situation intolerable. He had not been able to provide me with a coherent answer to the question: 'How is it that when Alex no longer met the criteria for secure accommodation at the Fulchester Centre, it had been conceded that he was "free" to come home to me; but then, in mid-conversation, after I'd made it clear that I would not be a party to his going back into a secure unit later, he suddenly no longer fitted the criteria for coming home?' He started to fumble his words and I could imagine his cheeks becoming flushed. I slammed down the phone. I felt I was being punished for refusing to toe the line, and Alex would be the one to suffer.

There was now, it seemed, only one way I could get my son back and that was via the High Court. My solicitors had advised me that I would have to broach this legal stronghold, which meant convincing a judge to rescind the care order in social services' favour and replace it with a residence order in mine. If my application was successful I would partly regain some of the rights most parents take for granted – as indeed Sharon and I had once done. The Fulchester Centre's report made it clear that in the long term Alex should be returned to me, and social services claimed that this was their objective too. However, when Sharon and I challenged them in the courts, their legal department went into overdrive.

In my ignorance, I wanted my solicitors to get this residence order immediately but procedures had to be followed. Before Alex had left the Fulchester Centre, social services had already obtained a fresh secure order to keep him for a further month in secure accommodation. They had in fact wanted a three-month order but my lawyers objected and made known my intentions to file for a residence order. In any event, they could legally keep Alex at Grange Court until 20 April. Sharon and I had no alternative but to accept this. We used the time between regular visits to Alex to prepare our case and did whatever our lawyers advised. But I couldn't keep still; I'd been distressed one time too many.

Fired up, I spent the next few days drafting an eight-page letter to the then Secretary of State for Health, Virginia Bottomley. When I thought I'd got it right I posted it to her. It was an impassioned plea for help, in which I strongly protested against the handling of my son's case. Desperate that it should reach her without delay, I did not get it typed as this meant imposing on friends and wasting valuable time. So it went off handwritten, grammatical errors included.

I knew it would probably take some time to get a reply, and I wasn't even sure if Mrs Bottomley would personally see the letter. In the interim I decided to make enquiries about what *I* could do to remedy the situation. Someone suggested that I should see my local MP. Then a female member of Grange Court's staff, appalled at Alex's treatment, took me aside privately. 'Complain in writing to the Ombudsman,' she advised.

I wrote to the Local Government Ombudsman, and also complained in person, in writing, or both, to my local MP; to the Chair of Social Services; to the Leader of the Council; to a Liberal Democrat councillor who, I was told, was deeply distressed by the mounting complaints against social services; to the Director of

Education; to the Principal of Grange Court Manor; and to everyone at social services involved in my son's case. I also requested from the education department, social services and Grange Court Manor copies of all paperwork they had on file relating to Alex. I updated my solicitors every step of the way, and they, in turn, kept the council's legal department on their toes. Above all I wanted Alex's sufferings to end and for him to get the help he needed.

As April and May unfolded, I believe that the true extent of my offensive must have surprised officialdom. Everyone connected with Alex's case became extremely defensive. It had become obvious that Sharon and I were now united as parents, which meant that no one could exploit our differences. Yet none of this stopped the local decision-makers from pursuing their fruitless aim to put Alex back in another secure unit. On the contrary, it seemed to have stubbornly consolidated and hardened their resolve; a determination that seemed to be coming from the highest level.

Social services now learned that the Moorcroft Centre for Children in the north of England could offer Alex a bed, possibly within a few weeks. They were absolutely delighted. Moorcroft would require him for a minimum of three months to carry out – wait for it – yet another assessment. A very concerned Vivienne Gill contacted Judith and bluntly set out the problems as she saw them, giving her recommendations as to how best they be tackled. In her view, social services was spending vast sums of money on institutions without any clear understanding of Alex and the outcome of such treatment. Alex's problems were multiple and *all* had to be addressed simultaneously if he was to be helped. She bemoaned that continued incarceration (or the threat of it) was the technique used to control Alex. This was pointless unless Alex associated earned rewards with positive behaviour. She saw me as pivotal to Alex's recovery and suggested that by far the cheapest way for them was to work with me. Her advice was ignored.

Back at Grange Court, Alex and Gary renewed their hostilities, and Alex got hurt; one of the managers beat him up – according to Alex – and a female teacher assaulted him in front of Gregory, the agency worker who rode with us in the police van to Fulchester.

The teacher expected Gregory to support her and was shocked when he spoke out in Alex's defence, rebuked her, and complained to the unit's management. I salute the Gregorys and Richard Evanses of this world. They have the guts, conviction and decency to speak up on behalf of children and to try to protect them. Without their added encouragement I might possibly have given up fighting for a better outcome for Alex; my efforts were all so very much up-hill.

During this period, Sharon, Jason and I, and other family members and friends, regularly visited Alex to support him. All he wanted was to come home, to get away from Gary and Grange Court. We told him that we would soon be going back to court to try to get the secure order lifted. Then in August there would be a big trial in front of an important judge. But Alex was an extremely unhappy 12-year-old boy. Our words of encouragement must have seemed empty and useless. Who could blame him for being despondent: he'd heard it all before.

The next court hearing was due on 19 April, one day before the existing secure order was due to expire. Social services needed to convince the judge not only to renew the order but to extend it to three months, since this was the minimum period Moorcroft had stipulated they would require to assess Alex. When Richard Evans heard that plans were afoot to send Alex to Moorcroft he was extremely concerned, since it had a reputation for being very violent. He thought it an inappropriate place for Alex, and encouraged me to do all I could to prevent him going. Even David Brookes, the secure unit's team leader and former advocate for sending Alex to Moorcroft, told me he should be returned home to my care.

Sharon and I sat in the High Court like muzzled pit bulls, angry but unable to say a word in our son's defence. Talking was strictly reserved for the barristers – all four, including the Official Solicitor's. Now this Official Solicitor was that mysterious chap who seemed only ever to pop up five minutes, metaphorically, before an important report was due to be written, or when some crisis had brought Alex's case back before a court, and who was supposed to be Alex's guardian *ad litem*. When Alex became a ward of court, he was the person appointed by the court to represent, and serve, Alex's best interests. I must ask: where was he when Alex needed him over the years? Now here he was, represented by his barrister, siding with social services to condemn Alex to Moorcroft, a place that seemed highly likely to do him harm.

The judge seemed absorbed by the case. The hearing, which should have lasted no more than an hour, took up the whole day. We watched helplessly as my barrister argued eloquently, but in vain, that Alex should not be sent to Moorcroft. He told the court about the negative media attention the place had attracted and highlighted the fact that it was under investigation by the Department of Health. All this made no difference. Then, during the lunchtime recess, we learned that, following yet another restraint and confinement at Grange Court, Alex had set fire to his bedroom after he himself had been locked inside it – such was his frustration. Both sides subsequently cited this latest incident as evidence to the judge: our opposers as proof that Alex needed to be locked up in Moorcroft, and our barrister to show the futility of it. I didn't understand all the legal jargon he used, but at some point towards the end of the proceedings the social services' barrister stood up and more or less told the judge that he had no option but to grant the secure order. The judged complied. Our solicitor, Cassandra, was disappointed and saddened by the order. Sharon and I were furious but took solace in the fact that in three months' time there would be a proper trial: a five-day hearing, at which we would finally get an opportunity to speak up on Alex's behalf.

Two days later, on 21 April, Alex was moved to Moorcroft. In desperation I phoned the National Children's Bureau, the Children's Legal Centre, and various other children's rights organisations, searching for help or advice. Eventually, someone asked whether I'd tried the National Association of Young People in Care (NAYPIC).

NAYPIC is a pressure group staffed by young people, all of whom have themselves been children in care. Some of them, like Alex, have been made to run the gauntlet of the care system, and have experienced at first-hand the same bureaucratic failings. I described

Alex's predicament on the phone to a young woman called Rosa. She listened attentively but when I mentioned Moorcroft she started to cough. Once she'd regained her breath, she told me she'd choked on the cigarette she was smoking in a mixture of shock and horror: 'Whatever you do, don't let them send him to Moorcroft.' She insisted I come and see her immediately.

'It's too late, they've moved him up there this morning.'

She asked which part of Moorcroft they were sending him to. I told her 'Huxley'.

'Oh my God, that's the worst one,' she exclaimed in horror. 'They've put him in with the murderers and the rapists. We've got to get him out.'

I was devastated.

Rosa was aged about 21, intelligent, articulate, spirited, and overflowing with enthusiasm. Because of her youth, I wondered if she could be of any real help; she assured me she could. Depressed as I was, her confidence gave me immense strength and encouragement.

She rang Moorcroft and made preliminary enquiries about Alex to try to head off any potential abuse. 'They might take it easy on him', she reasoned, 'if Moorcroft know NAYPIC's been approached.' She was quite determined to go to Moorcroft to see him for herself, to give him hope and encouragement. This impressed me, and I thought how different it is when someone genuinely cares; the contrast was obvious. All the judges, bar one, and most of the senior people who made decisions influencing Alex's life had made no effort to meet him. Rosa and I had several subsequent discussions about Alex's care and treatment at Moorcroft, and we planned strategies as to how best NAYPIC could support him.

Sharon got to Moorcroft the day before me. I first went there on Friday 23 April, two days after Alex's arrival. It was a long way up north, about 300 miles from my home in London, the entire round trip lasting eight or nine hours. I made this journey two or three times a week, and Sharon and Jason went once a week. If anyone thought we were going to leave Alex entirely to Moorcroft's mercy they were sorely mistaken.

The Moorcroft Centre for Children was one of the biggest children's homes of its sort in England, with boys and girls in residence at any one time from local authorities all over the country. It had both open and secure units. Some clients had committed no crime but were simply runaways or victims of sexual abuse. There was also a far more disturbing category which included some of England's most persistent and violent teenage criminals. This troubled me deeply.

The centre wasn't how I had imagined it. Grange Court could have been tucked away in one corner of the complex – Moorcroft was big. It was set in open land and abutted a main country road. Attractive to look at from the outside, it had plenty of pleasant staff houses and extensive 'open' residential facilities for clients. Moorcroft boasted schools and was very proud of its variety of sports facilities, including an indoor swimming pool, all set in lush green countryside. But Moorcroft's jewel in the crown was its spacious secure units, each with a maximum capacity of 14 clients. The taxi driver knew exactly where to go, and set me down at the relevant reception building. I signed in and was directed to the appropriate entrance.

Eventually they let me in and I entered a roundish foyer area with various doors leading from it. One led to the visitors' room, another to the toilets, and I could see that the one in the distance led to the locked clients' area. I had to wait in the visitors' room. I knew the routine.

When Alex saw me he ran to me shouting 'Daddy!' and hugged and squeezed me ever so tightly. I asked him how he'd been, and was taken aback when he started going on excitedly about how much better this place was than Grange Court. Apparently he'd been introduced to some of the centre's sports activities and liked them, but he also said there were some boys with whom he had problems. He'd already had a confrontation with two of them in which staff had had to intervene. Alex was, I believe, the youngest on the unit, which consisted of about eleven boys and two girls; his arrival brought the unit up to, or near, full capacity. He began to tell me more about his new peers. According to him, several of them were there for murder, rape and other serious crimes. One had boasted to him that he'd tried to kill his mother by setting fire to her. Apart from these revelations it was an uneventful first visit.

Participation in sports, competitive sports in particular, was an important feature of the Moorcroft curriculum: it was thought to be a safe way for youngsters to burn off excess energy or aggression. Alex loved sports.

During one of my early visits I made what for me was a remarkable discovery, which in many ways sheds light on Alex's story. Alex was torn between wanting to take part in a swimming session and to see me. I had just travelled a long way and he did not want to disappoint me, so he asked care staff whether I could accompany him as a spectator. They seemed quite amenable to this and I was allowed to enter the lounge area. This gave the clients their first close-up look at me, and I at them. They seemed like ordinary kids, yet it was an eerie feeling to know that I was standing in the midst of what was probably one of the most dangerous groups of teenagers in the country. They had to line up and be counted by the two female staff on duty. If any one of them behaved badly, swimming would be abandoned for the day.

The group looked eager, jittery with excitement, except for one very quiet young man of about 17. It reminded me of infant school, when 'Miss' lines up the high-spirited children before taking them on an outing – but these were going only a few steps into the courtyard outside. When the exit door from the residential building was unlocked, their excitement reached fever pitch, like young children on a coach trip. There was no turning back: they were going swimming. We walked across to the pool building. Again, a door had to be unlocked and we filed in. About ten boys rushed to change and then charged into the water, while the quiet boy, a girl, the two care workers and I looked on.

I was mesmerised. *'I've never seen so many Alexes under one roof before,'* I remember thinking.

How can I convey what I saw? These boys were extremely physical. Bodies were hauled and pushed and pulled about; for about an hour these lads turbulently wrestled and challenged one another in the water. They rushed in and out of the pool, pushed each other in, dive-bombed down dangerously close to boys in the water. They took turns in ganging-up to duck one another for a few seconds. I detected no sense of fear or danger. This was fun at Moorcroft, and Alex was right in the thick of it. Nobody swam, or seemed the least bit interested in doing so. It was as if these kids were on another planet, suspended in their own time warp. They hadn't grown up.

What I saw that day made a tremendous impact on me. These appeared to be heedless children with the mentality of 5- or 6-year-olds, but with the strength and bodies of teenagers. Now I could understand why some of them ended up as murderers – they simply acted without thinking, impulsively responding to the stimulus of the moment, as Alex had done all his life. And, like Alex, they were capable of thought when they were calm, but were usually so highly emotionally charged and easily overexcited that any little thing was able to trigger a disproportionate response.

If it had got out of hand in the pool there wouldn't have been much those two women could have done – or myself, for that matter. I could see no benefit – save for the fact they were *temporarily* removed from society – in locking up so many Alexes in one place. As it was, the two staff continually acted as mental prompts, shouting orders and blowing their whistles at the youngsters throughout what seemed to me a wild session, when they were in danger of going too far. I'd never seen anything like it before, though obviously they were used to it and the session passed without serious mishap. I later had opportunities to watch the group at football, and saw the same extremes and childish tendencies.

It came as no surprise when Alex began to complain about other clients; what I hadn't expected was that he would be faced with such a concentration of bigger, stronger and more deeply disturbed versions of himself. He'd barely managed to cope with Gary at Grange Court. Now he had to live with a whole tribe of them – there was no way that this would work out well. But what surprised me most was the staff. On the Sunday, following his arrival on Wednesday, Alex's honeymoon period at Moorcroft had ended. According to him, he was manhandled during a restraint, and suffered a bruised arm and an injured wrist. Later he told me: 'Dad, this man is racist!' The member of staff concerned denied any wrongdoing and claimed that Alex had struck him on the forehead first.

Over the next three months, Alex detailed to me a highly distressing catalogue of violence. One staff member grabbed him by the chest in a frenzied outburst, crashing his back from wall to wall. His feet were swept from the floor while he was standing with his back against the wall, so that he struck the base of his spine on the concrete floor, suffering excruciating pain; a manager did this because Alex defiantly refused to take his thumb out of his mouth when ordered. On more than one occasion he was dragged across the lounge like a rag doll until the carpet burned holes through his jeans and removed a patch of skin from each knee. His head was smashed against a wall by another client – a girl – and he bled until about a pint covered the room. He did not fight back because, as he later said to me: 'I remembered you said that I mustn't hit girls.' He received a vicious upper-cut punch in the jaw from a young man which split his tongue as his teeth went through it. He was given three stitches in hospital. He suffered restraint after restraint, during which he received head and face injuries, and bruises to just about every part of his body. He was kicked by both staff and clients. And on one occasion he was punched in the face four or five times by a teacher. Several of these incidents were witnessed by staff and other clients.

Naturally Alex retaliated, and sometimes he started the incidents, but not always. This was a war zone. The verbal abuse was prolific and the atmosphere volatile. The slightest event could trigger the next incident and they occurred almost daily. Trapped in that environment with no means of escape, he boasted that I would defend him physically. His hope, I suppose, was to keep his opponents at bay and take what comfort he could for himself, but this didn't work. Alex knew, deep down, that he was alone, and Sharon's and my visits offered him no protection. 'You're in Moorcroft now, and there's nothing your daddy can do!' 'Gonna run to your daddy, then? – ahh.' 'The cry-baby is going to tell his daddy,' some staff tormented him.

Alex's situation looked desperate and hopeless. Moorcroft, I learned, was regarded by many social workers around the country as the last stop before prison. The viciousness of the regime staggered me and still haunts my imagination. Alex himself summed it up for me on my third visit, when he asked: 'Daddy, why did they send me here? I haven't done no murders!' I had no answer for him. He looked like the loneliest kid in Britain.

I encouraged Alex to make formal complaints against anyone who assaulted him. I complained bitterly to social services on his behalf. They made telephone calls to Moorcroft but chose not to believe Alex's versions of events. 'But what about the scars and the bruises?' I protested, when they claimed Alex was simply acting up and would soon settle down. But nothing Sharon, Alex or I said made any difference.

I updated Cassandra and her colleagues regularly. This firm of solicitors appeared to have been deeply touched by Alex's case and were extremely supportive, listening to me and giving me advice way beyond what legal aid afforded.

Sharon and I used our visits not only to see our son, but also to try to advise him how best to cope with his predicament until we could get him out. 'Don't play with so-and-so! Stay in your room, read books and play by yourself.' We knew that this was unrealistic but what else could we say? We never encouraged him to fight; it would solve nothing, and Alex stood out like a sore thumb – one slight black boy in a sea of white faces, apart from one mixed-race male staff member who occasionally worked on the unit. When we brought up the subject of race, they responded by seconding a black boy from another secure unit in the complex to befriend Alex, who, according to one staff member, was in Moorcroft for 'very serious crimes'.

I learned that Alex was entitled to an independent advocate. He had been advised of this in writing by the manager of children's services at the centre following his mounting formal complaints. When he showed it to me I was upset that I had not been sent a copy. They must have realised that the letter would mean nothing to Alex, considering he was dyslexic, suffered from short-term memory, had the reading age of a 7-year-old, and wouldn't have the foggiest idea what the 'ASC Service' agency was. On his behalf I spoke to an advocate there who could represent Alex. As for that elusive Official Solicitor, he'd gone into hibernation again . . .

Alex's complaints had set in motion a formal procedure whereby the local social services department, the child protection team and the police sprang to action to investigate the alleged abuses. But when it mattered most, Alex clammed up. He refused to say a word. Nothing could be done if he was not prepared to make a statement. After the meeting he told me that a member of staff had spoken to him 'nicely' and told him he should 'forgive and forget', rather than be like his dad who didn't want to.

Then on one visit I arrived to find he had a long, raw superficial wound above his right eyebrow, and I insisted the police be called. This caused a bit of a stir on the unit. Alex was by now becoming very depressed and would not be consoled with more talk of what I or my lawyers were doing on his behalf. In reality, all the letters I'd written during April and the preparations for the High Court trial in August must have stirred my local authority considerably. They didn't seem to be taking any chances. A planning meeting was scheduled for 11 May at Moorcroft.

All the 'big guns' attended, some of whom were the decision-makers I'd never seen before and recognised by name only. I thought it extraordinary. Janice Lee, Chair of Social Services; Howard Lewis, Head of Division – wasn't he the one who had been responsible for having my son transported to Manchester in a police van? There were other councillors, a legal expert, social workers – they'd dispatched a platoon to confront me and I could not help but wonder why – but the one person whom I was particularly interested to see, Bertha Higgins, wasn't present. I had often heard it said that hers was the only view which really counted.

I begged the team to release Alex but they refused. They also refused to guarantee his safety while attempting to brush aside my fears. For me it felt like a trial whose outcome had already been decided. Alex had to remain at Moorcroft: for me, that much seemed predetermined.

A few days later came a bombshell revelation. I turned on the television to discover they were about to show a *World in Action* documentary on Moorcroft, entitled 'School of Crime'. I had to see it.

I watched without surprise as the narrator told me all the things about this children's home that social services hadn't bothered to. Moorcroft was indeed under investigation by the Department of Health for complaints of excessive cruelty against its clients, some of whom were only 10 years old. Evidently it had a long history of staff violence. Bones were broken. Limbs sprained or bruised during restraints. Some staff employed control methods used in adult prisons – headlocks, armlocks and the like – on these children. Both parents and children complained, but to little or no effect. Solvent abuse and sexual promiscuity were rife among the kids; some of them were absconding from the centre repeatedly, collectively notching up a monthly average of 130 such incidents, and the crime rate was sky high in the neighbouring community. A number of former clients, staff and experts spoke against the regime. They described and demonstrated how difficult children were treated at Moorcroft, and the injuries they received. With the exception of broken bones, all of them had happened to Alex. I was stunned that my son could have been sent to such a place and amazed that the Fulchester Centre had recommended it. It seemed that the whole Moorcroft establishment was underpinned by fear and violence.

As I continued to visit Alex, I sensed that he was beginning to give up. Despair was written all over his face and could be heard in his voice and in what he said. I used to recognise that glint in his eye, the one that meant trouble; now his eyes were without hope – beaten. He said he wanted to die and for the first time I actually believed him. With the profound resignation of a dying person making a will, he told me he wanted to write a book about all the things that had happened to him. He didn't want any other child to suffer as he had, and if ever he got out he'd buy a 'big house' and look after children like him, to 'stop them coming into these horrible places'. He spoke with the reflectiveness of an old man, full of knowledge and wise with experience. He gave me a piece of paper, which turned out to be the 'book' he had already spent the previous evening trying to write:

> When I go home I wait to get a dog. And go home to my Dady that will Be the Best Day of my Life Some day that will Happen to me when I go home If I go home I want to start all over agen start a new Life agen if it is not over Now Do you no waht my Bigest Wish is to go home
>
> The End

At the sight of this I found it difficult to stop the tears from welling up and started to cry silently. I tried not to show it and turned away from him to look out of the window. When he realised what was happening he became extremely concerned for me. Here was Alex – in prison – while I was free to leave at will, and for those moments he was far more interested in my wellbeing than his own. That's why I have always loved my son and will always try to do my best for him, because he has always loved me – without condition – come what may. He was deeply affectionate and supportive; he came over and hugged me. 'Don't cry, Dad, everything will be all right.' I thought how typical of Alex, but how few people could ever see this side of him. I put my arms around him and asked him whether I should help him tell his story. He said yes. I asked him whether I should write his book for him. When again he said yes, I vowed to him that I would, but explained that it would mean revealing some of the unpleasant events of the past. As I looked through the window I thought, 'Why not? People ought to be aware of the uglier side of these institutions.' Maybe this was the only way to help him, and others. This book represents the fulfilment of that promise.

Clients at Moorcroft either had to swim with the system or drown. After about six or seven weeks, Alex overcame his isolation and he learned to swim from the day he gained a victory over a teenager who had been terrorising him. His confidence grew as he began to fight back. From that moment on, Sharon and I lost a part of our son. He was heavily traumatised and started to reflect his environment. He was very far from being perfect before, but now whatever remaining boundaries he had were rapidly stripped away. In the equation of fight or die, he chose to fight – anybody and everybody. In response to my regular updates my solicitors had become so concerned for Alex's safety that they were threatening to bring the matter back before the courts early for a judicial review, and to subpoena Moorcroft's director Dr Hassan to appear before the High Court to explain why Alex was receiving so many injuries. That's how seriously the matter was being taken, for Alex had become suicidal.

I got the feeling that Moorcroft had begun to regret their decision to assess him. Maybe they thought our local authority hadn't fully briefed them on the level of our resistance to Alex's being placed there. I began to sense that the centre would not have minded if Alex were to vacate their facilities fairly swiftly, not least because they were already under the spotlight of negative media attention. I'd set the police on them and was keeping notes, my lawyers were putting on the pressure, and Alex himself continued to report complaints formally. Each complaint generated a lot of paperwork for the centre and caused outside agencies, including the local police, to poke around and ask questions – something Moorcroft could well have done without. Some of the staff now modified their behaviour towards Alex considerably and became much less confrontational. Even at this stage, some of them were honest enough to admit that Moorcroft wasn't the right place for him.

On 8 July the case conference was convened. Dr Hassan presided over the meeting and our local authority team was headed by Judith. This time Cassandra came with me and a more positive outcome to the meeting seemed intended. My impression was that the authority now wanted Alex to leave Moorcroft and were looking for a favourable opportunity to introduce this idea into the discussion, providing I co-operated. If I didn't allow them to continue with their care order, they would be absolved legally from the responsibility for funding a proper care plan for Alex.

I knew this would not have been in Alex's best interests as he was very disturbed at this stage and needed appropriate specialist help which I could not afford. With memories still fresh from my previous failure, I worked out that my options were: to pursue fully the residence order and get Alex back home with me, without any help or funds, and struggle on until I fell flat on my face; to anger social services and Dr Hassan by adopting a tough stance verbally, backed by further legal threats, and risk forcing them to defend their position via the courts to ensure Alex stayed put in Moorcroft; or to go along with social services' plan to place him into a boarding school, even though I had no confidence in what appeared to be a makeshift solution to move him off their hands. Hobson's choice, I know. For Alex's sake I had to co-operate. My hope was that now at least there would be redoubled efforts to find him an *appropriate* place. It was conceded that Alex could stay with me until that came on stream. My placatory stance paid off: Dr Hassan could see no reason why Alex could not come home with me immediately, but this idea was opposed by social services.

The five-day court case was due on 2 August, which virtually coincided with the end of Alex's assessment period. So though it was apparent at the July conference that he was *not* going to be recommended for long-term placement at Moorcroft, possibly for legal reasons social services decided he must stay there until the official end of the assessment. However, with Dr Hassan's approval they did allow him home for weekends from that point forward – a hard-won victory indeed. I was behaving myself and was now willing to comply with their future plan to send Alex to a boarding school of their choice, when they found one. Until then, he could return home to me with support. That was all I wanted for my son; I would have agreed to anything to accomplish it.

The big trial finally came and went. It fizzled out in about five or ten minutes. Everything had been previously agreed by the lawyers and needed only to be rubber-stamped by the High Court. Alex was free to leave Moorcroft. No apology was forthcoming from any local authority official, but I took comfort from a small incident: Wendy could no longer look me in the eye. I heard she left the adolescent team shortly afterwards and went to work in a department dealing with old people – less stressful, I suppose. I liked Wendy, she was a good woman. I don't think her conscience could stand it any more.

Compliance with the wishes of 'the department' was what it was all about, in my view. No matter how many times I have racked my brain since then trying to make sense of social services' action, I remain baffled as to why my son was forced to lose 190 days out of his life in secure units that weren't helping him. The 13-year-old child we got out of Moorcroft was far more disturbed than the one who had gone in – and all for the princely sum of about £3,000 per week, besides other ancillary expenses.

Answers

Fourteen

I FOUND THE whole experience of Moorcroft soul-destroying, but this does not begin to compare with what it did to Alex. His body resembled that of a soldier coming back from the wars rather than of a 13-year-old boy from a children's home. He was covered in scars old and new, and fresh bruises. His mind was in a far worse state. My son had been ripped away from his parents. In many ways we had lost him, for he now reflected the attitudes and thinking typical of children traumatised by institutional care.

The detailed narrative of Alex's life ends here. It would require another book to cover the turmoil-filled post-Moorcroft years. Social services did find a therapeutic boarding school for him – several in fact, each placement lasting a month or two before breaking down. None came near to meeting Alex's needs. Some had staff who would spend many hours attempting to reason with him after an incident, only to see all their endeavours overturned by the next fracas. No one could have spent more hours than Sharon and I in trying to help Alex work things through, but by now we knew that any seemingly positive results would last only until the next flashpoint. He needed specialist help, but how could he get it if no one in authority had the will to identify the problem? Some might ask: 'But what else could they have done with such a difficult child?' An understandable question, but Alex had demonstrated cause for concern from the very first day he entered the education system at nursery school, aged 3½.

Commenting upon Alex's case history, Dr Patricia Rouse, Consultant Psychologist, believed that since Alex was clearly presenting symptoms of developmental immaturity there should have been a multi-disciplinary assessment of his condition, so that it could have been accurately diagnosed and an appropriate plan devised to help him. Those involved would have included Alex and his parents, his teachers, a paediatrician and a psychologist. Had it been considered in Alex's best interest, he might also have received remedial help from a speech and language therapist, a physiotherapist and a special education teacher. Finally, she was concerned about the lack of medical intervention in Alex's case.

The tragic course of Alex's life continued when in 1994 social services arranged for him to be accepted by Goswell Care, a private-sector organisation based in London. Here, Alex seems to have the freedom to do virtually as he pleases, apparently with the full knowledge of the authorities. He has been sexually active since he was 14, which may have made him calmer for longer periods, but he still has a tendency to explosive outbursts. From this age he has roamed the streets at all hours of the day and night; he has attended all-night parties where drugs and alcohol are freely available; he moves with very dubious company and has been arrested several times. According to him, he has been kicked, verbally and racially abused, and otherwise assaulted on several occasions by the police, for whom he has developed a hatred. He also alleges that he has often been left totally unsupervised or in the care of incompetent, untrained staff, some of whom have also assaulted him. He is provided with his own video and television, and at one time satellite TV, so that he can watch movies of any description. 'Dad, I ain't got no education in my head. I am fed up of watching sex videos. I need an education. Please help me, Dad. Please!' Alex pleaded to me in one desperate phone call. According to Alex, since being placed at Goswell Care he sleeps till midday, or later, if he wishes, consumes alcohol, and has received no therapy and only sporadic, token education since September 1996. At the time of writing he remains at Goswell Care at a cost of about £2,000 a week, plus the added expense of an agency care worker who supposedly acts as an escort or guardian for Alex during regular working hours, wherever he happens to be, to prevent him from getting into trouble. The education department has never provided a *finalised* 'statement' of his special needs, which would make them legally liable to educate him. In this way he has become a stereotype of just another failing black youth.

Somewhere in Alex's heart he yearns desperately for something better. He knows he needs help and is not getting it. He feels trapped, cornered by the system, and finds it difficult to trust anyone. Life's cruel lessons seem to have convinced him that no one can in fact help him, whatever good intentions they may have – not even his parents. He feels he has only himself to depend on and so seeks his own short-term goals. He trusts no one. His pathway seems pre-determined: extremely poor education, little prospect of worthwhile employment, an escalating criminal record, more secure accommodation and, when he comes of age, prison – if he doesn't come to serious harm first. My fears are not exaggerated. During the year after Moorcroft, his life was fraught with dangerous incidents.

In one a child was left paralysed following a near-fatal road accident, and in another Alex could have been killed. His agency worker thought it safe to leave Alex outside his mother's home while she was still at work and was not expected home for at least an hour. Free to roam the streets, he went off on a bicycle and was hit by a car travelling on a dual carriageway. He went through the windscreen, suffering a fractured leg, damaged ribs and multiple severe bruising.

I was still desperate to convince the decision-makers that there was something specifically wrong with Alex, in the hope that they would offer constructive help. Time was against us. He was 13, and I didn't possess the academic skills needed to research and identify the problem.

Alex had shown considerable insight when he decided to write his story. He'd sensed the apparent hopelessness of his situation and, in his own way, wanted it to be a warning to other children like him. But his one-page 'book' could not accomplish that. Several friends had already concluded that the issues raised by Alex's treatment should be aired before a wider public, to try to prevent similar fates befalling other children.

Some urged me to write Alex's story, but at the time such a notion seemed like conquering Everest or sailing round the world single-handedly. Yet Alex's own pathetic attempt, and the fact that he himself saw the need for something drastic to be done, put me to shame, and I was also desperate to focus a spotlight on his enigmatic illness.

What did I know about writing books? Nothing. True, I had at the time been writing furiously on the train and late into the night when I couldn't sleep – after I started having those mysterious experiences and began to comprehend what was happening inside Alex's head. Since I'd become wholly convinced that a physiological explanation lay at the root of Alex's eccentric personality, I had wanted to convey this to the relevant authorities. Getting this message across became my absolute priority.

The more I thought about his tragic history the more it forced me to look closely at my own personality and behaviour, my father's and also Jason's. I noticed that we bore some remarkable personality similarities, over and above ordinary family traits, yet we were all very different characters. I was intrigued. I asked myself why Alex was afflicted with his condition. I concluded that Alex had inherited a biological brain dysfunction from my father, through me. (At least blaming it on my father seemed more palatable than saying he'd inherited his condition from me.) Gradually I developed my own theory based on those abstruse insights I'd had on the train.

I planned to share my new understanding and excitement with Vivienne, but unfortunately she succumbed to a critical illness, and died before I had opportunity to do so. Alex and I were devastated.

I eventually noted down a very rough version of my theory, which I stuck on the back burner in order to start the daunting task of drafting my book. It was by now January 1994 and telling Alex's story became my new priority. His problems were becoming worse and I had no sound basis for believing they would ever get better of their own accord, or that his troubled downward spiral would be arrested.

My hope was that, via the book, some expert or establishment would come forward with an offer of appropriate help. That seemed the shortest route. Developing the skills to write about such a specialist issue would take much longer.

Meantime I took word-processing and typing classes. I also feverishly tried to follow up contacts who might be willing to offer advice or provide care for Alex, some of which included privately run specialist organisations, teachers, therapists and care workers. Most were sympathetic but unable to help. Undaunted, I eventually drafted my own alternative care-plan for Alex, having found a few professionals who were willing to participate, providing I could organise it. In this, despite my very best efforts, I failed.

All the while, festering in the back of my mind was the fact that one day I'd have to find out how to get my book published.

One kind agent I contacted introduced me to a long-established writers' group, and I learned much from their meetings. This gave me my first insight into how far I still had to go with my new craft, before I could even think about getting into print. But fortune was on my side for I eventually met another agent who took compassion on either me or Alex, perhaps both, after reading the script. Much was wrong with it; but he tempered his advice with encouragement, and then it was back to the drawing-board for me. Never had I tackled anything so challenging and grievously vexing to my system; I would have gladly swapped it for fixing an old engine. Gradually my typing improved, and Richard, a computer-expert friend of mine, generously assembled a computer for me out of recycled parts. This meant I could practise more and, in time, I began to rewrite my book.

Concerned for Alex's future, I worried that his stagnant situation was becoming progressively worse. I wanted to meet the Director of Social Services in person to ascertain exactly what her plans for my son's future were, and to see whether I could reason with her. This meeting eventually occurred in August 1994. Now at last I would be able to look her straight in the eye, to see whether she could offer a justifiable explanation for my son's suffering. She didn't. Within minutes of the meeting's commencing I soon realised: all that was on offer was just more of the same, until he was legally no longer their responsibility. Poor Alex.

One day a couple of months later, I came across a magazine article about unruly children. It was well written and uncluttered with complicated jargon. Disbelievingly I read descriptions of various children's behaviour in a number of different settings: It was as if I was reading about Alex.

Something new also leaped from its pages. Evidently there was a medical condition called either Attention Deficit Disorder (ADD) or Attention Deficit Hyperactivity Disorder (ADHD), which was thought to be the *cause* of the abnormal or antisocial behaviour in such children. The article mentioned scientific research which suggested that children who suffered from ADD or ADHD had problems with the regulation of certain chemicals in the brain. I got very excited indeed. In fact, I was jubilant. This was the first time I'd heard anything about these syndromes.

Though the article did not enter into great technical detail I knew instinctively that this was what Alex was suffering from. My 'train experiences' had led me to the same conclusion as this article: that there was a biological deficiency in Alex's brain which affected his behaviour and learning abilities. I had called it the Dysfunctioning Brain Syndrome. The illness is identifiable primarily through a combination of behavioural and/or educational effects it produces within its host. These symptoms are not easily detectable, and are often misinterpreted or missed in standard medical or psychological analysis.

Since my conclusions were reached well over a year before I came across ADD or ADHD, so my heady excitement soon turned to indignation. Why hadn't any of the distinguished psychiatrists told me about this? Surely they must have known about it? A fire had ignited under me: I had to find out more.

The article mentioned several American doctors by name so I jotted them down. A little detective work followed. The American Embassy was helpful and provided me with addresses for three of the doctors, and by 31 January 1995 I'd obtained a fourth. I sent a long letter, full of specific questions grouped under subject headings, then hoped and prayed for some response. I thought: 'Even if just one of them answers my questions truthfully, at least I will have informed expert information at last.' I hoped this promising turn of events would mean that 1995 was going to be a good year. It was.

Before the end of January, Dr Mel Levine, Professor of Paediatrics and Director of the Child Development Research Institute at the University of North Carolina, replied. His letter was brief, but very encouraging – 'At all costs, it is of course critical to bear in mind that you are all innocent victims' – and he assured me that the questions raised in my letter were all answerable. He suggested I obtain a copy of his book *Educational Care* as it dealt with every issue I'd raised.

Some weeks later I rang Dr Levine, and he told me that he would be in England the following month to address a conference on learning disorders at Churchill College, Cambridge, and invited me to attend. At last I was going to meet an expert who understood my son's illness. I couldn't wait.

Days later a copy of *Educational Care* arrived. I noticed Dr Levine had dedicated it to 'Innocent children whose stifled struggles to succeed have been misinterpreted'. I started to read it straight away. After only a few pages I could no longer hold back my tears. I felt as if my prayers had been answered and kept muttering under my breath, 'So I wasn't mad after all. I wasn't mad. I was right all along.'

Dr Levine's books describes in eloquent detail the different effects that a range of brain deficiencies, including ADD and ADHD, can have on a child's learning abilities. It explains how these effects are easily misinterpreted by adults as anything from mental retardation to blatant antisocialism, and how this creates inner turmoil for the child. The deficiency or deficiencies – a child may have a cluster of them – can manifest themselves in a multitude of ways: from daydreaming and quiet isolation, to extremes of disruptive behaviour and violence. Most of these symptoms applied to Alex.

Dr Levine emphasises the need to build up an individual profile for each child, based on continual, informed observation by teachers and parents, so that consistent remedial action may be taken in all areas where the pupil is failing – both academically and socially. An essential, balancing ingredient within this profile should describe the positive side of the child's character and gifts, since 'the strengthening of their strengths becomes an indispensable part of their management'. The book is extremely practical, and describes many of the useful strategies that Dr Levine and others have developed to assist such pupils.

Perhaps I never did doubt my sanity, but the world becomes a rather lonely place when you feel that nobody understands your problem and you meet continual opposition. Under such circumstances it's easy to start doubting yourself. Some say I'm strong; determined, perhaps, would be a more accurate word. I couldn't, and wouldn't, allow myself to sink into complete despair. But even I must admit I came pretty close. Now, thanks to reading a few pages of Dr Levine's book, I knew no such thing could ever happen. My confidence was buoyed up a hundredfold. The book not only confirmed all that I'd already discovered for myself, but also enhanced my understanding of the whole subject tremendously. And I was soon going to meet Dr Levine.

Through my writing group I had also met a truly kind person: the author Paddy Kitchen, who came as a guest speaker. After the meeting we spoke for a while, and I was delighted when she offered to look over my attempts to record Alex's story, though I knew she couldn't possibly have had any idea of what she was letting herself in for. Shortly thereafter I sent it to her; the very next day came another welcome surprise.

I'd just about given up all hope of getting a response from any of the other American doctors when the most wonderful letter came from Dr Jan Mathisen, a paediatric neurologist from Birmingham, Alabama. If I had any vestige of doubt about my sanity after learning of Dr Levine's work, this letter dispelled it. In plain language, Dr Mathisen answered all my queries about ADD and ADHD. It was like the icing on a cake.

In response to my question, 'Are ADD and ADHD recognised medical conditions?' he wrote:

In the US, ADD with and without hyperactivity had been a well defined entity for the last 30 years. There has been considerable confusion about its etiology and treatment over time, but I believe that medical science is getting closer to the mysteries of this disorder. ADD is a condition that is well recognised throughout the world. Some societies do have greater difficulty dealing with the condition because of the overlap between psychiatry and neurology.

I had asked whether there were any recognised medical tests that would identify the condition, and at what age specialist help should be made available:

No specific medical test would identify a child with ADD. Typically, we evaluate children by going through a multitude of questions about their behaviour as well as their degree of inattentiveness and impulsivity and, based on clinical judgement, would make the diagnosis . . . In addition to this, complete testing to evaluate for any identifiable school or learning difficulties is also provided. Children with ADD may present at a very young age, occasionally with severe behavioural problems.

Responding to my question as to whether afflicted children can cope with mainstream education, he said:

Most children that have ADD in the US are in regular classrooms, occasionally getting additional learning assistance from tutoring or special education teachers . . . It has been noted that in children who are not identified as having this condition or who are not treated properly, many of them do seem to have more antisocial behavioural problems and may get into difficulties with the law at an older age. It is also obvious that if a child who has these features is ostracised or kept from joining in with other children who are normal in their behaviour, he would often participate in activities with children who have similar types of antisocial behaviour or the propensity for more violent activities.

His letter indicated that ADD was treatable and advised me to seek out the assistance of UK physicians who are interested in ADD.

The Cambridge conference to which Dr Levine had invited me was organised by the Helen Arkell Dyslexia Centre in Surrey. It stands fondly in my memory as a gathering that brought me immense joy as well as being an eye-opening experience. For 14 years I'd known there was something troubling my son; the last eight or nine years had been spent seeking professional help in the face of ignorance and, at times, opposition. With the exception of Bill Smart and Vivienne Gill, no effective help was to be found. This mysterious illness contributed to the breakdown of my marriage, home and business – all gone. My children's lives were shattered, each in their own way. I'd become almost a nervous wreck, dependent on all sorts of remedies that mostly failed to provide even an occasional decent night's sleep. And now, here I was, probably the only layperson in an auditorium of about 250 professionals, mainly teachers and psychologists, each of whom had encountered some aspect of Alex's illness in their schools and practices. They came from all over the country to listen to Dr Levine, and to discuss the latest developments in recognising, understanding and tackling learning disorders. I was somewhat overawed by the occasion, but for the first time I no longer felt alone in my immense struggle. In fact, I felt as if I was among friends, even though I didn't know a soul there.

In many ways it was a mirage, for everyone soon disappeared back to where they had come from and I was isolated again; but it was lovely while it lasted. I met many people and heard many stories about the intractable problems some children with learning difficulties faced and caused at school, and there was common agreement on the appalling way they were being failed. Dr Chris Singleton, Lecturer in Developmental and Educational Psychology and Director of the Dyslexia Computer Resource Centre at Hull University, outlined in clear detail the need for effective early screening of children with learning difficulties.

I left the conference on a high that lasted for some days. Almost overnight, the pressure of years of uncertainty had lifted and that was a good feeling. None of this had any immediate practical effect, however. Alex knew little of the profound efforts I was making on his behalf, and I couldn't share my discoveries with him. His life was utterly confused.

On 1 May 1996, via the ADD Support Group, I made contact with consultant child and adolescent psychiatrist Dr Finn Cosgrove – a UK expert who is familiar with my son's illness. That October, Dr Cosgrove diagnosed Alex as suffering from ADHD and prescribed appropriate low-dose medication. Alex is also receiving some tuition that has allowed him to 'strengthen his strengths' (related to music) and develop his basic numerical and literacy skills. An appropriate educational programme still needs to be set up for him, but resistance from the local education authority has to date scuppered this. Nevertheless, since Alex has been receiving modest medical treatment, everyone connected with Alex's care (including social services and education officials) has acknowledged the dramatic improvement in coping and interacting with him – when he takes his medication.

To help Alex further and prevent a breakdown, the problems relating to his care arrangements, education, therapeutic input and consistency in taking his medication all need to be resolved. My hope is that, together with Dr Cosgrove, other knowledgeable professionals who are willing to help will do so quickly. My son needs to salvage a life. He deserves it.

Fifteen

WHILE I'VE BEEN pursuing help for my son, my long journey has brought home to me the frightening reality that he is not alone in his experiences: there are many more Alexes out there, and they all need help.

Dear parents and readers
This book aims to obtain appropriate help for children like Alex – while they are still children. Many cases are less acute, though some are even worse.

I have come to know parents of such children and watched some of them reach the end of their tether, barely able to cope. Their whole lives revolve around the child and every setting becomes a virtual battlefield: home, school, the streets . . . We've all seen children wildly out of control when we are out shopping, passing a school or walking along the road. 'Little monsters', they are often called, or something similar. Usually others assume it must be their parents' fault and that they are not being brought up properly. Sometimes that may be true, and if the child also suffers from ADD it is so much worse. Owing to chemical irregularities in the brain, it is possible that these children do not have sufficient mental controls to enable them to improve their behaviour through experience alone. They are capable of some learning, but generally they will need considerable help. Love especially, along with patience and consistency, will contribute, but sometimes such qualities are not enough in themselves. Education tailored to children's individual needs may also be crucial. As is, in some cases, relevant medical therapy or prescription. If they receive this, many will go on to live useful, normal lives.

Unfortunately, many are failed by the system. Some may end up in mental institutions and be driven to mental illness. An unacceptably high proportion slide – sometimes irrevocably – into criminal careers. They must be identified early, preferably while they are under the age of 5 and still pliable enough to benefit fully.

It is beyond the scope of this book to discuss appropriate types of education and medical care for ADD sufferers. However, modest strides are at last being made in this country to emulate successes enjoyed by some American institutions who have recognised and coped with this type of child for many years. There is a growing wealth of knowledge in organisations such as the ADD/ADHD Family Support Group UK, the Learning Assessment Centre, the British Dyslexia Association, the Dyslexia Institute, the Helen Arkell Centre, plus many other small specialist educational groups scattered around the country (see Useful Addresses). Their members encounter such children daily. Most of these groups exist as charities or privately run organisations. This means that only relatively few children with ADD/ADHD, dyslexia or any other learning disability are ever fortunate enough to gain access to, and benefit from, their services. The vast majority of these children never begin to fulfil their educational potential. They are trapped in a system which, like a giant supertanker, can't change direction quickly enough to cater specifically for them. This is a shameful waste of talent. Either way, like Alex, these youngsters lose out. They are condemned, somewhat unfairly, by the very system that fails them.

Call it what you like: Attention Deficit Disorder, Attention Deficit Hyperactivity Disorder, Dyslexia, Mixed Emotional Conduct Disorder, Hyperkinetic Syndrome, Thought Disorder, Specific Learning Difficulty, Oppositional Defiant Disorder, or the name I chose to call it – these are all branches of the same tree. A word of caution, however: I agree with Dr Levine's view that such labels tend to limit the scope of this illness, which can manifest itself in any cluster combination. There is no doubt that, in its worst manifestations, it is frightening, for both the sufferers and those who live with them. When I eventually unravelled its nature my understanding was that, though specific at a biochemical level, it nevertheless manifested itself differently in each person – thus making itself highly individual in character, but with enough common denominators to make the illness identifiable to the trained eye. It cannot be cured at present, but can be managed successfully. In some parts of the world knowledgeable practitioners have been helping these children since the 1960s.

I don't pretend to know what can be done about adults and older teenagers who are severe sufferers, but I would like you to bear in mind, the next time you come across a horrific media report about some heinous crime committed by a young person, that *some* are driven to it. If, as a result of publicising Alex's plight, one disordered child can be spared at least a part of the suffering he has been through, then his ordeal will not have been totally in vain. After all, that was Alex's wish.

Lastly, this illness is not in the least bit prejudiced. It does not care whether you are black or white, rich or poor, male or female, tall or short, fat or skinny. Right now, you are quite likely to have an undiagnosed friend, workmate, aunt, uncle, son, daughter, grandparent or next-door neighbour who is afflicted by an aspect of this illness. You may even be a sufferer yourself. This illness is *not* new, but has only relatively recently been identified. In its worst form it can devastate a family without their ever knowing why. It might manifest itself in problems with a child's reading, writing, spelling, memory, poor sociability, hyperactivity or short attention-span. Poor Alex had the lot. Yet almost without exception those who get to know him well generally conclude that he's not such a bad guy. It remains my hope one day to share, in uncomplicated language, everything I've been able to learn about the 'mechanics' of this complicated but fascinating illness.

Dear parents of children with behavioural and learning difficulties
If you have a child in care or displaying characteristics similar to Alex's, please learn from my struggle. Get proper help for your child – early. Do not allow yourself to be fobbed off by unhelpful officials.

For your child's sake, understand your educational and legal rights, and pursue them vigorously. Remember, it was Alex's desire that your child should not suffer as he has.

I'm not encouraging you to be confrontational. You can see from Alex's case that this is not the best way; co-operation is much more desirable. But if you have no alternative but to threaten legal action, then for the sake of your child it might be worth considering. Try to get a good lawyer on your side. Try to gather as much data as possible about your child's condition; maybe a support group exists and will help. Remember, you are unlikely to challenge a local authority successfully unless you can provide evidence. Even then it isn't easy, and they will certainly defend their interests. Keep all written communications, and take notes after every phone call, logging the date, time, name of person(s) you spoke to, and what was said. Keep a separate log of events that concern you about the way your child is being cared for or educated – detail them. Always ask for confirmation in writing, and clarification of any terminology or statements that you don't understand.

Dear Government
Since the summer of 1988, my local authority, primarily via their social services department, have spent in the region of £1 million of public money, directly and indirectly, on my son. Imagine multiplying it by the growing number of similar children in care. In the case of Alex, and very likely many others, there is little doubt this money has been wasted. The result has been to turn him into a highly disturbed young man and to earn him a criminal record. Spending on him is therefore unlikely to stop when he reaches maturity. If only a modest proportion of that money could have been targeted effectively through the education and/or medical system(s) in his early years, he might have become a valued contributor to government coffers rather than a drain on them. Perhaps you may wish to reflect on the reality of this case when you are debating the rapid rise in the number of 'difficult' children excluded from mainstream education.

Speaking as a parent who has been an eye-witness to much of my son's *unnecessary* trauma, I believe that if you are truly to help learning-disabled children like him three fundamental areas urgently need your attention. They are (1) how to get separate institutions to act in unison (educational, social and medical authorities need to treat their pupil, client, patient as one entity, not three separate people – if damaging conflicting strategies are to be avoided; (2) early screening, which is critical and needs to be implemented nationally (as an alternative to a future of one-way, life-long expenditure – children's homes, special schools, young offenders' institutions, secure units, prisons and/or mental hospitals – early screening surely seem more rational); and (3) simple recognition, and acceptance, that *only the will of government* can set in motion the systems needed to correct the abominable weaknesses that exist at present.

Dear judges
Minors, ultimately, are at your and the law's mercy. I have no doubt that on the whole you serve them well. Indeed, it was one of you who ordered that the root of my son's disturbances be sought – someone whose insight I shall always respect. But this order has never been fully complied with. From this review of my son's case-history, as a body, even you may agree something needs to be done. My message to you is a simple one: vulnerable people, who depend on social services, will sometimes need your protection from a minority within that system. They do not always know best. Perhaps one of the reasons for this is the inbuilt, fundamental conflict: financial interest versus the needs of the child (or elderly person, etc.). Those who need help need only a one-tier social service – the real one. If you do not want to see some whom you met as children, by way of social and other professional reports, swelling the population of present and future secure units, prisons and mental hospitals, as dangerous, deranged teenagers or adults, ought not something be done about it *now*? Otherwise more trouble is undoubtedly being stored up for the future: an escalating crime rate, wanton acts of violence and even motiveless murders.

Dear social services
We need your services: you do a good job without which the quality of many people's lives would undoubtedly suffer. I know the maj-

ority of you are caring, committed people. This book criticises only a minority who physically and mentally abuse the weak and vulnerable in their care, and their superiors who either by acquiescence, or design, allow substandard or violent regimes to masquerade as social service. In furnishing these services to those who need them in our sprawling communities, many times you have to cope with some who have serious problems. Often you do a thankless, difficult job that nobody else wants; this is acknowledged. But please weed out those among you, at whatever level they exist within your organisations, who are damaging your reputation.

You took my beautiful son, aged only 7, and helped to set in train events that split my family apart. We love our son but he has been prematurely aged by exposure to too many adult vices, that have left him traumatised, degenerate and depleted of the good family values society needs. This can't be right. Society pays an unbelievably high price, and keeps on paying. Read my story again if you doubt this. I appeal to your consciences. If you can't help children like Alex, all I ask is that you have the decency to admit it, so that something constructive can be done about them. If there are specific problems in catering for the specialist needs of such children, surely the way forward is to raise these issues with all relevant bodies at a level that can cause change, rather than simply to continue to let these children be failed at taxpayers' expense.

Dear psychiatrists and psychologists
Please recognise ADD/ADHD – it's real. If you have any doubts, contact the ADD Support Group or similar organisations for more information. Additionally they will be able to tell you about many parents like Sharon and me, who have suffered for years because their child has this condition which nobody recognised or understood. Some of your colleagues in America are progressing by leaps and bounds in the management of this disorder. It cannot yet be cured, but it can, with accurate early diagnosis and mutual co-operation by all concerned, be managed successfully. Why not form links with them? ADD, ADHD – call it what you like – will be with us for a long time, and if you can become part of the network of

professionals with the skills to manage it, you can be assured you will be taking part in desperately needed, as well as rewarding, work. I would have loved to have been recommended to someone like you when Alex was 5 years old.

Dear education department
Please take on board that a range of educational difficulties can coexist within one child. It is your job to find out what they are so that you can fulfil your obligation to meet all that child's special needs. Maybe you were unaware of ADD and ADHD before; you are not any more. Please familiarise yourself with this disorder and be determined to help these children early. Get a copy of Mel Levine's *Educational Care* and read it from cover to cover; you'll find it an invaluable addition to your special education/learning disorder repertoire. There are children in your schools, undiagnosed, who need appropriate help now. Give it to them, and save the government heaps of unnecessary future spending in the process.

Dear professionals involved in my son's case
Is it fair or justified that a child, my son, Alex, should pay such a horrifically expensive price: a lost education, acute physical and mental abuse and trauma, a lost childhood? Why didn't you view the bigger picture? Because it was far easier to blame the parents, and accept that Alex wasn't suffering from a genuine medical problem, despite overwhelming circumstantial evidence that something medical *must* be wrong. You let us down! We've had to accept our portion of the blame – *so should you*.

Dear children (and adults) with behavioural, emotional and/or learning difficulties
I hope you can read this, or that someone can read it to you. *Do not give up on yourselves.* This might seem strange at first until you think about it, but be proud of your disability. You have talents that nobody else has. They are locked inside you and need only the right chance to come out. True, there will always be some things that you and I might never be able to do as well as others. So what? In exactly

the same way, there are things that you can already do, or will be able to do in the future, better than many others. You must believe that. Did you know that some of the most famous and talented people in the world are said to have the same type of special brain as yours – scientists, engineers, artists, writers, singers, musicians? Did you know that some businesses employ people because their brain is special, if they are trained in their line of work? Do your very best to get an education and let your special brain work for you.

There are experts who can teach you in the way that suits *your* brain. This sort of teaching is much better for you, and it's not a bit like how you've had to struggle at school. All it needs is your willingness to try and you can be successful. If you are a child, ask your parents and teachers to do their very best to get you this help. If you are an adult, you might have to try to get this help yourself. But you must be determined to find it. Be willing to listen and put into practice what your tutors or therapists say. If you recognise any of the behaviours or learning difficulties outlined in this book in yourself, contact a dyslexia or ADD support group. It will be a good place to start.

If you have been getting into trouble, you must decide to make a break with *all* bad company: male or female, young or old. You must no longer view what you have as a disability or weakness, but as a strength; and if you apply yourself it might even become a blessing.

Dear Sharon and Jason
I know you have both been through a lot and have suffered in your own way. Sharon, I know you have shed many tears over our sons, especially Alex, and the pain of heart you feel is extra great – no mother can bear to see or know that their child is suffering. Jason, you haven't had an easy life, my son; I love you, and admire the way you have survived despite the many obstacles. Few of your peers could endure similar. Not one of the four of us knew about this illness or how to cope with it; we were all victims. We can't undo the past, but life must go on. And Sharon, your instincts were right about, oh, so many things – especially the hyperactivity and dyslexia.

Dear Alex

My son, my son. I want you to know that I love you and always will; so do your mother and brother, as do the rest of our families. You know that I have never, and will never, approve of the wrong things you have done. But I also want you to know that *I do not blame you. NONE OF IT IS YOUR FAULT.* As Dr Levine said: 'You are innocent.' I know you have had a tougher life than most kids, and because of that you have been left confused and find it difficult to trust anyone. I want you to know there are many people out here who love and care for you, and who want to see you given the chance that you deserve. They are willing to help, if you let them. Please see if you can find it in your heart to forgive all of us who have so badly let you down, including me. Sometimes, son, when people don't understand something or someone, it makes them act in a way that they regret when they come to understand the matter fully.

I know you are a very bright and intelligent young man. Don't waste your special abilities, and I do believe that you can do anything that you want to in life. Put this behind you and try to get the education your special brain needs. I will help you.

Love,
      Dad

Epilogue

Weeks before the appointment (with Dr Cosgrove in October 1996) I was very apprehensive: would we make it there on the day?

Alex had insisted on seeing Dr Cosgrove, a move that at first was met with stiff opposition by social services. They relented when Alex told them: 'You can forget it, I am not seeing any one else.' We drove to Bristol the night before, to ensure he was well rested and able to keep to the time of our appointment. Dr Cosgrove interviewed Alex, skilfully answering all his and my questions about the treatment. We'd made it! Alex had finally received a diagnosis. The bonus for me was that he agreed to give the medication a try.

Staff at his new special school were soon commenting how much more teachable and easier to get along with he had become. Everyone accepted the drastic improvement. Some felt the transformation was nothing short of miraculous.

At the time of writing, however, Alex remains at Goswell Care. This seems to be working against his long-term best interests, and his co-operation with his medication has not always been forthcoming – a fact that has hampered his already meagre education and the efforts of staff at his school, not to mention undermining the success of the medical intervention. I hope this will one day be resolved, but it has proved to me that the *correct* medication can help – even in cases where the circumstances are less than ideal. Of course, for Alex to get maximum benefit from his medical treatment, all his needs must be adequately addressed. And the years of pent-up anger and frustration mean he will need therapeutic help to move on. Remember, he had *never* received the psychotherapy at the Tavistock Clinic that came so highly recommended by the Morgana Stanfield Foundation.

The stress caused to Alex by his care arrangements has continued to depress and traumatise him. Our family sometimes fears for Alex's future. Sadly, the recent accidental, drugs-related death of a close teenage friend – whose life at the hands of the care system uncannily mirrored his own and whom he loved like a brother – has hit him hard. He feels bitter and blames social services – 'Dad, it could have been me!' For weeks after he cried, and he still misses him. Nevertheless, at the time of this last update, three promising, positive developments coexist nicely, and on these, hope can be built: (1) *Alex wants to pursue a music-related career*, and he sings pretty well, too; (2) he is clean of all criminal activities and *wants to leave that lifestyle firmly behind him*; (3) *he wants a future* and, for the first time, with the impending departure of social services from his life, sees light at the end of the tunnel. My hope is that his wishes are realistic and that we can build on these developments, as a way of 'strengthening his strengths'. Besides, he is growing up and, with support, may yet turn into a fine young man.

In all this the most important lesson I have learned is to show your child love, love and more love, though this isn't always easy or enough. However the cookie crumbles, *your love* will be sorely tested for sure.

When I started to write this book I knew nothing of ADD/ADHD. Since then, the condition has received a lot of media attention. Typically the sufferers are reported as 'wild' kids whom no one can control. Much of the media debate is centred on the controversial use of the drug Ritalin. Many parents claim it has helped their children, though some medical practitioners are cautious. The same drug (prescribed with another) has brought about near-miraculous results with Alex.

Despite this developing media interest, I continued writing this book until I finished it in the autumn of 1997 because of my conviction that telling my story would help other families in similar situations. Holding on to this hope, I can perhaps begin to make sense of my son's immense suffering.

Useful Addresses

The ADD–ADHD Family Support Group UK
1A The High Street
Dilton Marsh
Nr Westbury
Wiltshire
BA13 4DL
Telephone: 01373-826045

ADD Information Services
PO Box 340
Edgware
Middlesex
HA8 9HL
Telephone: 0181-9052013

National Learning and Attention Deficit Disorder Association (LADDER)
PO Box 700
Wolverhampton
WV3 7YY
Telephone: 01902-336272

Helen Arkell Dyslexia Centre
Frensham
Farnham
Surrey
GU10 3BW
Telephone: 01252-792400

The British Dyslexia Association
98 London Road
Reading
Berkshire
RG1 5AU
Telephone: 0118-9662677

British Dyslexia Institute
133 Gresham Road
Staines
Middlesex
TW18 2AJ
Telephone: 01784-463852

Learning Assessment Centre
2nd Floor
44 Springfield Road
Horsham
West Sussex
RH12 2PD
Telephone: 01403-240002

Acknowledgements

Special thanks go to:

Dr Patricia Rouse – who through a gracious humanity, rare among her peers, was always there for me. She buoyed me up, willed me not to give up each time I was about to, when absolutely no one else was around. Unstintingly juggling time she could not afford, she gave me much sorely needed encouragement and was a tremendous source of sound, reliable advice, as well as a sympathetic listening ear.

DP – whose selfless compassion and extraordinary sage-like insight has taught me so much. You were a well of inspiration and believed in me when I could barely trust myself.

Jeffrey – whose input was the single pivotal factor in bringing this story to the public. Thank you for sending me back to that drawing-board again and again, when you could just as easily have banished me and my work to oblivion.

Paddy – who is one of the kindest, most unselfish, modest people I have ever met. Where can I begin to thank you? No words could do justice to the help you have given me. I know I fell way short of being your brightest pupil; nevertheless, with painstaking forbearance and expertise you taught me some of the skills of the trade and, in the process, became not only a teacher and mentor but also a dear friend. Sorry for the many hours spent twisting your ear; Alex and I will forever be in your debt.

Caroline, Grant and Nick of John Murray's – Caroline and Grant in particular for their faultless editing, sharp, critical eye and genuine support. Special thanks to Deborah for working so hard on my behalf. Collectively you have done far more than publishing a book; you have provided important information to those who need it, highlighted a subject that needs informed debate, and furnished the voiceless – a disadvantaged, neglected minority of children – with a voice.

Without the help of the above, FD, Michael A. – who enhanced my writing skills – Cheryl and several others whom space does not permit a mention, this book would never have seen the light of day. Thank you all very much.